Praise for

PIETY&POLITICS

"Lynn . . . has made a career of confronting leaders of the religious right . . . [he] doesn't dispute the need for moral values . . . he simply wants to assure that the government does not become the vehicle for imposing them."

—*Chicago Sun-Times*

"Lynn calmly demonstrates the twisted logic and outright hypocrisy of the right. While his opponents in the 'culture war' relentlessly fan the passions of their followers, offering the faithful a self-image of persecution and martyrdom, Lynn maintains a reasonable demeanor, largely forgoing cheap shots and one-liners. Essential reading."

—*Kirkus Reviews* (starred review)

"Lynn brings passion and a broad perspective to the national debate. . . . Whatever readers' religious or political beliefs, they will appreciate Lynn's well-considered examination of this contentious issue."

—*Booklist*

"In this political season, Lynn offers a sound alternative."

—*Publishers Weekly*

"For too long, quasi-Christian forces on the far right of the political spectrum have been bullying courts, legislators, and ordinary Americans under the guise of defending American values and religious freedom. It's high time that someone from the real religious community stood up to them. Hats off to the Reverend Barry Lynn for pushing back with this cogent and timely antidote to intolerance."

—Ron Reagan

PIETY &

The Right-Wing Assault on Religious Freedom

POLITICS

THE REVEREND Barry W. Lynn

 THREE RIVERS PRESS • NEW YORK

Library of Congress Cataloging-in-Publication Data
Lynn, Barry W.
Piety and politics : the right-wing assault on religious freedom / Barry W. Lynn.—1st ed.
p.   cm.
1. Christianity and politics—United States.   2. Religious right—United States.
3. Freedom of religion—United States.   4. Religious pluralism—United States.
5. Religious tolerance—United States.   I. Title.
BR526.L96   2006
323.44'20973—dc22   2006012878

ISBN 978-0-307-34749-7

Printed in the United States of America

Design by Helene Berinsky

10 9 8 7 6 5 4 3 2 1

First Paperback Edition

In memory of my late parents,
Edith and Harold Lynn,
who introduced me to the church and
to the value of thinking critically about issues

ACKNOWLEDGMENTS

This book could not have been written without the lifelong experiences and expertise of many people whose names do not always appear in this volume.

I want to thank the entire past and current staff of Americans United for Separation of Church and State, with a special nod to Rob Boston, whose clarity and research have been a tremendous asset.

Looking over my career, so much of it devoted to First Amendment protection, I am thankful for several great supporters and mentors, including the Reverends Paul Kittlaus, Larold K. Schultz, and Cal Didier, as well as John Shattuck, Morton Halperin, and the late Dr. Foy Valentine. All gave me extraordinary opportunities to work and go out on more than a few limbs—where I always found them when I needed them.

Two professionals from the world of television who have left us in recent years were inspirations to me and helped me understand what effective communication is all about: ABC anchor Peter Jennings, who gave me the right words of encouragement several times when I needed them, and Warren Steibel, longtime producer of William F.

Buckley's *Firing Line,* who arranged for me to be a regular panelist for the last few seasons of the show.

One needs muses every once in a while, and I have often taken a break to listen to the songsmithing of Guy Clark, Kris Kristofferson, and Billy Joe Shaver. They all have a passion for life and a sense of the "spiritual" that more than a few television preachers would benefit from hearing.

My family has always supported me (even when I occasionally headed in the wrong direction). To this day, I miss my late parents, Edith and Harold. My wife of thirty-six years, Joanne, and my two wonderful children, Christina and Nick, are constant reminders of the value of family.

This book would not have come to pass were it not for the guidance of Connie Zweig, Candice Fuhrman, and Ivory Madison. I also appreciate the vision of Shaye Areheart and her staff at Harmony Books.

A short time after I started working in Washington, I realized that when you win or lose battles to protect the rights of the people, there is nothing abstract about it. It helps or hurts unique individuals you will probably never even meet. That is a responsibility people who think of themselves as activists must bear. I hope I've lived up to that call.

When I had worked on social justice for only about six years, former Attorney General Ramsey Clark introduced me to a group in New York City as "a young man who I believe has signed on for the long haul." I'm no longer so young, but I can't stop re-enlisting in this work because despair and pessimism are death wishes for our country, our Constitution, and our communities. I'm not going to contribute to that atmosphere when I look around me and see so many other folks gearing up to do whatever it takes to bring justice a little bit closer.

CONTENTS

INTRODUCTION

Why Does a Nice Minister Like You Support the Separation of Church and State?

THE LATE REVEREND JERRY FALWELL doesn't like me. How do I know? Let me count the ways.

On January 23, 2003, Falwell told me on CNN's *Crossfire* that if I really read the Bible I'd be a conservative. I told him I did read it, and to prove it I'd be happy to come down to his church in Lynchburg, Virginia, any Sunday and preach at all of his services. Falwell replied, "I wouldn't trust you to preach the gospel out on the corner."

Even Bob Novak, the curmudgeonly conservative cohost of *Crossfire,* told me after the show that he was "shocked that Jerry didn't take you up on it."

And then there was the time Falwell called me a "left-wing thug" and the time he said I was a "rancher without any cows"—a bucolic allusion that I had to research on the Internet.

Finally, there was his strangely paranoid comment right before a live side-by-side appearance on yet another *Crossfire* episode. To get me, Falwell, and then cohosts Pat Buchanan and Geraldine Ferraro into the shot, the producers made us sit very close together at a table. About fifteen seconds before airtime, Falwell complained to Buchanan, "Barry's knees are touching mine!" Buchanan quickly responded, "No time to do anything." Quickly picking up on his apparent fear of human (or was it demonic) contact, I waited until we were live and Falwell was complaining about a Disney movie with images he found disturbing to reach over and pat his hand, saying, "If it bothers you, don't watch it." There was a brief moment when I thought Falwell was going to turn to stone.

Pat Robertson is not joining my fan club either. On his daily cable program, *The 700 Club,* he has referred to me as "a ferret," "an intolerant jerk," and "lower than a child molester."

Nevertheless, Robertson and I sometimes have more measured discussions. He even invited me to be one of three liberal debaters at the twenty-fifth anniversary celebration of his Regent University. I was paired with Harvard law professor Alan Dershowitz and American Civil Liberties Union president Nadine Strossen in what was billed as "Clash of the Titans." The conservative titans were Ann Coulter, Jay Sekulow (certainly the best legal mind on the Religious Right), and syndicated columnist David Limbaugh, a kind of poor man's version of his famous brother, Rush.

Dr. James C. Dobson of Focus on the Family seems to see me as a bully. Dobson once groused about me, "Every time I turn around, he's whacking me for something."

Whether I'm a "thug," "ferret," or "titan," the Religious Right finds itself mightily disturbed by my simple affirmation that as a minister (in the United Church of Christ) I stand foursquare in support of a clean and clear separation between religious institutions and government entities—in other words, a sharp demarcation of church and state.

To the Religious Right, separation of church and state is a myth, a dangerous, anti-Christian principle imposed on the nation by judicial fiat in 1947. The results of church-state separation, they contend, have been rampant immorality, plunging SAT scores, increased godlessness in American society, and the literal "persecution," as the aforementioned Limbaugh titled his book, of "people of faith."

To this I can only ask, "What planet are members of the Religious Right living on?"

I've spent nearly my entire adult life defending the separation of church and state from Religious Right attacks. Their history is wrong. Their analysis is wrong. Their attacks on the church-state wall are wrong.

I'll go further: Their agenda for America is wrong. They have hijacked Christianity and claim to speak for all people of faith. They don't. The Religious Right represents a narrow, but powerful, segment of fundamentalists who have had the audacity to wed their faith to ultraconservative political movements. In recent surveys, between 14 percent and 18 percent of Americans proclaim themselves adherents of the Religious Right. Obviously, this means that not all Republicans and not all evangelical and theologically conservative Christians are members of this movement. For the sake of power in the halls of Congress and the White House, they have sold the Savior many of us hold dear down the river and now seek to use the power of the federal government to impose their theology on the rest of us as if we were still stuck in the Middle Ages.

It's time to take the Savior back, repudiate the Middle Ages and rebuke the power-hungry theocrats among us. It's time to rescue religion from the death grip of the Religious Right. It's time to reassert the wisdom of the Founding Fathers who gave us the separation of church and state.

It's time to rally all Americans around that standard. And when I say all Americans, I mean everyone—Christians, Jews, Muslims, Buddhists, Wiccans, pagans, nonbelievers, humanists, the unaffiliated, and others.

That's what this book is designed to do. The separation of church and state is in trouble. It needs your help.

I make no apologies for defending the separation of church and state as a member of America's richly diverse community of faith. In fact, my status as a member of that community is precisely why I do it.

I don't hesitate to rebuke those religious leaders who have gone astray. Those of us who defend church-state separation need to speak up more. We need to challenge the politics of division, the misinformation, and the crude attacks that too often not only mar the Religious Right's perspective but serve as their only perspective. For a few years, I cohosted a radio show with Pat Buchanan on NBC/Mutual Radio. He said in an infamous speech to the Republican National Convention in Houston in 1992, "There is a religious war going on in our country for the soul of America. It is a cultural war, as critical to the kind of nation we will one day be as was the Cold War itself."

Buchanan's rhetoric was strident and his remedies unthinkable— but he was right about the existence of this "war." Our side did not start it, but it does exist. Efforts to act like this isn't a real "war" (as opposed to just one hyped on television) or that a get-along philosophy is the only appropriate approach from any side will increasingly prove disastrous. We'll end up whistling past the graveyard of our Bill of Rights and religious freedom if we take that road.

To find the ideas of the Right reprehensible does not mean that we hate everybody who espouses them. That is truly both an erroneous waste and placement of moral energy. Some years ago, after a particularly tough week, I taped John McLaughlin's *One on One* television show. On it as well was a Religious Right lawyer named Seamus Hasson. At the end of the taping, John said to me, "Barry, your side isn't as passionate as his side." I thought to myself, "That's true, and today even I had run out of it." I've never felt that way since.

To me, church-state separation is the only principle that can protect our legacy of religious freedom. I want no interference with your religious freedom, mine, or the guy's down the street. I want no efforts by the government to "help" religion get the job done.

Religion doesn't need the government's assistance. If we can't do the job on our own through our use of moral persuasion and argument, we have nobody to blame but ourselves.

We can pay for our own schools and social service projects. If the believers in the pews support an idea, they should (and do) put out the money for it. Far from being a radical notion, this is an obvious one.

Our doctrines can be taught in the home and the church. We don't need public schools to spread our message. The men and women who teach and administer public schools may not agree with my view of religion or Christianity. Furthermore, they are not trained in theology. Why on earth would I entrust them with any oversight of the religious life of my children?

There is an appropriate vehicle for spreading religious messages to children, one that is staffed by people who have been trained to do the job right and who have been screened by each house of worship for doctrinal purity: it's often called Sunday school (and characterized by those who accept that the Sabbath, the day of rest, is Saturday by a similar name).

We religious leaders must reject relying on the raw power of the state to enforce our doctrines. No one was ever brought to a genuinely deeper understanding of faith through force or coercion. No one—in any nation on the earth.

We treasure our symbols, our signs, our deeply felt religious language. We are happy to share them with others—but we don't need the state to do it for us. To me, few things could be worse. Our symbols of faith communicate a deep message of what is to us spiritual truth. The government does not have a spiritual truth. Thus, our symbols belong in our homes and in our churches, temples, synagogues, and mosques. They are out of place festooning our courthouses, city halls, and state legislatures.

I look at the current attacks on church-state separation from members of the clergy like Falwell, Robertson, D. James Kennedy, and others and hang my head. Have they no understanding of history?

Don't they even know the history of their own church? Christianity's alliance with governments, from ancient Rome down through the Middle Ages, spawned only oppression of other faiths and led gradually to state control of the clergy.

Religion often seeks an alliance with government, believing it will gain the upper hand. The problem is, it never has. Modern governments especially are too powerful and all-encompassing to cede power to any rival institution. What begins as a partnership soon becomes domination and a co-opted church.

I see an echo of this in modern-day America. President George W. Bush has unveiled a "faith-based" initiative that would award huge government grants to religious groups for social service work. Already some pastors have shifted political allegiances in the hopes of winning a grant. Robertson was an early critic of the idea. He stopped complaining after the federal government gave one of his charities $1.5 million. Another minister, Luis Cortés of Philadelphia, frankly told the *New York Times* that his support was for sale.

"This is what I tell politicians," Cortés said. "You want an endorsement? Give us a check, and you can take a picture of us accepting it. Because then you've done something for [us]." That's candor, but it is also selling your soul.

Thomas Jefferson, James Madison, George Mason, Benjamin Franklin, and other framers knew why we needed to separate church and state. It wasn't because religion is a force for evil. The framers did not believe that. It was because religion, united with the raw power of government, spawns tyranny.

For Jefferson, Madison, and other framers, this was not a theoretical concern. They had seen up close the dangers of an injudicious mixing of religion and government. As a young man, Madison witnessed Baptist preachers languishing in jail because they had dared to preach in public a religious doctrine that conflicted with government-imposed orthodoxy.

The framers knew that people in some colonies enjoyed religious freedom while those living in others had to struggle under the yoke of state-imposed faith. They knew which scenario was better and which one would become the model for the new nation.

They also knew that merely banning an official church was not enough. The First Amendment's religion provisions do not say there will be no state church. They say, "Congress shall make no law respecting an establishment of religion or prohibiting the free exercise thereof." Earlier drafts did indeed simply prohibit the designation of one religion as the official one for the new nation. They were rejected because the framers understood the need to be expansive in their prohibition of aid to religion.

Why such curious language? To the framers, an "establishment of religion" meant laws funding, supporting, or advocating religion. That's why, as president, James Madison vetoed legislation that would have given surplus federal land to a church. Madison wrote in a veto message that it violated the First Amendment.

Madison ought to know. He helped write that provision.

Madison also opposed chaplains in the military and official federal government proclamations calling for days of prayer and fasting. Today's Religious Right acts as if anyone who holds these views is some kind of antireligion extremist. Maybe, like Madison, those who hold these positions simply realize that religion retains its purity and effectiveness when it is far removed from state power.

Too many politicians today not only want church and state closer together, but they also seem to think the government has some role to play in Americans' spiritual lives.

In this book's chapter on faith-based initiatives, I discuss President

Bush promoting his faith-based initiative in New Orleans in January of 2004. Bush told church members that he wants to fund groups that "save Americans, one soul at a time."

Waving a Bible, Bush added, "This handbook is a good go-by . . . Faith-based programs are only effective because they do practice faith . . . only [they] conform to one set of rules, and it's bigger than government rules."

His words sent a shiver down my spine. I do not want, nor need, to be "saved." I cannot imagine a more dangerous role for the government to assume.

I have seen thousands of people whose spiritual lives were enriched or changed through interactions with clergy, churches, temples, mosques, and synagogues. The hard work of bringing a willing participant to faith is never achieved by government fiat or through the actions of a bureaucrat. As a member of the clergy, I frankly resent government's intrusion on my turf. My church doesn't pass appropriations and tax bills, and in return I expect the government to stay out of the business of saving souls—literally or metaphorically.

I was once on FOX News Channel's *Hannity & Colmes* alongside a man named Dan Patrick, who had penned a book titled *The Second Most Important Book You Will Ever Read: A Personal Challenge to Read the Bible.* Patrick seemed to have little interest in discussing the topic of the evening, but he did want to bash me. He noted that he had searched the Nexis news database and found that during the previous year, I had given well over one thousand statements to the media, but in not one of them had I urged people to convert to Christianity. I told him I was glad he found the time for such research (if nothing else, it proves that I am one of the most quoted nonpoliticians in the country) but explained that the reason the press calls me is the part of my life where I work to preserve religious freedom. I do spiritual counseling on request—but not through the newspapers.

If Patrick wanted to hear me explain my theological beliefs, he could have found out where I was preaching a sermon or offering some type of religious service, things I do as a minister unconnected to my work at Americans United. Frankly, I gave up trying to have any intelligent conversation with Patrick. (Well, I did suggest that before he wrote his sequel, which I assumed would be titled *The Third Most Important Book You Will Ever Read,* he might want to read a few on the topic of religious history and the U.S. Constitution. Sometimes the brief length of these television debates can be a true blessing, even if not a divine one.)

From another angle, I sometimes hear interesting comments from nonbelievers because I do speak to many nontheistic gatherings. At the end of an address to the American Humanist Association in Las Vegas, one of the first questioners asked me if I knew the well-known Episcopal clergyman Bishop John Shelby Spong. I replied that I admired Spong's work but had only spoken to him on a few occasions. The questioner continued, "He is a very bright man. You are a very bright man. Since you are both bright, how can you both be stupid enough to believe in God?" The audience sounded shocked, but it is certainly a fair question. I told him this was not the place to address it, though, because I was discussing constitutional issues. Afterward, we did have a perfectly nice conversation where I explained some of my religious ideas and gave him the names of theologians who had been important to my spiritual development.

Sometimes people are surprised to hear a minister so strongly defend the separation of church and state. They shouldn't be. As I explain in chapter 1, members of the clergy, working in conjunction with colonial-era thinkers inspired by the Enlightenment, gave us that separation.

True, some have today strayed from supporting that principle. Ministers beholden to the Religious Right proclaim church-state separation a myth or say it is a recent invention by the Supreme Court.

The more perceptive among us can only be befuddled by such

attacks. We realize that church–state separation has been a great boon for religion. U.S. religious diversity and vitality far outstrips anything found in countries that retain state-established churches. Europe is known for its lackluster religious atmosphere. Countries that have official churches (like Great Britain) or systems of taxpayer-supported religion (like Germany) also have populations who say, by and large, that they regard faith as irrelevant to their daily lives. In Italy, the government negotiates separate agreements with each religion to "accommodate" their special needs, which only works until two groups' "needs" collide. In the United States, secularism is mandated for the government, but religion still pervades the culture with a strong and vibrant voice. In much of Europe, there is no government mandate of secularism, but the cultures are effectively secular. The irony is rich. I don't think there is a better model for the relationship between religion and government than what we have forged.

There is another path, of course: outright theocracies. Sadly, we know such things do still exist. Saudi Arabia is one example, along with several other hard-line Muslim nations. In Saudi Arabia, Pakistan, Iran, and other nations, blasphemy remains a capital offense, and public dissent from an orthodoxy imposed by religious leaders through the state bureaucracy is not permitted.

Except for an extreme radical fringe known as Christian Reconstructionists, few would argue that government enforcement of harsh religious/legal codes is desirable in modern-day America. That leaves us with separation—and I for one am glad to have it. I deplore the attempts to take it away.

I do not mince words. This book speaks without apology for the separation of church and state. While discussing issues such as school prayer, faith-based initiatives, Ten Commandments displays in courthouses, and others, I will return often to a central argument: *Efforts by government to "help" religion don't help at all. They are as unwanted and unnecessary as they are unconstitutional and unwelcome.*

This book speaks to why faith does not need state support. I won't make a specifically theological argument. It is my belief that Jesus Christ did in fact support church-state separation (see Mark 12:13–17), but even if he had remained silent on the subject, I would still contend for that division.

I would do so for two reasons. First, although I was a long time ago persuaded by the doctrines of Christianity, others have taken different spiritual paths and have come to different conclusions. I respect the fundamental human right to make a spiritual choice different from my own. Only church-state separation can guarantee that.

Second, I realize as a religious leader that reliance on government funds or support makes the church lazy. Will members sitting in the pews dig deeper and give their last dollars if the possibility of a government grant is dangled before them?

Religious Right leaders like Falwell have accused me of being "anti-Christian." My support for separation comes not because I hate faith but because I embrace it. Yet I acknowledge that some are moved to support church-state separation because they don't particularly like religion and want to be free of its influences.

To me, this is not a particularly radical point of view. Even the most fervent believer wants to be free from imposed religion—especially if that religion is not his or her own. A conservative Protestant would probably not support school prayer if the prayers were Wiccan (or even Roman Catholic) in nature. A scheme to channel tax funds to a religious group to provide social services would quickly lose support if the body in question were the Reverend Sun Myung Moon's Unification Church.

If there are certain religious perspectives that conservative or orthodox believers are unwilling to support, why are they offended when nonbelievers wish to be free of them all?

Furthermore, I am happy to take the support of nonbelievers and work alongside them to buttress the separation of church and state. I am aware that their goal is not to shut down religion but merely to oppose government-mandated faith. That's the same thing I want. I recognize that church-state separation protects all forms of religious freedom—and that includes the right to reject all faiths.

So, even though I speak in these pages as a man of faith who remains convinced that separation of church and state is healthy for religion in America, I do not wish to commit the offense of excluding anyone else from the cause. People are motivated to support church-state separation for many reasons. Those reasons are less relevant to me than the energy, ideas, and commitment they bring to the cause.

This book will be part manifesto, part call to arms—with some history along the way. I expect I'll step on a few toes, as I've never been one to hide any light under a bushel, especially when it comes to confronting those who oppose and attack the wall of separation between church and state. These days, that means the Religious Right.

Occasionally claims are made that those of us who support church-state separation have overstated the significance of the Religious Right. It's hard to take this argument seriously.

As I was writing this book, a school district in Dover, Pennsylvania, became embroiled in a lawsuit over its decision to offer instruction about "intelligent design," the theological belief that humans are so complex that they must have been designed by God. The Dover School Board lost its case in court when a federal judge, in a sharply worded 139-page decision, struck down the policy. Undaunted, state boards of education in Ohio and Kansas vowed to press ahead with plans to undermine the teaching of evolution, although Ohio later backed down. The governors of Kentucky, Florida, and Texas promptly endorsed intelligent design.

As I was writing this book, news reports chronicled the federal government's practice of restricting sex education funding in public high schools to groups that advocate abstinence-only programs. This funding, heavily lobbied for by Religious Right groups, continues even though studies have shown that abstinence programs do not reduce the rate of teen sexual activity, are often medically inaccurate, and are sometimes rife with sectarian dogma. Things got so bad that the American Civil Liberties Union sued over one group, the Silver Ring Thing, whose program was clearly little more than an extended Bible study. We also learned that one-fourth of all AIDS-related money was going to religious groups. As an Associated Press story that ran in *USA Today* on January 29, 2006, noted, "President Bush's $15 billion effort to fight AIDS has handed out nearly one-quarter of its grants to religious groups, and officials are aggressively pursuing new church partners that often emphasize disease prevention through abstinence and fidelity over condom use."

As I was writing this book, a huge flap erupted about the proper role of religion in the military. Charges that the Air Force Academy had improperly favored evangelical Christianity infuriated Religious Right groups. Efforts by the federal government to enact common-sense regulations for chaplains that respect the healthy religious diversity of the military were attacked as another form of persecution of Christianity. Thanks to the Religious Right, the guidelines were watered down to the point of being useless.

As I was writing this book, the U.S. House of Representatives was embroiled in a debate over allowing religious groups to accept taxpayer money and still engage in forms of religiously based employment discrimination. Prodded by the Religious Right, Congress sought to change civil rights laws so that fundamentalist Christian groups could literally take millions in taxpayer support and then hang out signs reading, "Help Wanted. Catholics, Jews, Muslims, or Atheists Need Not Apply."

As I was writing this book, President Bush had begun reshaping the U.S. Supreme Court with two new appointments who received strong backing from TV preachers and ultraconservative fundamentalist religious groups—justices who clearly seem to be more conservative than moderate, shifting the balance of the court to the right.

These are just a handful of stories plucked at random from headlines at the time. Having monitored the church-state scene for so long, I am well aware of the power of the Religious Right in the halls of Congress, the White House, and the state legislatures.

I disagree with the Religious Right's agenda. I try to disagree with my opponents respectfully, but disagree I do. When they are wrong, I don't hesitate to say so.

In short, if he gets through this book, Jerry Falwell's not going to have any reason to like me any better than he does now—but I hope he'll at least understand where I'm coming from.

1

Freedom of Religion
WHAT IT IS AND WHAT IT IS NOT

I AM A CHRISTIAN MINISTER who strongly supports the separation of church and state—and some leaders of the Religious Right simply cannot deal with that. You've read about some of their personal attacks already.

TV preacher Pat Robertson regularly calls me names. He has also asserted, on numerous occasions, that I take things so far I believe that if a house of worship catches on fire, a municipal fire department cannot extinguish the blaze. (For the record, this is crazy, and I don't believe it.)

The Reverend Jerry Falwell routinely tells reporters that I'm not a real minister. I received my master's of divinity from Boston University School of Theology in 1973 and was ordained in the United Church of Christ later that year—yet Falwell says I'm a phony cleric because right now, instead of pastoring a church, I run Americans United for Separation of Church and State, a national advocacy group based in Washington, D.C.

By Falwell's rather rigid standards, his crony Robertson isn't a real preacher either. After all, Robertson also does not pastor a church and hasn't done so for many years. These days, he mainly claims to heal people over the television.

In fact, as Falwell well knows, a minister does not have to pastor a church to be considered fully ordained. Every year, I preside at weddings, speak at funerals, and deliver sermons as a guest minister in pulpits all over America. Unless Falwell knows something I don't, I have not forfeited my ordination, and my denomination has not revoked it. This means I have the right to function as a minister regularly and consider that a part of my identity. I also hold a law degree, and although I have not argued a case in court for a number of years, being an attorney is also part of who I am.

So what's going on here? Why the personal attacks? Why the need to (literally) put words into my mouth and attack my credentials?

The principal reason is that the Falwell-Robertson line of argument has little support in law, history, or culture. I support complete religious/philosophical freedom for all and believe that only the separation of church and state can give us that. Falwell and Robertson want to see a state based on a religion—theirs.

It's an old story. The Religious Right desperately wants to shift the focus of the debate. The plain truth is that Falwell is angry that any of his fellow Christians would dare to publicly support the separation of church and state, a principle he despises. That a man who believes in God and long ago accepted Jesus Christ would do it outrages him. Therefore, he'd rather attack me personally instead of responding to my views and engaging in a vigorous debate over specific issues. It's called an ad hominem attack—shifting the discussion from issues to personalities—and it's one of the oldest tricks in the book.

What's really bothering guys like Falwell, Robertson, TV preacher D. James Kennedy, and James C. Dobson of Focus on the Family is that the wall of separation between church and state stands as a bulwark against their schemes to force all of us to live under their narrow view of Christianity. They know that. That's why they work overtime to undermine that wall and discredit those who defend it. They want it to collapse and don't care that when it falls, so will the very religious liberty that gives America a special place in the world.

Why is the wall so important? That wall means no one can force your children to pray in public schools against your wishes. It means schoolchildren will learn modern biology, not Bible stories masquerading as science. It means religious groups must rely on moral suasion, not the raw power of the state, to convince people to adopt their views. It means religious organizations must pay their own way in this world, not rely on government-provided handouts coerced from the taxpayer.

All of this drives Falwell and his pals up some other metaphorical wall. What they are really after is a type of theocratic state—with themselves as chief "theo," of course. That may sound harsh, but I mean it. I am convinced that these folks would have felt better in the world of the Puritans, where heretics could be labeled witches and hanged. (This is probably why the late Arthur Miller's play *The Crucible,* about parallels between the Salem witch trials and 1950s McCarthyism, is so frequently the target of censorship efforts.) I've studied the tactics of these groups for more than thirty years. I know what they want. They want to run your life, mine, and everyone else's as much as they possibly can.

Amazingly, Religious Right groups that now claim to control both houses of Congress, have an open line to the White House, and have four or five ideological cohorts on the U.S. Supreme Court still carp about being victims of persecution. Are we seriously to believe these groups are somehow marginalized and frozen out of American society?

Far from being cast out of public life, the Religious Right all too often seems to dominate our national dialogue, bringing to bear only a loud voice of intolerance and division. Issues like same-sex marriage, legal abortion, and the proper role of religion in public schools and government are marred by abrasive Religious Right leaders whose rhetoric usually simplifies complex issues, providing far more heat than light.

Falwell rode a wave of political activism in the early 1980s. By all rights, he should be considered a has-been today. Yet he practically lives on the FOX News Channel and visits CNN and MSNBC as regularly as you'd drop by a friend's house. Falwell is constantly sought out by the media as if his narrow, fundamentalist version of Christianity, which in my view has little in common with what Jesus taught, sets the gold standard.

Pat Robertson, too, routinely says things that can only be described as bizarre and offensive. Two days after the horrific terrorist attacks of September 11, 2001, Falwell and Robertson joined forces on Robertson's *700 Club* to muse about how the nation had finally gotten what it deserved for turning its back on God. The two blamed the horrific attack not on cold-blooded terrorists but on liberals and the ACLU, opining that the assault was a form of punishment from God.

"What we saw on Tuesday, as terrible as it is, could be minuscule if, in fact, in fact, God continues to lift the curtain and allow the enemies of America to give us probably what we deserve," Falwell said.

Robertson replied, "Jerry, that's my feeling."

There was an uproar, but it did not last. Those comments should have forever exiled Falwell and Robertson from polite society. Instead they soon returned and still retain access to the halls of power.

Robertson's track record in this area is long and strange. He is a wealthy man, and it's a good thing for him that he is; otherwise, he would have been marginalized a long time ago. This is a man, after all, who believes that God punishes communities that displease him with hurricanes, floods, and meteors; who asserts that demons control major U.S. cities and who thinks Harry Potter books lure children into practicing witchcraft. Most recently, he advocated assassinating the democratically elected president of Venezuela and told his national television audience that God smote Ariel Sharon with a stroke because Sharon gave land to the Palestinians. Robertson's views come straight out of the Middle Ages but are disseminated worldwide by twenty-first-century technology.

Robertson is a big booster of the "poor persecuted Christians" line. Here's one of his gems from the *700 Club:* "Just like what Nazi Germany did to the Jews, so liberal America is now doing to the evangelical Christians. It's no different. It is the same thing. It is happening all over again."

Oh, really? Six million evangelical Christians have been sent to concentration camps and gassed to death? The fact that Robertson would equate the alleged "persecution" of evangelicals in America with the Holocaust shows how deeply twisted his worldview really is. What Robertson calls persecution is really the attempt by the courts to enforce a reasonable separation of church and state so that theocrats are not permitted to employ the engine of the government to run and ruin the lives of the rest of us.

Let's take a closer look at the so-called persecution Robertson, Falwell, Dobson, and other Religious Right honchos must labor under:

Jerry Falwell Ministries took in $15,266,689 tax free in fiscal year 2004. Falwell runs his own university, several political groups, and is aligned with a legal organization called Liberty Counsel. When you add it all up, these Falwell-related organizations, all of which enjoy tax-exempt status, pulled in $95,348,265 in twelve months alone.

Robertson, like Falwell, oversees a powerful Religious Right octopus with many tentacles. His Christian Broadcasting Network reaches one million viewers a day and collected $186,482,060 tax free in 2004. Operation Blessing, a controversial charity run by

Robertson, has received millions in direct government grants and in-kind aid. After Hurricane Katrina, the Federal Emergency Management Administration Web site listed recommended groups that were helping provide relief. Operation Blessing was number two, right after the American Red Cross.

Robertson runs his own graduate-level university and a legal group, the American Center for Law and Justice. Adding it all up, Robertson's tax-free empire in 2004 took in $461,475,115. Robertson's CBN has an endowment of $2 billion—ensuring that the operation will live on even after Robertson is gone.

James Dobson, a powerful Religious Right broadcaster and psychologist, reaches five million U.S. radio listeners *every day.* Dobson's Focus on the Family broadcasts worldwide, even in countries like China that are not usually welcoming to evangelicals. He presides over not a building but a campus in Colorado Springs. In 2004 Dobson groups brought in $150,017,629 in tax-free donations.

Even smaller Religious Right outfits do quite well. The Family Research Council, a Washington-based political lobby started by Dobson that still works hand in glove with him, has an annual budget of $10 million. D. James Kennedy's Coral Ridge Ministries collected $37,403,206 in fiscal year 2004. Even the Reverend Louis P. Sheldon, who along with his daughter runs an outfit with an antigay focus called the Traditional Values Coalition, brought in $8,795,084 in 2004.

So this is persecution—unlimited access to the airwaves, huge, tax-free empires, and direct-mail operations that bring in millions annually. Get me in line for some! I should also note that especially in the case of TV preachers, there is virtually no government oversight of the activities of these religious organizations. Many TV preachers and their top lawyers and advisers lead flashy lifestyles, own several homes and fancy cars, and continue to collect millions tax free every year.

The fact is, far from being persecuted, religious organizations in America enjoy substantial benefits and reap great respect. Tax exemption, in and of itself a very desirable benefit, is extended to religious groups by virtue of their very existence. Under special legislation and unlike other nonprofits, houses of worship don't have to apply for tax-exempt status and deal with cumbersome paperwork. They are assumed to have it as soon as they form. Federal law also makes it exceedingly difficult to audit a church, but secular nonprofits can be audited more or less at the discretion of the Internal Revenue Service.

Nor are religious leaders barred from speaking out on moral, social, and political issues. They do it all of the time, and nothing in the law prevents it. All nonprofit groups that hold the 501(c)(3) tax exemption are barred from endorsing or opposing candidates for public office, but this ban does not extend to discussion of issues. Houses of worship not only deliberate issues, they act on them. Denominational lobbyists troll the halls of Capitol Hill and statehouses, lobbying legislators alongside defense contractors, tobacco industry representatives, and advocates for labor unions. People have mixed feelings about the appropriateness of church lobbying, but the fact that it is so common clearly debunks ludicrous claims that religious voices are crying out in the wilderness, unheard by anyone but forest animals.

Whether through culture or custom, the law often treats religious groups with kid gloves. A wide-ranging scandal over child sexual abuse engulfed the Roman Catholic Church in the 1990s. Evidence abounds that church officials covered up allegations of abuse and reassigned suspected priests to keep them one step ahead of the law. A corporation whose leaders did the same would have been shut down, its leaders put behind bars. Yet while a few individual clerics have been imprisoned, the U.S. leadership of the Catholic Church has never been held accountable by law enforcement officials. The only way some victims could get justice was through civil lawsuits.

Persecuted groups have no political capital and are despised by the government. Does that sound like evangelical Christianity? The very idea is absurd. Evangelical groups enjoy more political influence now than they ever have and meddle in our personal lives in unprecedented ways. Conservative Christian organizations hold a veritable veto power over Supreme Court appointments, for example. President George W. Bush was forced to replace Court nominee Harriet Miers after complaints from the Religious Right. Ironically, White House strategist Karl Rove had even called Dobson to tell him of Miers's nomination in advance of a public announcement, specifically noting that she attended a conservative church with a history of "pro-life" activism.

Political analysts agree that the Religious Right holds the Republican Party in a type of headlock. Only candidates who submit to the Religious Right's ideological litmus test—anti–legal abortion, anti–gay rights—can make it through the GOP primaries. Dobson roams the country, endorsing candidates and bragging about his political power. He claims to have played the decisive role in the defeat of U.S. senator Thomas Daschle in 2004 and pressures other "red state" Democrats to do his bidding, lest they meet the same fate.

Megachurches dot our landscape. Religious television and radio broadcasting is a multimillion dollar business. Religious publishing rakes in millions more; Tim LaHaye's *Left Behind* series of apocalyptic potboilers topped the bestsellers lists for months. On any given weekend, about half of the adult population attends a religious service of some type, and more than 90 percent of Americans say they do not doubt the existence of God. Most people think well of religion. They certainly have no desire to persecute it.

Religion has invaded our political system to such an extent that it befuddles and sometimes even alarms Europeans. Politicians trip over themselves to talk about what their faith means to them, and no candidate or officeholder in his or her right mind dares to end a speech with any phrase other than "God bless America." During the 2000 primary season, the GOP contenders were asked during an Iowa debate to name their favorite political philosopher. When George W. Bush replied, "Jesus Christ," subsequent speakers generally gave a thumbs-up to the Savior also, although even some fundamentalists found Bush's description of Jesus as a political philosopher a little strange.

When asked to name a favorite book, political hopefuls know that answers other than the Bible are unacceptable. This has led to several embarrassing incidents. President George H. W. Bush once read a speech in which he cited John 16:3 as a favorite biblical passage. He had obviously meant John 3:16, a passage favored by evangelicals. In 2004 former Vermont governor Howard Dean, then seeking the Democratic presidential nomination, told a questioner that Job was his favorite book in the New Testament. Of course, Job is an Old Testament book.

This is persecution? This is a government-approved drive to eradicate religion from public life? Hardly. Religion in America is alive and well, and it prospers thanks to, not in spite of, the separation of church and state.

At its root, the Religious Right will not come to grips with some of the essential truths of the Constitution, American history, and the nature of our judicial system. These are three big strikes against them. Here are a few ways this confusion plays out in their approach to power:

First, members of the Religious Right are angry because the government will not enforce their religious dogma and extend preferential treatment to fundamentalist forms of Christianity. What they fail to understand is that freedom of religion means you have a voice in the public debate—not a guarantee of control. Religious groups, like every other organization in society, get a place at the table. What the Religious Right wants is the power to control the table and saw the legs off the chairs of the people they don't want sitting at it.

The Religious Right has a confused definition of freedom of religion. Movement leaders seem to believe that natural resistance to their schemes is an attempt to deny them the right to worship. Not so. Freedom of religion means lots of things: It's the right to worship or not worship as you see fit. It's the right to join in communion with a like-minded body of believers free from undue intermeddling and regulation by the state. It's the right to evangelize and spread the doctrines of the faith even in public spaces with private resources. It includes the right to approach government officials and advocate for causes and concerns. It doesn't mean the right to run everyone else's lives.

In a famous passage in the 1947 case *Everson v. Board of Education,* the U.S. Supreme Court explained how the First Amendment bar on laws "respecting an establishment of religion" protect religious liberty. The court observed:

> The "establishment of religion" clause of the First Amendment means at least this: Neither a state nor the Federal Government can set up a church. Neither can pass laws which aid one religion, aid all religions, or prefer one religion over another. Neither can force nor influence a person to go to or to remain away from church against his will or force him to profess a belief or disbelief in any religion. No person can be punished for entertaining or professing religious beliefs or disbeliefs, for church attendance or non-attendance. No tax in any amount, large or small, can be levied to support any religious activities or institutions, whatever they may be called, or whatever form they may adopt to teach or practice religion. Neither a state nor the Federal Government can, openly or secretly, participate in the affairs of any religious organizations or groups and vice versa. In the

words of Jefferson, the clause against establishment of religion by law was intended to erect "a wall of separation between Church and State."

It's a sensible definition. Had the Court itself fully adhered to it and the American people had its uniquely American significance explained to them, the nation would have been spared a lot of heartache. But the *Everson* language has been vociferously opposed by the Religious Right and their champions on the Court for close to sixty years. The Religious Right opposes it precisely because that language, if consistently applied, would block their efforts to control society. And control of society is what the Religious Right wants, not some generalized religious freedom or freedom of conscience for everyone living here.

The Religious Right seeks to change the definition of religious freedom and convince the American public that religious freedom means things it was never intended to encompass—mainly, that government has some sort of duty or obligation to "help" or promote religion, and if it does not do so, religious freedom is violated.

Nonsense. The *Everson* court had it right. The Religious Right's definition of religious freedom is upside down. While the parameters of religious freedom can be difficult to pin down sometimes, there are certain proposals, activities, and demands made by the Religious Right under the guise of religious freedom that, if enacted, would actually lessen religious liberty and defeat the whole purpose of the First Amendment. For example:

Religious freedom does not mean the right to employ the machinery of the state to achieve theological goals. Religious groups must use moral persuasion and good arguments to convince people to voluntarily adopt their positions on matters of faith and personal morality. If people choose not to, the principle of religious freedom does not mean that the government can or should act as religion's enforcer.

Religious freedom does not mean the government must financially subsidize religious organizations or houses of worship. Mandatory, taxpayer-supported religion is the antithesis of religious freedom. No one who is forced to support religion against his or her will is truly free. Religious freedom gives all faith groups the right to exist and contend for their views and to seek new members and support. But if the people do not choose to support a certain group, its leaders have no right to expect a bailout from the state. This principle should not be negated merely because a group does good work or is well liked in the community or throughout the country.

Religious freedom is for everyone and every group—period. Religious groups that are large and have millions of members do not have more freedom or rights than smaller organizations. Religious groups with doctrines perceived to be unusual have the same rights as long-established groups. All religious groups must abide by certain secular laws. All are equal in the eyes of the state. A benefit extended to one must be extended to all. There is no hierarchy of favored religions and unfavored ones. When it comes to religion, the majority does *not* rule!

This last point has been especially difficult for the Religious Right to grasp. Its leaders often argue that the United States is a "Christian nation," and therefore Christians should have more influence over the government or even receive some type of favored treatment. This fallacy is a prime example of their second major area of ignorance: American history itself.

The Christian nation argument suffers from several flaws—fatally, that nowhere does the Constitution state that the country is Christian. In fact, the Constitution contains no references to Jesus Christ, Christianity, or even God for that matter. The fact that above the signatures is the phrase "in the year of our Lord" is purely stylistic and not theologically significant.

There are only two references to religion in the Constitution: the

First Amendment, which bars laws "respecting an establishment of religion or prohibiting the free exercise thereof," and Article VI, which guarantees that no American will be banned from or favored in holding federal office on the basis of his or her religious beliefs. (This article states that "no religious test shall ever be required as a qualification to any office or public trust under the United States.")

Some conservative ministers of the founding era were aware of the Constitution's secular nature, and they considered it a defect. Many blasted the document from their pulpits and asserted that a country that did not proclaim its faith in Christianity front and center could never survive. They were not pleased either when in an early treaty with Tripoli, President John Adams and the U.S. Senate signed off on a passage that read, "As the government of the United States is not, in any sense, founded on the Christian religion."

In the post–Civil War period, conservative ministers grew so frustrated that they actually formed a political lobby to pressure for rewriting the preamble to the Constitution to include specific references to Christianity and Jesus Christ. Congressional committees deliberated the amendment for several years, but it never came close to passage.

Frustrated over the lack of references to Christianity in the Constitution, today's Religious Right activists have had to rely on other documents to pitch their case. Some point to the Mayflower Compact. This document inspired the Puritans' avowedly theocratic colony and cannot seriously be seen as a model for the First Amendment or looked at as something worth emulating today.

Still others point to the Declaration of Independence, but again they find no comfort here. The Declaration refers not to Jesus Christ or God but a deistic "Creator" from whom rights flow. In this view, God, much like a clock maker, set things in motion and then went on a perpetual family vacation. The term sounds somewhat jarring today because Deism is a barely noticed religious system, but to the educated eighteenth-century resident, it was perfectly acceptable to speak of a higher power in these completely abstract terms. Enlightenment-era values sought to merge religious thought with a rationalistic approach that stripped religion of its more exuberant features and miraculous claims.

Thomas Jefferson, the author of the Declaration, was himself convinced that much of the Christianity of his day relied too much on superstition and claims of miracles. His mind-set was far from evangelical, and he once expressed his belief that a form of rational-based Unitarianism would become the general religion of the country. Jefferson rejected belief in the Trinity, calling it "an unintelligible dogma," and saw Jesus as a great moral teacher but not the son of God.

After leaving the White House, Jefferson for years tried to find someone who would rewrite the New Testament, stripping away what he saw as fantastic claims and unnecessary appeals to divinity. Unable to find a suitable candidate for the job, Jefferson undertook the project himself. His "Life and Morals of Jesus of Nazareth" is a remarkable document, more for what it says about Jefferson than Jesus. Jefferson's Jesus makes no claim to divinity and performs no miracles. Jefferson sought a faith anchored in reason and would be appalled at the idea that religion must go to war against science and modern thought.

Jefferson was not an atheist, but he was never afraid to subject the claims of religion to harsh scrutiny. He once advised his nephew, Peter Carr, to "question with boldness even the existence of a God." If there is a God, Jefferson opined, he must approve more of reason than of "blindfolded fear."

Imagine if Jefferson were alive and running for office today. His bold dismissal of miracles, his rejection of the Trinity, and his advice to his nephew would make him the Religious Right's public enemy number one. It is a great irony that Jefferson, the man who helped birth our republic, could not today be elected to any office in it. It is doubly ironic because when a phrase or action of Jefferson serves the purpose of the Religious Right, the core of his life and thinking is ignored, and he becomes a "hero" to them. Some of these examples are wrenched from context. For example, Jefferson did not object to federal buildings being used for religious services since Washington, D.C., was still being built during his presidency and churches had not yet been constructed. To the Religious Right, this mundane fact becomes reason to assert that Jefferson must not have really supported church-state separation.

Despite the plain language of the Constitution, a Christian nation myth retains great power among the Religious Right. It's powerful to them because it feeds a common form of collective delusion that has plagued societies since ancient times, that of the stolen legacy. The stolen legacy myth holds that a certain group of people once founded or helped to shape a great nation but that their achievements have been either covered up, denied, or systematically eradicated by usurpers.

The usurpers, this myth holds, have suppressed the "real" history of the people because if it becomes known, the usurpers will lose their grip on power. Usually the usurpers are portrayed as having evil designs on the society or some type of nefarious end goal. In the case of the Religious Right and the proponents of the Christian nation myth, the usurpers are usually described as the "far left," "radical secularists," "secular humanists," "anti-Christians," or some other descriptive term. The goal of these groups, according to the myth, is the eradication of Christianity and its positive influences on society.

Adherents of the myth assert that the usurpers have rewritten history or suppressed certain facts to create a distorted view that backs the usurpers' agenda. Thus, Christian nation advocates often argue that today's advocates of church-state separation lie about Jefferson's real views. Some Religious Right leaders and activists attempt to argue that Jefferson was really a conservative, almost fundamentalist, Christian who would today cast his lot with Falwell and Robertson.

Myth backers often go to great lengths to create an alternative, though completely fictitious, "history" that supports their view. For example, the claim that Jefferson was a fundamentalist is easily disproved by an examination of his voluminous writings on religion and specifically Christianity. In one 1819 letter, Jefferson actually listed the features of Christianity he could not accept. These include the resurrection, the Trinity, the divinity of Jesus, the New Testament miracles, and the immaculate conception, among others.

Obviously, someone who rejects the core tenets of Christianity cannot be accurately described as a fundamentalist. How do myth advocates deal with this? They simply ignore this letter, relying instead on an anecdote that has been making the rounds on the Internet lately. According to this story, Jefferson was accosted while attending a church service one Sunday and asked why he was there when he obviously did not accept the doctrines of Christianity. Jefferson, the story goes, went on to praise Christian theology and insist it was the best form of religion.

There is one problem with this story: it was told many years after Jefferson's death by a man who claimed to have been about ten when he heard Jefferson say it. Obviously, a secondhand, single-source tale that cannot be confirmed does not compete with a letter in Jefferson's own hand plainly stating his views. Yet myth advocates elevate the story while ignoring the letter. Since the letter is not in common currency and is known mainly by those who have studied Jefferson's life, it is easy to overlook or suppress. The story about Jefferson going to church, meanwhile, has strong imagery and conveys the power of oral tradition. Many such tales are false—consider young George Washington's chopping down of the cherry tree—but they retain currency in the culture and continue to be handed down and believed by many. Simply put, facts often cannot compete with a good story.

A similar fate has befallen Jefferson's famous 1802 letter to the Danbury Baptist Association of Connecticut. This is the missive in which Jefferson employed the famous metaphor of the First Amendment, creating a "wall of separation between church and state." This letter is a great embarrassment to the Religious Right because in it Jefferson speaks so plainly of the need for a division between religion and government. Thus, Religious Right revisionists have taken to adding passages to the letter that are not in it or simply making up stories about why Jefferson wrote it. For example, Religious Right activist and "historian" David Barton of Texas for many years insisted that in the letter Jefferson spoke of the wall as being "one directional," meant only to protect the church from incursions by the state. Mainstream historians have debunked this folderol, but Barton's claims still circulate widely among the Religious Right.

Any historian who has studied the letter can easily debunk Barton's wild tales. But most Americans lack this background. They may have heard of Jefferson's letter, but few have actually read it. Fewer still have read the Baptist letter to Jefferson that sparked his famous reply. Having not read the Baptist epistle, they lack the context for Jefferson's response and have no idea why he employed the wall metaphor and fail to grasp its significance.

The facts are easy to ascertain: The Baptists of Danbury, Connecticut, wrote to Jefferson because they lived in a state that still had an established church—Congregationalism. This angered the Baptists, and rightly so. In their letter, the Baptists pour out their frustrations but also express hope that a Jeffersonian view of religious liberty will one day pervade the nation.

Jefferson's reply includes the famous phrase "Believing with you that religion is a matter which lies solely between man and his God, that he owes account to none other for his faith or his worship, that the legitimate powers of government reach actions only, and not opinions, I contemplate with sovereign reverence that act of the whole American people which declared that their legislature should 'make no law respecting an establishment of religion, or prohibiting the free exercise thereof,' thus building a wall of separation between Church & State."

Jefferson saw the reply as important. He also knew the letter would become public, as missives from prominent figures generally did at that time. Thus, Jefferson consulted with his attorney general before sending his reply to the Danbury Baptists, stating clearly that he saw his answer as an opportunity to make a major public statement on church-state relations.

A figure like James Madison is even more susceptible to abuse at the hands of Religious Right myth advocates. Although he wrote the Constitution and the Bill of Rights and helped establish religious freedom in Virginia, Madison is a shadowy figure to most Americans. His accomplishments are neither understood nor appreciated. In many ways, Madison was just as powerful an advocate for separation of church and state as Jefferson, but this is not widely known. Madison lacked Jefferson's dramatic flair and failed to cut such a romantic figure. He remains to most people a fairly obscure person, overshadowed even by his own wife, the reportedly vivacious Dolley.

Thus, it is easy to put words in Madison's mouth, and this is just what the myth boosters have done. A quotation frequently circulates on the Internet, attributed to Madison, that lauds the Ten Commandments as the basis of American government. The problem is, no one has been able to produce an original source for this statement, and it appears nowhere among Madison's papers. The statement is also incongruous with just about everything else Madison wrote concerning church-state separation. To anyone familiar with Madison's writings in this area, the Ten Commandments quote is jarring, ill fitting. It is almost certainly a fabrication. Yet it appears in newspaper columns, letters to the editor, and Web postings constantly, attributed to Madison.

The irony is that the real achievements of Jefferson and Madison in the arena of religious freedom are considerable and in no need of embellishment. This is not a history book, and I do not intend to recap that struggle for religious liberty and church-state separation here. But I do want to note that while some conservative Christians of the day attacked Jefferson and opposed his view on religious liberty, by no means did all do so.

Many colonies had established churches and compelled everyone to support them. Virginia's established religion was Anglicanism, and government officials there would not allow ministers from other denominations to preach in public. Baptists, who were just as theologically conservative then as they are today, strongly opposed this system of partnership between church and state. They joined forces with Jefferson and other thinkers inspired by Enlightenment values to press for the complete separation of church and state.

The story of how these two camps put aside their theological differences to work together has been told many times. I won't recount it in detail here. My point is that the creation of the separation of church and state had strong involvement from the religious community. It would not have happened without religious leaders. When, in 1784, Patrick Henry proposed taxing all Virginia residents to pay for the propagation of Christianity, opposition letters poured in from all corners of the state—from pastors and their congregants. Madison had penned a powerful document, the "Memorial and Remonstrance Against Religious Assessments," to rally opposition to the Henry proposal, but it would have remained mere fancy words on a page had not the state's religious leaders spearheaded a campaign to circulate it, collect opposition signatures, and get them back to the state capital.

Thus, separation of church and state was not the brainchild of forces opposed to religion. Rather, it was the heartfelt desire, and eventually the demand, of devoutly religious people—people who were weary of being told by the government that their religion was unimportant, unpleasing to God, and even corrosive.

One of the first advocates of separation of church and state in the colonies was Roger Williams—a Puritan minister who briefly became a Baptist and then drifted into a more idiosyncratic spirituality. Nearly every argument Williams made was couched in religious terms. Forced religion, he insisted, was an affront to God. State-mandated faith, he opined, "stinks in the nostrils of God." Churches, Williams insisted, were corrupted by alliances with governments and became spiritually bankrupt, lethargic, and irrelevant.

In defense of religious liberty, Williams often employed language that sounds strident to today's ears. "I must profess," he once wrote, "while Heaven and Earth lasts, that no one Tenet that either London, England, or the World doth harbor, is so heretical, blasphemous, seditious, and dangerous to the corporal, to the spiritual, to the present, to the Eternal Good of Men, as the bloody Tenet . . . of persecution for the cause of conscience."

Williams was hard core. He would have offended Falwell and the entire news staff at the FOX News Channel. When he found out that Massachusetts's leaders had decided to require all men to swear a loyalty oath ending in "So help me, God," Williams protested sharply. Requiring a man to take a religious oath that he did not believe in, Williams pointed out, would be "to take the name of God in vain."

Perhaps Williams thought he was being helpful. The religious/political establishment of Massachusetts had other ideas. They kicked Williams out. He lived among the native people for a time and eventually founded the colony that became Rhode Island.

Williams was no freethinker. In fact, he tended to be somewhat dogmatic in his personal religious views and often criticized members of other denominations. Williams chided members of other faiths for their dogma, but he did not try to suppress them. Williams did not think much of Quakers, but Quakers worshipped unmolested in Rhode Island on Williams's watch. Williams believed that the best way to correct someone who had adopted theological error ✓ was through dialogue and spirited debate, not the torture rack or the raw power of the government. It was a remarkable and uncommon view in the seventeenth century.

Yet it was not to remain so unusual. More than one hundred years after Williams, Baptist minister John Leland echoed many of his sentiments. "Government should protect every man in thinking, and speaking freely," Leland once wrote, "and that one does not abuse another . . . [A]ll should be equally free, Jews, Turks, Pagans and Christians."

Leland also abhorred the notion that a man should have to believe certain Christian doctrines as a condition of holding public office. "If a man merits the confidence of his neighbors in Virginia—let him worship one God, twenty Gods or no God—be he Jew, Turk, Pagan, or Infidel, he is eligible to any office in the state," he once asserted.

Leland said these things, yet he was a devout Christian and today would probably be considered quite far to the right on a theological scale. How many Religious Right leaders today would stand up for the right of a pagan or atheist to hold public office? How many would publicly endorse the right to worship twenty gods?

Leland had absolutely no problem working with Jefferson, despite Jefferson's unorthodox religious views. In fact, Baptist clergy around the country looked to Jefferson as their champion. Celebrating Jefferson's election to the presidency, Leland on January 1, 1802, arrived in Washington with a gift for Jefferson from Massachusetts Baptists. It was a giant wheel of cheese accompanied by a card that read, "The greatest cheese in America for the greatest man in America!"

A fellow Massachusetts Baptist, Isaac Backus, was so infuriated over the combination of church and state that he refused to pay a church tax and was tossed in prison. He once wrote, "[R]eligion is a concern between God and the soul with which no human authority can intermeddle."

Conservative Christians and religious skeptics are often today portrayed as bitter enemies. This is ironic, as historically they were partners and the best of friends. Were it not for their cooperation, our nation might not have the full measure of religious liberty it enjoys today.

What happened? In a nutshell, theologically conservative religions began to grow in numbers in the new nation. Jefferson's vision of a Unitarian America never came to pass. Instead, a series of "Great Awakenings" in the early nineteenth century made conservative forms of Christianity dominant. A generic form of Protestantism, generally conservative on theology and social mores, took hold and became a type of de facto established faith.

Having tasted power, many of the conservative Christian leaders decided they liked it. Their support for religious freedom for everyone—even for denominations they disagreed with on doctrine—began to erode. In the mid-nineteenth century, many Protestant leaders violently opposed immigration from Roman Catholic countries. They used the power of the government to impose Protestant forms of religion on Catholics, especially youngsters attending public schools (see more on this in chapter 2). Arguments were made that the United States was meant to be a "Christian" (that is, Protestant) nation and that the Constitution should reflect this. This led to the rise of the National Reform Association, a post–Civil War pressure group and type of proto–Religious Right organization.

The conflict over religion's role in society was spirited, even violent on occasion. Some political leaders inflamed the situation, but others sought solutions. During his tenure in office, President Ulysses S.

Grant offered what we can now see was a sensible compromise. Grant recommended ending sectarianism in public schools, that is, mandatory Protestant instruction, and also opposed government aid to religious education. Grant proposed codifying these features in a constitutional amendment. His thinking was that secular public schools would welcome Catholics as well as Protestants and end political battles over extending tax aid to denominational schools.

It didn't work out that way. Conservative Protestant groups had an agenda that went far beyond "Christianizing" public education and were in no mood for compromise. Led by the National Reform Association, they continued to press for this wide-ranging agenda.

A time-traveling Jerry Falwell would fit right in at a National Reform Association meeting. The group, as I mentioned earlier, pressed for a "Christian nation" amendment to the Constitution and also advocated laws curtailing commerce and other activities on Sunday. Its members, drawn from eleven major Protestant denominations, turned their backs on their own history and sought alignment with the government as a way of achieving a theocratic state.

Naturally not everyone who belonged to these denominations agreed. There are still Southern Baptist moderates today who celebrate the legacy of John Leland and back the separation of church and state. But as years passed, the leaders of these denominations became increasingly conservative—some might say reactionary—and this had a clear effect on the men and women in the pews.

The Christian nation myth became stock in trade for the nineteenth-century theocrats and has reverberated down to the present today. Thus today's Religious Right leaders do hearken back to a past time when they launch their crusades—but it is a past that would be alien to Jefferson, Leland, and other religious and political leaders of the founding era.

Finally, aside from promoting poor history, the Religious Right also seems to fail to respect the very rule of law itself. This is much more than having an occasional pastor on the political right or left, after careful consideration of options and consequences, decide to break a law deemed "unjust." (On the left, this could include a pastor sitting down at a lunch counter segregated by law or burning a draft card; on the right, it might involve refusing to send a child to mandated sex-education class or using a church for an activity proscribed by zoning laws.)

The Religious Right's argument lately is phrased as the absence of "authority" of the courts. That is, they assert that the courts simply do not have the power to issue the rulings they do. You will read later how this played out in the cases of Judge Roy Moore and Terri Schiavo. In those cases, there seemed to be a virtual contempt for the very framework of legal justice. Yet even Jesus conceded the essential validity of the social order, reminding people that they should "render unto Caesar the things that are Caesar's and unto God the things that are God's" (Matthew 22:21). Moreover, in the rest of the New Testament, with the possible exception of the letter of James, there is strong support for the civil government, even when it is opposing Christians.

After the election of 2000, many on the Religious Right hoped to see President Bush appoint "godly" men to the federal courts who would end what remained of the ideas expressed in the *Everson* case. Sadly, some went so far as to pray "imprecatory" prayers against members of the Supreme Court with whom they disagreed on reproductive choice and church-state issues, calling on God to bring down death or illness.

By 2005 the Religious Right was claiming that virtually any federal court nominee proposed by Bush who didn't get immediate consent from the Senate with a vote of approval was probably being waylaid because of "antireligious" forces. One example, William Pryor, former attorney general of Alabama, was nominated for a slot on the U.S. Court of Appeals for the Eleventh Circuit. Pryor had made some astounding comments in the past, and some of us thought this raised serious doubts about his ability to distinguish his personal, deeply felt religious beliefs from his obligation as a federal judge to make decisions rooted solidly in constitutional values and Supreme Court precedent.

For example, Pryor once called *Roe v. Wade* "the worst abomination of constitutional law in our history" and, during a rally in support of Judge Moore, told the crowd, "God has chosen, through his son Jesus Christ, this time, this place for all Christians—Protestants, Catholics and Orthodox—to save our country and save our courts."

In light of these comments, I did not think it was too much for the Senate Judiciary Committee to clarify that nothing in Pryor's background would preclude him from making an objective analysis of cases. When a few senators simply acknowledged that such questioning was reasonable, they were immediately labeled religious bigots or anti-Catholic. (I hadn't even known Pryor held to that faith.) They were accused of advocating a "religious litmus test" on would-be judges. All of this just because a few senators wanted to give Pryor a chance to say, "I'm objective; my personal views are not what I will use as a judge."

This issue became even more of a focus when President Bush announced his intention to elevate federal judges John Roberts and Samuel Alito to the Supreme Court. In a "dueling op-ed" I did with Jay Sekulow, Robertson's top legal eagle, he accused me of denying judgeships on the basis of religious belief. Again, all I thought was that a clarification would be useful. In all of those cases, we'll be able to assess a few years down the road whether personal religious views have indeed trumped basic constitutional principles.

All of this talk about "religious litmus tests" was particularly hypocritical because the president himself, in an unguarded moment, essentially admitted he had one: no nonbelievers on federal courts. Bush, while attending an economic summit in Canada, attacked a federal court that had declared recitation of the phrase "under God" in Pledge of Allegiance public school exercises unconstitutional, remarking, "I believe that points up the fact that we need common-sense judges who understand that our rights were derived from God. And those are the kind of judges I intend to put on the bench." Did Bush literally "vet" every judge's theological views? He would never say, but no administration official can ever give me one name of a freethinker on the president's judicial selection list.

As these debates were playing out, the Family Research Council was holding a series of three "Justice Sunday" rallies, which were nationally broadcast on Christian radio and television networks, where Religious Right luminaries consistently used words that described the federal judiciary as filled with "unelected," "black-robed," and "activist" judges.

Why such inflammatory rhetoric? These Religious Right leaders know that the Constitution mandates that federal judges be appointed, not elected, so they are not subject to majoritarian whims or political pressures once in office. They know they wear black robes as a symbol of the soberness of the courts—even though the Religious Right constantly uses the term to imply that black is somehow equivalent to immorality and evil. Finally, they know an "activist judge" is simply a judge who writes an opinion the Religious Right does not like. If the outcome is favorable to adherents of the Right, they don't care how ingenious a judge is in reaching his or her conclusion.

I had the privilege of speaking in a large African-American church outside Memphis at a counterpoint to Justice Sunday II. I told the gathering this: "It is those judges in black robes who stopped the cowards in white sheets and their political allies from killing the advance of educational and voting rights for all Americans. It was those judges who said that we as parents had the right to direct the religious upbringing of our children, not to have the government write prayers that our children would feel forced to recite. It was those courts that said women had both the moral authority and responsibility to make choices about childbearing, not to be second-guessed by men in political office. There is nothing to be ashamed of in those actions."

Most of Bush's judicial appointments—even the ones with extreme views like Pryor—waltzed onto the courts. (Bush used a maneuver called a recess appointment to bypass the Senate and put Pryor on the Eleventh Circuit.) Bush appointees now sit on the federal courts at all levels, yet the Religious Right still is not satisfied. This leads them to suggest sweeping changes to our system and to promote even more bizarre proposals.

For example, many Religious Right leaders are now enamored of "court stripping"—a concept not nearly as interesting as it sounds at first blush. This scheme would deny power to the federal courts, even the U.S. Supreme Court, to adjudicate controversies on contentious questions like the government-backed display of religious icons, statements, and symbols or the language used in the Pledge of Allegiance. Eliminating the jurisdiction of federal courts is a fundamental violation of the idea of a separation of powers among the branches of the federal government as well as an effort to relegate fundamental constitutional questions to the whim of fifty different court systems. It is difficult to imagine a more anarchy-friendly approach to governance than to allow basic constitutional rights to be interpreted by each state's highest court so that freedom of speech or freedom of religion would change as you crossed the bridge from Bristol, Virginia, to Bristol, Tennessee, or from California into Nevada.

At a Religious Right conference on the courts that took place at the time the Terri Schiavo affair was playing out, Michael Schwartz, chief of staff for U.S. senator Tom Coburn (R-Okla.), conceded that the Constitution does not allow Congress to cut off a federal judge's salary, but he opined judges can be denied office space, staff, and supplies.

"If we had a clear standard, and if it is breached, then the judge's term has simply come to an end," Schwartz said. "The president gives them a call and says, 'Clean out your desk. The Capitol Police will be in to help you find your way home.' That's the end of it. We don't need any trials, we don't need any impeachment."

Talk about extreme views! I cannot overestimate the hostility against the neutrality of judges one hears from the Religious Right.

Over the years, rhetoric like this and extreme solutions have become not the exception but the rule at gatherings of the Religious Right. In some ways, this is the logical fruition of a movement that has constantly flirted with zealotry. When theologically conservative Protestants ended their partnership with religious skeptics in the post-Jeffersonian era, they embraced a government-based solution to moral and social concerns. This means they did more than turn their backs on tradition. They stopped supporting meaningful religious liberty.

Those are strong words, and today's Religious Right activists would deny them, of course. I back up my assertion by pointing to the words and actions of Religious Right leaders and the followers they have radicalized. Every time I appear on national television to defend the separation of church and state, I receive a torrent of mail from supporters of the Religious Right thoughtfully pointing out that I am full of it and that the United States is a "Christian nation." By this, of course, they mean their version of Christianity. Other faiths are not to be afforded even a modicum of respect.

Pat Robertson's track record in attacking and even insulting other faiths is long and troubling. Robertson goes beyond mere disagreement with points of doctrine; he assails the separation of church and state and insists that a certain version of Christianity (his) receive favored status from the government. Robertson's 1992 book, *The New World Order,* is based on a host of 1920-era anti-Semitic sources, and his characterizations of Islam and Hinduism are crude and marked by an appalling form of ignorance, coming as they do from a man who claims to have studied religion as an academic subject.

Robertson has accused Hindus of worshipping demons, telling viewers on July 4, 1995, "Demons work behind the Hindu and other Oriental religions, and as well behind the teaching of mind control." Islam fares no better. On November 11, 1997, Robertson told his viewers, "To see Americans become followers of, quote, Islam, is nothing short of insanity . . . Why would people in America want to embrace the religion of the slavers?" The American Muslim Council was not amused and issued a statement criticizing Robertson. I also found Robertson's revisionist history pathetic. After all, many of the ship owners who brought slaves to America from West Africa were Christians. One such man, John Newton, had a change of heart and stopped transporting slaves after surviving a violent storm at sea. Newton later wrote the hymn "Amazing Grace" about his spiritual reawakening.

At the most extreme end of the Religious Right spectrum sit a group of out-and-out theocrats called Christian Reconstructionists. They argue that their version of fundamentalist Christianity is the only acceptable faith and assert that the government has not just a right but a duty to extinguish "false" religions. They are reminiscent of two other movements that saw no need for separation of religion and government: the Roman Catholic Church of the Middle Ages, which asserted that theological error has no rights—a fancy way of saying other religions have no right to exist—and modern-day Islamic extremists whose interpretation of the Koran as a manual for global religiopolitical terrorism frequently lapses into a horrifying form of spiritual fascism.

The irony is, Religious Right activists have spent years building a political machine to get close to the seat of power under the impression that religion will trump the state when the opposite is much more likely. Indeed, if historical models offer any parallel, the state will toss the Religious Right table scraps. There is a tendency to get caught up in trivialities. Religious Right leaders find themselves going to the mat over issues like the usage of "under God" in the Pledge of Allegiance, which they insist is "traditional" despite its 1954 birthday. Religious Right groups will declare war over the right to display a religious symbol on the steps of a government building for two weeks, never stopping to ask themselves how such a display helps religion.

Undoubtedly, some leaders of the Religious Right have become so intoxicated by their proximity to political power that they believe long-sought goals are within their grasp: a ban on all abortions, a rollback of gay rights, the power to censor books, movies and the Internet, the return of formal religious exercises to public schools.

What usually happens is that the reigning power structure in Washington uses these issues to excite Religious Right voters and get them to the polls—and then focuses on other things once in office. Some of what the Religious Right is asking for it cannot legally have. The Constitution, for example, does not permit censorship. Other goals may be obtainable, but at an extremely high cost. The Supreme Court, as remade by President Bush, may in fact overturn legal abortion. Religious Right groups will celebrate, but they will do so completely unprepared for the political blowback that will soon engulf them.

As conservative Christianity nuzzles ever closer with the state, it runs another risk: irrelevancy. Churches in many European nations enjoy state subsidies, access to the corridors of power, and all the trappings of power and influence. They want for only one thing: congregants. A church in alignment with the state is a co-opted church. It may have the ability to influence legislation—although churches in much of western Europe long ago lost even this—but it will never win the hearts of the people. Hundreds of years of church-state partnership has all but killed Christianity in Europe. It will do the same here.

The intersection between church and state need not be a cold and sterile place ruled by legal aphorisms. As I will point out elsewhere in this book, the public square can accommodate a vibrant religious voice. What it cannot accommodate is theocracy, and the reason it cannot accommodate it is because the Constitution does not allow it.

Because I publicly defend the separation of church and state and worship as a Christian at the same time, I have been called many names by Falwell and his ilk. One of these is "antireligion" or "anti-Christian." It's almost amusing to be called an antireligious fanatic when I look around and take stock of my rather normal life. My house is in the suburbs. My wife and I have been married for thirty-six years and have raised two children. I became a member of Bethany Church in Bethlehem, Pennsylvania, when I was in the eighth grade and have never wavered from that foundational commitment. I certainly don't feel anti-Christian when I'm preaching as guest minister in a church or leading the congregation in reading a passage from the New Testament.

I suppose I looked a little wild in the 1960s—who didn't? I've seen old photos of Falwell with sideburns that would make Elvis Presley envious. Still, this is no reason to assume I'm a radical. What I do is call for religious liberty, the real thing, undergirded by the separation of church and state. It is precisely because I take my faith so seriously that I don't want the government to have a say in it.

Falwell and I read the same Bible. I read it as an inspiring collection of stories and parables, with some history, that gives a message of God's undying love for his world. I acknowledge that God would not seek to bring anyone his message by force. Falwell reads it as a set of instructions for how to run society along narrow sectarian lines; he reads it as a type of political operations manual, something issued as a supplement by Republican Party strategists in a dank and smoke-filled room where political careers are made or broken. He sees it as a club with which to bash those unlike himself.

I leave it to you to determine which interpretation better serves our republic and its tradition of genuine religious liberty.

2

Religion and Public Education
THE UNNECESSARY CONFLICT

I HAD JUST FINISHED up a debate over school prayer with U.S. representative Ernest Istook (R-Okla.), a leading proponent of adding a school prayer amendment to the Constitution, when a man who introduced himself as Sam approached me from the audience with a strange request: he wanted me to look at his nose.

I complied. There was definitely something amiss with this nose. Before I could say anything, Sam, who looked to be in his sixties, asked me, "Do you see my broken nose?"

It was impossible not to. Sam proceeded to tell me how he got it. As a child, he had attended a Chicago public school. His teacher was determined to convert her pupils to her conservative brand of Christianity. She ignored a state supreme court ruling barring school devotionals and held Christian prayer every morning.

Sam was Jewish, and his parents demanded that he be excused. Every morning he had to stand up, file past everyone else's desk, and leave the room. What's worse, the teacher often instructed the rest of the class to remember to pray for Sam.

All this did was reinforce the message that Sam was somehow different. One day, a bunch of kids decided to teach the different kid a lesson. They jumped Sam on the playground and beat him up. The broken nose was among the results.

I've heard similar stories from people over the years. They don't always involve physical assault. Some people merely stood in silence feeling awkward and humiliated while alien religious rituals played out around them and their own faith was insulted or denigrated. I can always hear the pain and embarrassment these old memories dredge up for many people. It's clear these incidents left a mark.

A lot of people have been down this road. During President Ronald Reagan's first term, he pushed for a school prayer amendment to the Constitution. Reagan invited U.S. senator Arlen Specter (R-Pa.) to the White House to try to gain his support for the measure, which would have allowed government-sponsored religious exercises in public schools. Specter was known as a leading moderate, and Reagan undoubtedly thought if he could win over Specter, other GOP moderates would follow.

It didn't work out. Specter told the president he could not support the amendment and recalled, decades earlier, feeling like an outcast as the only Jewish student in his native Kansas public school. The amendment failed on a 55–43 vote, gaining a simple majority but falling eleven votes short of the two-thirds vote required for constitutional amendments.

Stories like this are why I'm left cold when I hear a TV preacher or Religious Right activist act like school prayer is no big deal. It's a very big deal. Prayer—the intimate effort to connect with the Divine and the Eternal—is always a big deal.

How did we get to where we are today, to a point where our nation seems to fuss constantly over the role of religion in public education? It's a story nearly as old as the country itself, and one of the key players is a man whose name will probably not ring a bell: Ellery Schempp.

Schempp was a resident of suburban Philadelphia in the late 1950s when he and his family challenged a Pennsylvania law requiring public school students to listen daily to ten verses from the King James Version of the Bible and recite the Lord's Prayer. Note that the law *required* this. It was not voluntary. It was not a matter left to each student's conscience. These exercises came wafting over the loudspeaker every day. You had to take part. I attended Pennsylvania public schools at the same time as Ellery. I remember these exercises.

The members of the Schempp family were Unitarians who believed the government should never impose religion on anyone. They believed in the right of individual students to pray on their own but insisted the state should have no say in the matter.

This was not a popular position to take in cold war–era America. Ellery recalls his family being called communists. Rotting fruit was often lobbed at their home. The family cat disappeared and was later found hanging from a tree.

As a young man, I had never heard of Ellery, but today I count him as a friend because he has remained active in the fight to maintain the separation of church and state all of his life. Occasionally he gives talks about his experience to interested groups of Humanists or church-state separation activists. His father, Ed Schempp, who died in 2003, also remained an activist all of his life on religious freedom and other issues.

Yet the family's story remains largely unknown to the public. Most people, when they think about prayer in public schools, focus on the name Madalyn Murray O'Hair, the late atheist leader who boldly proclaimed herself the woman who got prayer "kicked out of schools."

The story is not that simple, and to portray it as such does great injustice to history and overlooks the contributions of many others who had the courage to stand up to the practice of allowing government to impose prayer on children.

The mythology surrounding the school prayer cases—the belief that they were the work of one woman with an axe to grind against religion—has sparked serious and unfortunate fallout. Large numbers of Americans continue to believe that young people cannot, under any circumstances, pray in public schools. Religious Right groups fan the flames of hysteria by spreading wild, usually apocryphal, tales about zealous public school officials determined to stamp out all vestiges of religion in the classroom. The result has been more than forty years of fighting and bitterness. Public schools, instead of being permitted to focus on educating our children, are too often fronts in a misguided culture war. In fact, I blame the Religious Right not only for spreading lies about what happens to students who want to express religious sentiments but also for their failure to inform students of what their rights are.

It doesn't have to be this way. Recent polls show that the majority of Americans don't favor coercive forms of religious worship in public schools. A 2001 poll by the New York City–based Public Agenda found that only 6 percent of respondents believe public schools should sponsor Christian prayers every day. Most people—53 percent—backed a moment of silence.

Few want to go back to the days of mandated scripture reading and government-written prayers. What do the people want? Ironically, they want a right students already have—the right to pray voluntarily in public school according to the dictates of conscience. The issue, it would seem, has been resolved.

Someone, however, forgot to tell the American people that. Communities continue to wrangle over the proper place of religion in public schools, and no end seems in sight. It's a shame because emotions run high and schools are divided when they don't need to be. Resources and energy are spent on these battles that could be applied elsewhere to much better effect.

Because we have no sense of where we have been, we cannot see our way through to a solution now. In my experience, no church-state issue is more dogged by mythology and misinformation than the issue of prayer in schools. When people base their current views on a platform constructed of a smorgasbord of lies, myths, and misinformation, they will never reach a coherent conclusion. It is simply impossible.

We need to take a brief look backward. This is important because one of the core myths of the Religious Right is that religion and public education for many years got along fine. Everything was going along swimmingly, the Religious Right tells the American people, until that mean old Supreme Court, prodded by an atheist, intervened and threw prayer out. The country has gone downhill since then.

How a story this at odds with history has gained such currency is beyond me. A simple review of the facts exposes it as specious.

To begin with, the concept of public education in America—the idea that every child deserves to be educated at taxpayer expense—is a post–Civil War invention. It did not truly take off in America until well into the twentieth century. Laws mandating that children be educated are of even more recent vintage. As any history of the nation will attest, children of previous generations entered the workforce at a frighteningly young age. Many received little education, if any.

Reformers worked for years to change that, and some quasi-public schools do go back as far as the founding period. As long as there have been public schools in the United States, there have been battles over the role of religion in them. Late-nineteenth-century America was generically Protestant in a cultural sense, and this stance had great impact on the legal system as well. Public schools tended to reflect Protestant teachings, and religious exercises were often part of the school day.

Far from creating a sense of unity, these state-sponsored religious exercises usually sparked dissension. Roman Catholics were coming into the country in record numbers at this time, and many of them chafed at the Protestant flavor of the schools.

Public education became a battleground for Catholic-Protestant tensions. The country saw numerous protests over official school prayer, led not by atheists but by Roman Catholics.

Tensions over religion in public education rode so high in Philadelphia that in 1844 a riot erupted after rumors circulated that the local schools were going to remove Protestant religious exercises. In fact, the school board only planned to adopt a policy allowing Catholic children to skip the daily prayers. But as misinformation spread, violence erupted. People took to the streets and battled police for three days. When it was all over, thirteen people lay dead. Numerous houses, shops, and a Catholic church had been burned to the ground.

While tension over school prayer occasionally erupted in violence, the more common course was courtroom action. Catholics challenged mandatory prayer exercises in Cincinnati's public schools in 1869. The case reached the state supreme court, which ruled that the local school board was under no obligation to sponsor religious activity every day.

In language that still stirs today, the Ohio Supreme Court ruled, "United with government, religion never rises above the merest superstition; united with religion, government never rises above the merest despotism; and all history shows us that the more widely and completely they are separated, the better it is for both."

State supreme courts in Wisconsin, Nebraska, Illinois, and other states also struck down coercive programs of school prayer in the late nineteenth and early twentieth centuries. In many other states, particularly in the West, official prayers were not part of the school day. In spite of this landscape, many Americans today believe no court had acted until the high court's first ruling in 1962. That's clearly not true.

Complicating matters was that education officials in some states persisted in using religion as a tool of discipline or to achieve goals not related to faith. Thus, people argued that school prayer was necessary to calm kids down at the beginning of the day or provide a sense of order. Occasionally, one still hears these arguments today.

The problem is, the purpose of prayer is to communicate with God. It's not a tool of discipline or a punishment to be inflicted on fidgety first-graders. But as this sentiment grew, some educators and lawmakers came to believe that a dose of prayer, even the most generic and watered-down form, could tackle nearly any social ill. Thus, in the late 1950s, educators in New York State got the bright idea to draft religion in the battle against juvenile delinquency and communism.

The somewhat naïve faith of the New York Board of Regents seems almost quaint today. Its members asserted that a brief "nonsectarian" prayer would keep kids on the right path and prevent them from falling into the hands of the Soviets. The board wrote an allegedly "nonsectarian" prayer it hoped all students would recite.

This is a pattern I've noticed over and over again when it comes to school prayer. Proponents tend to treat it as a magic bullet with the power to overcome nearly any social ill. Whether the issue is teen sexual activity, "goth" fashions, or drugs, we're told that a watered-down prayer that few would recite at home or at church will fix everything up just right.

But many people don't want to recite nonsectarian prayers. As a minister, I can't say I blame them. I don't say them at home or at church, and I would never teach them to my children. Such prayers manage to combine the worst of both worlds. Seriously religious people don't recite such pabulum. The nonreligious find them merely irritating. Far from being an acceptable compromise position, nonsectarian prayers end up being the most useless form of religion known to humankind—the kind that doesn't say anything. "To whom it may concern" prayers aren't worth reciting.

In a landmark 1962 case called *Engel v. Vitale,* the U.S. Supreme Court struck down the New York Board of Regents prayer—a "prayer" that was actually written by committee!

The plaintiffs in this case were a group of parents on Long Island, New York, whose school board had voted to adopt the prayer. Madalyn Murray O'Hair was not involved in the case. It's more than a little interesting that the woman who claimed to have gotten prayer kicked out of schools played no role in the first federal school prayer case.

O'Hair entered the picture about a year later. At the same time the Schempp family was pursuing its case against Pennsylvania's school prayer law, O'Hair was fighting a similar practice in Baltimore's public schools.

Since the two challenges were nearly identical, the Supreme Court consolidated them. If you go to the Supreme Court and look up the cases today, you will see them styled as *Abington Township School District v. Schempp.* In this decision the Court, with only one dissenter, ruled that public schools have no business sponsoring prayer and Bible reading.

The Schempp family, having won their case, went back to southeastern Pennsylvania and went on with their lives. O'Hair became the nation's most visible atheist, often characterized as "the most hated woman in America."

Like the Schempps, O'Hair was attacked for challenging school prayer. She was a single mother at the time, and it could not have been an easy thing to do. O'Hair became notorious for her combative approach and in-your-face style of activism. She yelled at me on a number of occasions, but I do not question her commitment to the cause. I merely point out that she alone did not spark these rulings. The families on Long Island and the Schempps played an equally important role.

I should also note that many religious people strongly opposed mandated public school religious exercises. A longtime associate of mine, Robert S. Alley, emeritus professor of humanities at the University of Richmond, recalls being pulled out of daily prayer rituals in the public schools. Alley's family was Southern Baptist, and his father opposed all government intervention in religion. Alley ended up sitting outside in the hall with a Catholic classmate.

The nation lost nothing of worth when these types of religious activities were removed from public schools. The court did not rule, and never has ruled, that students cannot pray on their own. It merely declared that state and local laws *requiring* participation in religious activity are unconstitutional. This promotion of religion by an arm of the state, the court ruled, violates parental rights. Mothers and fathers, custodians and guardians have the right to determine what, if any, religious education the children they are responsible for will receive.

I want to be clear about what was going on in many parts of the country prior to these rulings: students were being forced to take part in religious activity against their will. Ellery Schempp, for example, was repeatedly expelled for refusing to take part in the morning prayer ritual. On one occasion, Ellery pretended to have a change of heart and offered to read the morning devotional over the loudspeaker. He began reading from the Koran. Furious, the principal expelled him yet again.

What we have here is a case of education officials stepping outside their proper bounds. In Abington Township, the public school was being used to further Protestant forms of Christianity. (Note that the Pennsylvania law required readings from the King James Version of the Bible.) No other religious texts could be read.

With this background, it may be easier to understand why current efforts to amend the Constitution to "permit" prayer are so cleverly worded and deviously explained. Since 1962 there has always been a school prayer amendment pending in Congress. Some get more attention than others. The leading proposal in recent years was authored by Congressman Istook. It has changed little over the past ten years.

The House voted on Istook's amendment on June 4, 1998. It was rejected, 224–203, falling sixty-one votes shy of the two-thirds majority required for passage. Undaunted, Istook has reintroduced it every term since then.

The current version reads: "To secure the people's right to acknowledge God according to the dictates of conscience: The people retain the right to pray and to recognize their religious beliefs, heritage, and traditions on public property, including schools. The United States and the States shall not establish any official religion nor require any person to join in prayer or religious activity."

This proposal would dramatically shift the way religious speech is treated in the United States. It would not only subject children to coercive religious worship in public schools, but it would also permit government to display religious iconography in schools, libraries, and other government institutions. All of this would be legal under the guise of acknowledging our "heritage."

Note the language stating that no one will be required to join in any prayer activity. That's cold comfort when you are seven years old and the only one who does not want to take part. What is to be done with these children? I fear they will end up back out in the hall. Children should not have to single themselves out in this manner.

Don't think it won't happen. In 1988 a Jewish family named Berlin protested prayers before football games and other school events in Crestview, Florida. The son found this note on his locker: "Max Berlin is one dead Jew. Hitler should have gassed you too."

I've heard too many stories over the years to believe that compulsory school prayer is benign and doesn't hurt anyone. I've listened to the pain in people's voices as they conjure up what are clearly traumatic memories. As a religious man myself, I can only hang my head in shame when I reflect on what some people will do to others in the name of religion.

It especially infuriates me when young children are involved. Who could seriously contemplate a scenario in which two first-graders are told to get up and leave the room, to go stand in the hall, while everyone else prays? How cold would your heart have to be to think this is a good thing? I do not believe that God would smile at the children praying. God's sympathies would be with the two exiled to the hall.

When all is said and done, this is my real beef with school prayer: I don't believe God honors ritualized prayer that comes through compulsion. I believe God hears all prayers, but prayers based on force and compulsion, prayers recited merely as part of a mandatory ritual, give him no joy, and he turns to them a deaf ear.

Formalized school prayer quickly becomes a ritual, a thing to get through so that the day's learning can begin. Students, in unison, chant words by rote without even thinking about what they mean. This activity cannot possibly provide spiritual sustenance.

In fact, it's the antithesis of prayer. Real prayer comes from the heart. Real prayer is backed with meaning, with power and force. Real prayer is a solemn event, an approach to the awesome power of God. It is not taken lightly. It is best undertaken when the mind is clear and focused. Believers know that this type of worship can be a unique, powerful, and intimate experience. What are the chances this is going to happen in a crowded classroom where a nonsectarian prayer is recited for forty-five seconds every day?

I am amazed that any parent would willingly expose a child to such "religion." Parenthood is a demanding job that presents numerous challenges. One of the most difficult of these, but also among the most rewarding, is the passing on of religious, ethical, and moral precepts to children.

No teacher, no public school administrator, no government bureaucrat can take the place of parents in the transmission of these values. Why would any parent surrender this crucial task to a public school teacher—a teacher who may not believe what the parents believe or who indeed may not even be a believer at all? Ritualized school prayer schemes force teachers to act temporarily as clergy—a role they are ill-suited to assume.

I would argue that prayer is only the beginning of the religious experience. Prayer opens a door, a line of communication with God. How you exploit that, where you go from there, is the next crucial step. Religious leaders exist in part to illuminate that path. They are the only ones who can do that, who were specifically trained to do it. A public school teacher is great for helping students learn the ABCs and how to do long division. Questions of the ultimate—why are we here, how did we get here, is there meaning to our existence— belong in the realm of theology. Prayer can engage those questions and lead to a deeper understanding of the purpose of our lives. It is too awesome a force to be turned over to an untrained part-timer who probably does not want the job.

Corporate, formalized prayer by rote is meaningless as an expression of true religion. No less than the founder of Christianity knew this. While Jesus did pray publicly at times, he never forced participation on anyone and reminded his followers that the purest religion comes in private. The best place to pray, Jesus said, is in a closet, behind a closed door (see Matthew 6:5–6). God, Christ told his followers, disdains ostentatious public displays of piety by hypocrites. But the believer who prays in private pleases God, who knows what is in that believer's heart.

Compulsory, state-sponsored prayer and religious worship in public schools is unworkable, violative of basic human rights and spiritually empty. Good riddance to it.

None of this means, however, that public schools must be religion-free zones. Far from it. In recent years, workable models have emerged that provide a place for truly voluntary religious expression in the schools while protecting the rights of those who do not wish to take part.

All we need to do is keep in mind a few ground rules. The first is that truly voluntary prayer is protected in public schools. Students may pray on their own in a nondisruptive fashion, at any point during the school day. Some students like to say grace over meals or recite a prayer before taking a test. Even a group of students praying nondisruptively together does not violate constitutional parameters. This activity is protected in our public schools.

Religious Right groups often claim that public schools are intolerant of even this type of voluntary religious expression. Stories are often told of students who are disciplined or warned by school officials to stop saying grace before lunch.

I hear these stories a lot but upon close investigation they are either apocryphal, little more than Religious Right "urban legends," or gross exaggerations of simple human errors that are easily remedied. In other words, these stories are either completely made up, or certain facts have been conveniently omitted. There are roughly fifteen thousand separate public school districts in America, some with dozens of individual schools. Of course, some school officials may make missteps on occasion. If that happens, the proper response is to educate them, not assume that every public school in America harbors bias toward religion. If you tell that to the Religious Right, though, its leaders will claim the examples illustrate persecution of Christians. David Limbaugh's book *Persecution* even has a lion on the cover, an effort to equate today's "anti-Christian" bias to the murder of the early Christians in the Roman Colosseum.

Aside from voluntary prayer during the school day, students in secondary schools may meet with their peers for worship and the study of religious doctrine through voluntary clubs that meet during noninstruction time—usually defined as before and after school.

These clubs began forming after Congress passed the Equal Access Act in 1984. The legislation allows students to form a variety of clubs not directly related to the curriculum so long as all such voluntary clubs are allowed to meet. Junior high and high school students all over the land have used the act to form Christian, Jewish, Muslim, Buddhist, and other religious clubs.

These clubs are supposed to be governed by strict statutory rules. Teachers or other school employees may not participate but may only serve as "monitors," which are often required by insurance providers. Because these clubs are formed and run by students, there is no coercion. No one has to attend, and the schools may not pressure anyone to go. At meetings, students can pray and read the Bible or other religious texts. They can be as religious as they want to be in communion with fellow believers. The setup is much preferable to half a minute of nonsectarian prayer every day, as it allows for genuine religious experiences as determined by the students.

Remember, school officials must permit students to form many types of clubs. The act prohibits public secondary schools from barring clubs on the basis of "religious, political, philosophical, or other speech content." The only ones that can be curbed are groups "that are otherwise unlawful." This has been interpreted to mean groups that might cause a serious disruption at school, not just groups that are deemed "controversial." This means students can form Scientology clubs, atheist clubs, and gay-straight alliance clubs alongside the Christian clubs.

It can be difficult to get some school administrators to accept this. Educators in Utah were so worried about gay-themed clubs a few years ago that they banned all non-curriculum-related clubs—a rather extreme overreaction. Some hypocritical activist-advocates for the Equal Access Act, who wanted "religious free speech" in schools, turned a deaf ear to the groups discussing human sexuality. These folks wanted "speech for me but not thee"—making them far from First Amendment purists. In 1998 a school in Grand Blanc, Michigan, refused to allow a student to form an atheist club, even though Christian clubs were meeting on campus. The student, Micah White, was actually told he could form a comparative religion club, but his basic response was that he did not believe in any religion, so clearly he didn't want to compare them. Americans United negotiated a resolution wherein White was permitted to form the club he wanted. The controversy, of course, generated far more student interest in the club than he would have gotten otherwise.

Students have the right to talk with their peers about religion. A student may invite a friend to worship with him and distribute religious material in a nondisruptive manner. Can this ever reach the point of illegal harassment? Consider a would-be suitor who asks a young woman to a Saturday night at the multiplex. If she says no several times, more persistent inquiries could become harassment. The same kind of test should apply to a request to accompany one to church, synagogue, or temple. Admittedly, it can be difficult to determine when too much is too much. But sometimes the calls are not even close. A Jewish parent once told me that her elementary school daughter was surrounded every day by a "prayer circle" of classmates, telling her she must accept Jesus or go to hell. Incidents like this should be stopped by responsible school officials.

Public schools may also teach about religion as an academic subject. An American history course, for example, can (and should) examine the role religion has played in our past. A literature course can examine biblical allusions in classic works of fiction. Public schools can even offer courses in comparative religion.

The approach here must be educational, not devotional. Good educators know the difference. Over the years, I have seen curriculum materials that claim to teach about religion but in reality promote fundamentalist views of Christianity.

Such material is usually not hard to smoke out. As a general rule, curriculum material that begins with certain assumptions—that Jesus was the son of God, that the Bible is literally true—belongs in a Sunday school, not a public school.

A North Carolina–based group, the National Council on Bible Curriculum in Public Schools, portrays its curriculum as appropriate "teach about" religion material. In fact, the group is closely tied to right-wing TV preachers and its curriculum parrots the fundamentalist view. A more recent book, *The Bible and Its Influence,* published by the Bible Literacy Project, avoids some of the obvious pitfalls of the National Council's material but still tends to offer an oversimplified, sugarcoated view of religion in America that fails to offer a truly balanced look at the role the Bible has played in our culture. I'm a minister, but I'm comfortable acknowledging that the Bible has not always been used in positive ways. Civil War–era Southerners, for example, used it to buttress slavery. If a course book is not willing to look at the good, the bad, and the ugly in its subject matter, it is unlikely to pass any test of objectivity.

Frankly, any school board considering expanding the curriculum to include an objective study of the Bible faces real challenges from conservative and liberal Christians, as well as minority religious groups. Some theologically conservative parents object to the presentation of events like the crucifixion as if they may not be true. They teach their children that the event was real during Sunday school. They may not appreciate a class on Monday that casts doubt on its validity. In *The Bible and Its Influence,* one exercise for students is to debate whether God was fair to Adam and Eve by expelling them from the Garden of Eden. This is pretty heady stuff for most high school students and is not typically what a fundamentalist parent wants examined by his children.

At the same time, other parents wonder why a school should pick out for special study the holy scriptures of only one faith—particularly the majority faith in the country. Doesn't that send a message of special approval for that religion? It makes better sense to discuss religious references when they naturally arise in art, music, or history class. A discussion of Puritan Massachusetts without looking at the underlying religious impulse of that society would be useless. Likewise, any fair discussion of the civil rights era must discuss the religious beliefs that motivated so many to seek change.

Students can also incorporate religious themes into their class work and homework when it is relevant. A student who is assigned to write a paper on any writer could, for example, produce a report on C. S. Lewis. In recent years, some students have claimed teachers rejected their assignments for raising religious themes. I have looked into many of these cases, and I find them wanting. One girl told her teacher she was going to produce a paper on drama but then turned in a report on the life of Jesus. The assignment was to research a topic the students knew little about (and the girl had earlier tried to proselytize her teacher to accept Jesus), not produce a biography of a person, so she received a failing grade. A federal lawsuit failed to change that. In another incident, a student cried foul when she received a bad grade after she showed a videotape of a Christian choir in communication class. Had the class been about audiovisual communication, she might have had a point. The whole point of the assignment was to give a speech before an audience.

At the end of the day, I believe we need to give as much latitude as possible to teachers so they can manage their classrooms and determine what constitutes meeting the parameters of an assignment. Federal courts are poor vehicles to grade any student's homework.

Public schools can also discuss values and even offer values instruction as long as it does not become an excuse to push religious dogma. The world's great religious and ethical systems share certain precepts, and public schools can discuss these in a manner that does not tie them to any one specific faith. Schools can and do impose values in other ways. When students receive poor grades for sloppy work or get suspended for breaking the rules, that is an example of the furthering of a school's value system. Most public schools promote certain messages—advising students to stay away from drugs, urging them to work hard and aspire to get accepted into college—that clearly reflect a values-laden thought system. The very treatment of students by teachers and administrators generally gives those students important lessons (good or bad) about respect, due process, freedom of expression, and fundamental fairness.

It's easy for the Religious Right to portray public schools as anarchistic, "anything-goes" institutions where concepts of right and wrong are alien. As usual, it's a simplistic mischaracterization. Many Religious Right activists either homeschool their children or send them to private academies. They go inside public schools about as often as they visit the surface of Mars. Yet they never hesitate to judge the schools they have no regular contact with.

Since so much religious activity is legal in public schools, and since religions can be discussed in so many different ways, why do Americans keep fighting over religion in the public schools? Reasonable people should be able to find middle ground over many of these issues. Unfortunately, reasonable people are not controlling the debate. It has been monopolized by extremists who have ulterior motives. Religious Right organizations, for example, aren't really interested in finding common ground. Their goal is to bash public education.

Late in 2004, for example, a startling story captured headlines nationwide: a public school in Cupertino, California, was accused of ordering a teacher to stop using the Declaration of Independence in class because of its reference to "the Creator."

The FOX News Channel practically offered team coverage, and

the teacher, Stephen J. Williams, made the rounds of inflammatory far-right TV and radio talk shows where he presented his claims without being challenged. It was taken as a given that his story was true, and in short order a Religious Right legal group, the Alliance Defense Fund, filed suit on Williams's behalf.

The case, however, turned out to be a completely dishonest distortion of events. Several parents at Stevens Creek Elementary School were suspicious from the start and launched a Web site to refute Williams's claims. The site included a photograph of a classroom in the school, with a copy of the Declaration of Independence hanging on the wall. It turned out that Williams had been accused of inappropriately proselytizing in class. His case quickly began to fall apart.

Less than a year after it was filed, the lawsuit was quietly withdrawn. The school admitted no guilt and did not change any of its policies. A local newspaper, the *San Jose Mercury News,* charged in an editorial that the case was the product of "conservative lawyers who drummed up a bogus claim of religious persecution. They had badgered and ridiculed the district to try to push religion into the schools."

The case collapsed, but in a way, the Religious Right still won. Williams's inflammatory claims received wide coverage in the media. Stories with headlines like "School Bans Declaration of Independence" were carried nationwide. The school was flooded with hate mail and phone calls from people who saw these stories and got worked up. The media soon moved on to something else, and few reporters outside the area bothered to follow up when the case was withdrawn. Many people who read the original stories probably never saw the later developments. Thus, the far right's goal, to implant the idea in people's minds that public schools are so religion phobic that they would even censor the Declaration of Independence, was achieved. Thank you, Sean Hannity and Bill O'Reilly!

Religious Right groups employ a similar strategy every year as the December holidays approach. Many public schools, in an effort to be inclusive and welcoming of all in the community, have re-named Christmas concerts something like winter concerts or holiday concerts. These performances often include a mix of religious and nonreligious holiday songs.

These would seem to be rather unremarkable changes, ones that merely indicate that more than one holiday takes place late in the year. But Religious Right groups continue to throw a fit, equating these minor alterations with a widespread persecution of Christianity. Groups that have nothing better to do than whine about what a school calls its December concert can be hard to take seriously, yet they have the potential to inflame passions and divide communities.

Religious Right groups seem unable to grasp the fact that American society has changed since the nineteenth century. What once might have made sense no longer does. A public school, which by law serves young people from many faith traditions and none, isn't the place to go to celebrate Christmas as a religious holiday. A Christmas pageant where little children dress up as New Testament characters and reenact the story of Jesus' birth is charming and appropriate in a church. It has no place in a public school. Programs consisting of all-sacred music sound great blaring forth in church. They don't belong in the school auditorium.

This latter point is an important one. No federal court anywhere has ever said that public schools cannot include *some* religious music in their holiday concerts. Courts have recognized that religion plays an important role in American culture and have stated that public schools can acknowledge that. Thus, most schools these days sponsor winter concerts that include Christian, Jewish, and secular songs. It's hard to turn this into the worst persecution of Christianity since the days of the Emperor Nero, but the Religious Right never stops trying. FOX News Channel host John Gibson actually told me on his syndicated radio program that if a child brings home the school calendar with the December break labeled a winter holiday, she is going to feel that Christianity is being repudiated!

Public schools can teach about the importance of Christmas, Yom Kippur, Ramadan, and other religious holidays from an educational standpoint. Such instruction can be useful, especially in the case of holidays that are becoming more popular but whose tenets may be misunderstood.

But public schools cannot celebrate these or any other religious holidays as religious events. To do so would entangle the school in worship and raise all of the same objections that felled school-sponsored prayer. In short, if you want to celebrate Christmas as a religious holiday and rejoice in the birth of a figure you believe was sent by God to redeem humankind, more power to you—just don't expect your local public school to join in. There are places where that can be done. They are called churches.

The failure of public schools to celebrate Christmas as a religious holiday infringes on no one's rights. In fact, it merely puts the job where it rightfully belongs—in the hands of the religious community.

I will concede that not every church-state issue that affects public education is open to easy compromise. In recent years, many states and local school districts have been polarized by battles over the teaching of creationism, or its most recent variant, intelligent design.

Unlike traditional creationism, intelligent design does not maintain that the earth is young or that the biblical Book of Genesis must be read literally. Intelligent design proponents insist their ideas are not religious. But at its core, intelligent design holds that life on this planet is so complex and diverse that it must have been designed by an intelligent force. And the only plausible candidate they offer for this course is God. That sure sounds like religion to me.

As I was writing this book, Americans United for Separation of Church and State and the American Civil Liberties Union of

Pennsylvania had just won a case in Dover, Pennsylvania, where the local school board had voted to introduce intelligent design in biology classes. Biology teachers were told to read a kind of disclaimer clearly designed to cast doubt on evolution. It read: "Because Darwin's Theory is a theory, it continues to be tested as new evidence is discovered. The Theory is not a fact. Gaps in the Theory exist for which there is no evidence."

The move tore the community apart. Reporters and camera crews from all over the world descended on this town of fewer than twenty-five hundred residents to report on the fight. It was a good example of how a relatively obscure corner of the county could become a flashpoint overnight thanks to one misguided action.

The trial lasted about six weeks in the fall of 2005. A few days after the case wrapped up, a curious thing happened: voters in the town went to the polls and tossed out every pro–intelligent design advocate on the ballot, replacing them with a proevolution slate. This led TV preacher Pat Robertson to rant on his *700 Club* show, "I'd like to say to the good citizens of Dover, if there is a disaster in your area, don't turn to God. You just rejected him from your city. And don't wonder why he hasn't helped you when problems begin, if they begin. And I'm not saying they will. But if they do, just remember you just voted God out of your city. And if that's the case, then don't ask for his help 'cause he might not be there." (This comment was a blunt reminder that all of the antievolution rhetoric is rooted in a religious belief system.)

I am a Christian minister who accepts evolution as a fundamental principle of science. I also happen to believe that such acceptance of evolution does not in any way either contradict or preclude the real possibility that God uses evolution for a divine purpose. This is pretty much the same belief expressed by the late Pope John Paul II, who, in a 1996 address to the Pontifical Academy of Sciences, said, "In the domain of inanimate and animate nature, the evolution of science and its applications give rise to new questions. The better the Church's knowledge is of their essential aspects, the more she will understand their impact. Consequently, in accordance with her specific mission she will be able to offer criteria for discerning the moral conduct required of all human beings in view of their integral salvation." He then added, "Today, almost half a century after the publication of the encyclical, new knowledge has led to the recognition of the theory of evolution as more than a hypothesis."

I can only be dismayed by these battles over evolution. They have done nothing to ensure the proper education of our children, and their harm is incalculable. It has been difficult to get the Religious Right to understand that as far as the scientific community goes, the theory of evolution is no longer in doubt, no longer controversial. Its tenets have achieved wide acceptance, and while there is still some debate and discussion over certain aspects and minute details, the big picture of evolution is as widely grounded as the theory of gravity or the theory of electromagnetism. In science, theories are not guesses or hunches; they are testable principles that explain a large number of events. We know more about all of these theories than when they were first proposed by Charles Darwin, Sir Isaac Newton, and Enrico Fermi. "Filling out" theories is the very essence of a scientific approach.

People in the religious community have everything to lose and nothing to gain by continuing to stand in opposition to modern science. Creationism, no matter what form it may take, is a poor substitute for science and even worse theology. It sets religion up for a fight it cannot win and guarantees that some of the faithful will wind up with egg-covered faces, whether the chicken preceded or followed the egg.

As a Christian, I believe that the Bible speaks to us in many voices. It frequently employs the language of metaphor. Far from draining the Bible of its power, this device was intended to add a sense of universality to the ancient texts. Creationism demands a literal adherence to the Bible, a controversial position of surprisingly recent vintage that is rejected by many Christians.

Consider Jesus' parables from the New Testament. It's unlikely Jesus actually knew a man who sowed some seed on fertile ground and some on rocky ground. That wasn't the point. Jesus was not relating actual history or even telling a story about something he had witnessed. His parables were teaching aides.

So it is, I believe, with many of the Old Testament passages that the fundamentalists stubbornly insist describe actual historical events. Why do so many ancient cultures retain a flood myth? It's possible that a catastrophic flood struck much of the known world in ancient times and that stories about it were handed down through generations. It's also possible that stories about the destruction of the world by water and the redemption of a select few speak to something at the core of our shared humanity.

Either explanation is more satisfying than the alternative offered us by the fundamentalists: an insistence that the event took place exactly as described in the Old Testament. To accept this, we must make a mental journey that simply requires too much in the way of brain gymnastics. Literalism also misses the point. Noah's flood is not about history; it's about God's covenant with his creation and his promise that even a sinful people can be redeemed. Ironically, by insisting that the story be literally true, fundamentalists drain it of all its power. The tale becomes an all-or-nothing proposition. Either you swallow the whole story, including the improbable bits, or you can get nothing from it.

I refuse to accept this false choice whenever fundamentalists thrust it at me. So it is with the creation of the world. The idea of a young earth, a mere six thousand years old, and dinosaurs strolling around alongside cavemen is absurd in the face of modern science.

The Bible, I believe, does not even claim such nonsense occurred. Those who read it and say it does have the right to that belief, but it is neither science nor history and cannot plausibly be passed off as such.

By denying the obvious reality of evolution, fundamentalists paint themselves into a corner of scientific illiteracy. They remind me of church fathers at the time of Galileo. Galileo's embrace of the system of Copernicus, that is, the heliocentric universe, led to his appearance before the Inquisition and sentencing to a type of house arrest. Galileo was forced to sign papers renouncing his ideas, but he didn't mean it. The Inquisition could force Galileo to sign the papers, but it did not have the power to change what was really in his mind. More important, it also lacked the power to make the earth the center of the universe—thus, it was embarrassed in the end.

More than five hundred years later, Pope John Paul II offered a type of apology to Galileo. He was able to keep a straight face while doing so. But the notion of a religious leader acknowledging accepted science five centuries after the fact could not help but dredge up the impression of the church as backward and medieval.

Science marches on, and religion threatens to be left behind if it does not find a way to reconcile itself with modernity. The tragedy is that none of this is necessary. Science and religion are not enemies.

Science and religion are perhaps best thought of as silent collaborators. Both systems seek to answer questions—but usually not the same ones. Science questions how evolution provided us with the diversity of life on earth and seeks to find ways to fight disease, improve living conditions, and exploit new technologies, among other things. Religion asks why we are here. It ponders how we are to live. It ruminates on the source of our ethics and morality.

Science asks "how." Religion asks "why." Those who choose to partake of both can piece the systems together for a coherent and satisfying worldview that draws on the best both have to offer. The Religious Right chooses to make them fight.

The evidence for evolution is overwhelming and so persuasive that to dismiss it with one wave of the hand, as many fundamentalists do, is to court anti-intellectualism. In the face of the growing body of evidence, creationism advocates are forced to adopt increasingly bizarre assertions—that fossils were planted by Satan to mislead us, that "lower forms" of life do evolve but not humans, that space aliens or time travelers may have "seeded" the earth to begin life here.

The rest of the industrialized world has long since stopped playing these games. Support for creationism in western Europe, Canada, Australia, and New Zealand is in the single digits. People in those countries can only laugh when they see residents of the United States, supposedly the most technologically advanced society on the globe, embrace pseudoscience and justify it by resorting to biblical literalism.

U.S. support for creationism remains high mainly because the battle here plays out on political grounds, not scientific ones. As far as the scientific community is concerned, there is no controversy. Go into any public university in the country and ask the chair of the Biology Department what is taught in freshman biology. You won't hear discussions of intelligent design, creationism, or "evidence against evolution" there. The academic community long ago moved on. It's time for the rest of society to do the same.

Over the years, I have attended many gatherings of Religious Right groups, under the theory that it's good to know your opponent and be familiar with his arguments. I've heard many creationists speak and present their ideas. One sobering fact hits home: the major creationist groups in America are religious organizations. If you doubt that, look them up. They are incorporated as ministries. Many are run by members of the clergy and have explicitly religious mission statements posted online that reflect fundamentalist tenets. The

Nicene Creed is a nice start for a religious denomination; it makes for lousy science.

The proliferation of preaching, statements of faith, and tips on how to be saved found on the creationist sites are a sure sign we're not dealing with a science here. Scientists don't sign documents stating what they believe up front and then go out looking for evidence that supports only that point of view, rejecting everything that does not fit. Creationists do. This attitude is not surprising for a religious ministry. It's alien to science.

Among a friendly crowd, creationists speak openly about evangelizing and using their attacks on evolution to persuade people to adopt fundamentalist forms of Christianity. They argue that Darwinian evolution promotes atheism; the end result of their program is a religious conversion, hardly a scientific goal.

It is much the same with advocates of intelligent design. Although paraded about by its proponents as something new and cutting edge, intelligent design is in reality an old and discredited idea. The argument for design predates Darwin. Indeed, the idea that the world is so complex that it must have been created by a designer was one of St. Thomas Aquinas's "proofs" for the existence of God in the thirteenth century. More recently, Christian apologist William Paley advanced the argument in the eighteenth century.

Much has been learned about the operation of the natural world since then. Yet we still see advocates of intelligent design relying on miraculous explanations for things they cannot explain. Some forms of bacteria, for example, have a type of propeller attached to them that pushes them through muck, helping them feed on microscopic particles within.

No one is really sure how these flagella developed their propellers—yet. Some ideas have been floated. The advocates of intelligent design argue that the propeller is evidence of design. They are advancing a supernatural answer to cover for their own inability to posit a natural explanation. This is the old argument from personal ignorance that in effect says, "I can't figure out how this got here, so it must have been a miracle."

Arguments like this, as well as the idea of "gaps" in the fossil record, are the starting points for intelligent design and creationist hokum. Once, during a two-hour PBS debate on William F. Buckley's *Firing Line*, intelligent design advocate and mathematician William Dembski started complaining about these alleged "gaps." When I pointed out that scientists had recently found three intermediate fossils between horses and whales, he said that was not enough. I responded that if this was insufficient, would five or fifty suffice? Dembski's lack of a response demonstrated that he would never be satisfied, that any "gap" was enough to justify his weird conclusions. "New math" or old, that's just preposterous.

In time, science will explain the bacterial flagellum's propeller. There will be no need to resort to supernatural explanations, which, after all, lie outside the realm of science. Intelligent design advocates will then move on to something else, hold it up as a great mystery, and propose divine intervention. Real scientists will eventually solve that as well.

The goal of intelligent design is not to break new ground in science. It can't do that simply because it is not properly equipped. You might as well try to fix a broken motor with a broom. Intelligent design is merely the latest twist in a long-running fundamentalist con: instill doubts about evolution, use that as an opening for fundamentalist proselytism, gain a new convert. An entire book has been written exposing this strategy—*Creationism's Trojan Horse: The Wedge of Intelligent Design* by Barbara Forrest and Paul R. Gross.

Phillip Johnson, a former law professor who is a guru of the intelligent design movement, admitted to a religious strategy during a February 1999 gathering of followers of the TV preacher D. James Kennedy. Addressing this friendly venue, Johnson was uncharacteristically candid. His main goal, he admitted, is to persuade people to accept Christ as their personal savior.

To that end, Johnson said, intelligent design should be used to instill doubts about evolution. People are then introduced to "the truth" of the Bible and the "question of sin." Finally, they are ready to be "introduced to Jesus."

In two recent Americans United legal cases, we have seen the evidence of this religious agenda firsthand. In Dover, Pennsylvania, pro–intelligent design board member William Buckingham made his religious motivations clear, stating at one meeting, "Two thousand years ago, someone died on a cross. Can't someone take a stand for him?" He also said, "This country wasn't founded on Muslim beliefs or evolution. This country was founded on Christianity, and our students should be taught as such."

And then, just weeks after the Dover decision was handed down, a high school in Lebec, California, decided to initiate a between-semesters elective course called "Philosophy of Design." It was supposed to be taught by Sharon Lemberg, a soccer coach at the school and wife of a local antievolution Assemblies of God minister. Her intent did not appear to be strictly pedagogical. The original syllabus promised that the course would "take a close look at evolution as a theory and will discuss the scientific, biological, and Biblical aspects that suggest why Darwin's philosophy is not rock solid . . . physical and chemical evidence will be presented suggesting the earth is thousands of years old, not billions." Lemberg proposed using a series of videos in class. Twenty-three of twenty-four were produced by creationist religious ministries. She also told the local newspaper, "I believe this is the class that the Lord wanted me to teach."

After Americans United filed a lawsuit, the school board voted to terminate the course—they changed it to a class on "ethics"—and agreed never to offer it again. Regrettably, even these court victories have not stopped other school districts from considering adding intelligent design to the curriculum (thus waving giant red "Sue Us Soon" signs).

In the public school arena, Johnson and his cohorts talk about intelligent design because teaching standard creationism has been declared unconstitutional by the Supreme Court. Intelligent design is merely the latest manifestation in a long-running crusade by the Religious Right to undermine Darwinism. There is nothing new here. Prior to intelligent design, the idea was called the theory of abrupt appearance. Before that, it was evidence against evolution. And before that it was scientific creationism—as if simply adding the word *scientific* would give the idea credibility.

Johnson and the other advocates of the intelligent design form of creationism will lose in the long run. They will almost certainly lose when most courts rule against their ideas, but they will lose more because their ideas are not science. A law of economics states that bad money drives out good money. Laws of science flip the equation: good science drives out bad.

Science is a self-correcting process. When ideas are proposed that do not pan out and that cannot be replicated in the laboratory by other independent researchers, they are quickly dropped. (Remember cold fusion? How about alchemy—turning base metals into gold?) From a research standpoint, intelligent design is a blind alley. It's a nineteenth-century notion walking around in an ill-fitting lab coat. That will be enough to do it in at the end. Some fundamentalists have once again insisted on picking a fight with science they cannot win. As biotechnology industries become more prominent, as businesses continue to invest in these ventures, parents are going to realize that the kids who were not taught adequate science in high school will be left behind in college, unable to pass a basic biology course because they were not taught about the underlying theory of the biological sciences in high school. Those kids will see doors slam in their faces. They will be denied access to certain well paying high-tech jobs. They will be left behind. Simply put, there is no money, no jobs, and no future in studying intelligent design. There's a bundle to be made if you understand evolution and can isolate a gene mutation that causes a rare illness. Scientific technology corporations around the world understand this.

Few parents are so wedded to a dogmatic faith that they would willingly consign their children to hopeless ignorance and chock off avenues for advancement. Fundamentalists will continue to try to shield intelligent design, but they can't save it from one of the most powerful forces known to humankind: the natural evolution of knowledge.

Before leaving this topic, there is one related issue that must be discussed. People sometimes ask why, if Americans feel so passionate about their religious beliefs, we do not simply establish a system of taxpayer-funded religious schools for those who want them. Indeed, many Religious Right activists, including Jerry Falwell, have argued for the complete dismantling of the public school system and its replacement by a government-supported network of Christian schools. They love the controversy generated by the issues I have just discussed because the misinformation spread by their side, they hope, will weaken public support for funding quality public education.

Among other things, this idea is wholly impractical. About 90 percent of American schoolchildren attend public schools. Despite the attacks on the system by the Religious Right, polls show that most Americans who have children are happy with the school they attend (even though they are more skeptical of the quality of "other" public schools) and do not want to put them somewhere else. Most Americans support public schools and do not want to move to a privatized system. In more than two dozen state referenda on public funding of private schools, all such proposals have been defeated.

Public schools are also one of the few places where children of many different religions come together. This is a healthy trend, and we as a society should encourage it. Segregation along religious lines can be dangerous. As a former high school teacher in a multifaith culture, I know that children are taught tolerance and mutual respect by osmosis as they learn alongside peers of many other faiths and none.

But perhaps most important, the idea should be rejected because it forces taxpayers to foot the bill for the propagation of religion. Religion and all of its projects should always be funded voluntarily by its supporters. Any other system results in taxation for religion and ends up putting a stranglehold on faith.

Many European nations have a long tradition of granting government subsidies to religion or religious schools. Over the years, this policy enabled the government to gradually assume control of the religious schools and begin imposing regulations on them. As a result, many of the schools have lost much of their distinctive religious character.

In the fall of 2005 a Vatican official, Archbishop J. Michael Miller, criticized the United States for its policy of not subsidizing religious education. Miller, secretary of the Vatican's Congregation for Catholic Education, said the refusal to extend such aid put America in the same company as Mexico, North Korea, China, and Cuba.

I was amused at what came next: Miller, a native of Ontario, remarked that Catholic schools there were given taxpayer support and gradually pressured by the province to cease hiring only Catholics. The resulting influx of non-Catholic teachers, he said, "was disastrous . . . many schools ended up by seriously compromising their Catholic identity."

What did Miller expect? Generally, the government regulates the things it subsidizes. There is no reason why a religious school should be able to accept generous subsidies from the taxpayer every year and then say to some of those involuntary supporters, "Sorry. You can't work here. You're the wrong religion."

A few American states have experimented with vouchers, a form of taxpayer aid to private schools. In 2002 the U.S. Supreme Court, in a 5–4 ruling, upheld the constitutionality of private school vouchers in Cleveland, Ohio. The swing voter, former Justice Sandra Day O'Connor, argued that vouchers for private schools were just one alternative to other educational services provided by the state. Among the others were after-school tutoring, charter schools (less regulated but still publicly controlled institutions), and regular, old-fashioned public schools. Finally, she and a few other justices seemed confused by the real-world facts of the case.

I don't want to belabor the legal argument because at the Supreme Court, as in baseball, the side with even one more vote or run wins. However, in deciding whether to initiate voucher programs, there is a commonsense logic that should dictate that they not begin.

Vouchers are not just a kind of aid to children or their parents. If, say, the state of California were to give every parent a voucher for $2,000 to be used in any school of their choosing, and the parent then takes that voucher to the local Christian fundamentalist academy, and that school then takes the voucher to the state treasurer and says not just "show me the money" but "hand over the money," that looks, smells, and feels like a direct subsidy to a religious school. The parent is nothing but a pipeline, a conduit, that runs from the taxpayers' pockets to the coffers of the religious school.

Unlike a state-loaned math textbook that is pretty much only useful for math, cold cash can be used directly to fund anything, from hiring a new religion teacher to purchasing Bibles or sacrificial goats.

This argument remains important because thirty-seven states have specific state constitutional provisions that do not permit any aid to religious institutions, ministries, or schools. In these states, voucher schools can and will be successfully challenged on state, not federal, grounds as the "money trail" argument is made. State supreme courts in Colorado and Florida have already struck down voucher plans on these grounds.

So much for the legal argument. A more practical question is, do these plans work? Milwaukee and Cleveland have had voucher plans for years. The results have been less than spectacular. No study to date has shown voucher students outperforming their public school counterparts. In Milwaukee, site of the nation's first-ever voucher experiment, legislators got so embarrassed by annual reports showing no improvement among the voucher students that they passed a new law; it did not end the program but dropped standardized testing for the kids in voucher schools! Studies in Cleveland have shown no academic improvement among participants. A 2003 study of the Cleveland plan by researchers at Indiana University's Center for Evaluation found that claims of incredible gains by voucher students had not materialized.

"There are no consistent, significant differences in achievement between scholarship and public school students by the end of third grade," wrote researcher Kim Metcalf in the executive summary of the analysis. "This finding holds across all of the available achievement measures (reading, language arts, mathematics, social studies, science and total battery)."

One year later, Metcalf's team issued another report on the Cleveland plan, again finding no academic improvement for the voucher students. "After adjusting for students' minority status and family income, there is no consistent pattern either of enhanced or diminished academic achievement for students who have used a scholarship to attend private schools from kindergarten through fourth grade," read the report's executive summary. "Further, students who exit the program to return to public schools often experience a comparative drop in achievement during their first or second year after leaving the program, but return over time to levels of adjusted achievement that is [sic] comparable to other students."

Both Milwaukee and Cleveland have been plagued by the problem of fly-by-night schools being established to cash in on the taxpayers' largess. In Milwaukee, a school that called itself an "excellerated" academy subjected students to endless drills and accepted student reports copied word for word from newspapers. The school received $414,524 in taxpayer aid in 2005.

Another Milwaukee school, Carter's Christian Academy, serves kindergarten students. Its owner told the *Milwaukee Journal Sentinel,* "The curriculum that we have is so basic that someone with just a plain high school diploma is able to teach it." The newspaper reported no toys or educational materials in sight.

One Cleveland voucher school, an Islamic academy, hired a convicted murderer to teach history. It operated out of a rundown building with no working fire alarms. The school eventually shut down in the wake of revelations that it had bilked the state by claiming to have enrolled students who did not attend, but not before collecting more than a quarter of a million dollars in tax assistance.

Another Cleveland voucher school, which called itself a Christian academy, taught children primarily by having them watch videos all day. School officials actually defended the program, as if it were somehow innovative. The academy received $150,000 in taxpayer support.

Then there is the problem of who will be admitted to these private, yet state-subsidized, schools. The Supreme Court did not really address some extremely important issues: Can a religious school give preference to persons of the same religion? Must a school funded with tax dollars comply with the Americans with Disabilities Act? What about civil rights laws?

These are not theoretical problems. Let's go back to Milwaukee, the site of the first voucher experiment. The plan there theoretically requires that students with vouchers be admitted to private schools through a "random selection" process, on a nondiscriminatory basis.

However, during one year of the program, about one-third of the religious schools either failed to file any random selection plan or filed one that appeared on its face to allow discriminatory admissions. For example, the Mount Calvary Lutheran School's plan required applicants to fill out a form that asked whether the interested student was baptized, the name of the church his or her family attended, why the parents wanted their child in a Christian school, and what the family planned to do to help the school give the child a good Christian education. This might be construed as random selection—but only in another dimension.

A reporter for a Baptist news service visited schools in Milwaukee and found one two-story high school with a very proud principal. The reporter asked about students with disabilities and was told they were welcomed at the facility. When the reporter noted that many of the school's labs and special classrooms were on the second floor and pointed out that a lack of elevators would preclude anyone in a wheelchair from getting to them, the principal responded, "I said we welcomed children with disabilities; I didn't say we could accommodate them." I don't think she was being venal; she was demonstrating, though, just what "choice" means in voucher programs. It is the schools that do the choosing. They choose if your child gets in, and they choose if he stays. And, if he is asked to leave over some minor disciplinary infraction, the good old public schools pick up the slack. After all, public schools are required by law to accommodate all children no matter what their needs.

Obviously some public schools in America are troubled. Many schools in inner-city areas or rural regions marked by extreme poverty suffer from a lack of resources. Shuffling these children over to private systems that are not accountable to the government is not the answer.

Free market "privateers" often make the curious assumption that if there is a new flow of state or federal money for schools, competitive, high-quality facilities will pop up all over America's inner cities. Where in south central Los Angeles or inner-city Memphis is this phenomenon occurring with any other institution? Banks have opened branches in inner cities only because federal law forced them to. Where are the department stores, grocery stores, or high-end retailers in these neighborhoods? New money might lead to new construction somewhere, but it won't be in the same neighborhoods now missing groceries and malls. It simply won't be viewed as cost effective. This argument that vouchers will help low-income folks is absolute poppycock.

It's important to remember how vouchers got started. The movement was launched after the Supreme Court handed down *Brown v. Board of Education,* the key school integration case, in 1954. Hardcore segregationists in the South pioneered "massive resistance" to integration, and taxpayer-funded private "whites only" academies were one component of that. At the time, courts struck down these schemes. In Milwaukee, the Democratic state representative who originally pushed the voucher plan, Annette Polly Williams, has begun distancing herself from the program because it did not help the poor and was used mainly by affluent suburbanites who could have afforded private school tuition. A Harvard University study released just a day before the Supreme Court issued its ruling on Cleveland's plan found that the most segregated schools in the country were private religious academies.

Perhaps the most pernicious argument about vouchers is that if we don't allow them, we are consigning children in the worst schools to a life of perpetual failure and frustration. This is a false dichotomy. The choice is not between providing vouchers and doing nothing. During the Clinton administration, House Republicans proposed a $7 million program of vouchers for two thousand students in Washington, D.C.—which they called opportunity scholarships. The secretary of education at that time was Richard Riley. He pointed out that assisting at most two thousand students and leaving seventy-five thousand others without extra funds simply made no sense. His alternative was a good one: use half of the money to match fifty-eight district schools with proven educational success programs like the Laboratory for Success developed at Temple University or the "Success for All" programs at Johns Hopkins University in Baltimore. These are track-proven programs that can turn around troubled inner-city schools. Riley then proposed using the other $3.5 million to support seventy new after-school programs to keep kids out of trouble between 3 p.m. and 6 p.m., statistically dangerous times for children. We must never accept the premise that it's vouchers or nothing. As a minister, I think Americans need to demand a quality education for each and every child within our borders. That is a moral necessity, whether one is religious or not.

The United States has not traditionally extended tax support to religious education. This isn't because of hostility toward religion but because, historically, taxpayer-supported religion has been anathema to Americans. Forced support for religion created so much dissension in the colonies that it was barred by the First Amendment to the Constitution. The idea was that religious groups would have to pay their own way if they wanted to survive and prosper, not turn to the government for assistance.

Benjamin Franklin once observed, "When a religion is good, I conceive it will support itself; and when it does not support itself, and God does not take care to support it so that its professors are obliged to call for help of the civil power, 'tis a sign, I apprehend, of its being a bad one."

Religion does best when it relies on voluntary support. Demands for tax support should be resisted, as should attempts to reintroduce devotional religious practices in the public schools. As a nation of more than two thousand faiths, we would quickly find that any attempt to subsidize them all or bring all faiths into the public schools on some type of rotating basis would be unworkable.

There is a better way: Support your religion on your own. Don't expect any branch of government, especially the public school system, to do the heavy lifting of instilling moral and religious training in young people. The schools are not only ill equipped to do the job, it is not theirs to do.

3

Religious Icons and Public Property
THE ULTIMATE TRIUMPH OF SYMBOLISM OVER SUBSTANCE

FORMER ALABAMA SUPREME COURT chief justice Roy Moore was out of options. A string of federal courts had rejected his argument that he had a legal right to display a two-and-a-half-ton Ten Commandments monument in the state Judicial Building. Moore had defied the courts, vowed not to remove the monument, and had been removed from his post by a judicial oversight body. Moore's beloved (and, note to whoever does intellectual property work for Moses, copyrighted) monument was hauled out of the court foyer and placed in a storage closet.

In case you don't remember the ins and outs of the Moore saga, here's a quick recap: Moore was elected chief justice of the Alabama Supreme Court in November of 2000 after making a name for himself throughout the state thanks to litigation against him by the American Civil Liberties Union, which sought to force Moore to remove a hand-carved Ten Commandments plaque from his courtroom in Etowah County. Moore vowed that if elected to the state high court, he would bring the Ten Commandments to the Judicial Building in Montgomery, which houses the Alabama Supreme Court. He soon made good on that promise. Without bothering to consult with his fellow justices, Moore commissioned an artist to create the enormous display and, long after working hours on July 31, 2001, had the monument hauled into the rotunda of the Judicial Building. Thankfully, Moore thought to tip off a Religious Right television crew, which captured footage of Moore, in a T-shirt, helping bring the monument in.

The next day, Moore unveiled his monument to the general public. With just a touch of pomposity, he told the crowd, "May this day mark the beginning of the restoration of the moral foundation of law to our people and a return to the knowledge of God in our land."

Actually, the only thing that day marked was the beginning of my plan to sue Moore. The litigation against Moore, spearheaded by Americans United for Separation of Church and State, lasted more than two years. During this time, I repeatedly signaled my willingness to debate him in any public forum or cable TV talk show. Moore always dodged me. It's not that he was media shy. Moore was happy to appear on friendly programs like FOX News Channel's *Hannity & Colmes*—but without an opposing point of view.

I had heard Moore speak many times at Religious Right gatherings. I had listened to him distort American history and even recite snippets of his own poetry to adoring crowds of fundamentalist Christians who idolized him as a type of folk hero.

But I had not met the man face to face, and I wanted to. I wanted to meet Moore in person, to shake his hand, look him in the eye, and size him up in an attempt to figure out what made him tick. When I finally got the opportunity to do that, in some anonymous FOX News Channel green room long after the case had been settled, I couldn't help but feel disappointed.

"I've followed your career," I told Moore as we shook hands. His reply, delivered through a tight grin, was brief. "I've noticed," he said.

I'm not sure now what I expected to get from Moore that day. Generally speaking, whenever a politician starts talking about religious symbols and religious codes and expressing some desire to unite them with government, a little alarm goes off in my head. Over the years, I've seen too many politicians extol the virtues of the Ten Commandments while breaking as many of them as possible. Patriotism, it has been said, is the last refuge of a scoundrel. Now it seems to be religion. Indeed, religion is frequently the first. I suppose I wanted to see if Moore fit that mold.

I can't say that he did. When it was all over, I concluded that Moore's motives were sincere and driven by zealotry—but still terribly misguided. Moore's crusade wasn't so much about the Ten Commandments as it was the symbolic effort to merge them with the power of the state. He seemed to have a deeply felt need to send a message reinforcing his belief that the Ten Commandments are the basis for all moral and civil law. He was wrong legally, theologically, and historically.

As a minister, I'm expected to extol the Ten Commandments and I do—up to a point. Looked at in the context of their time, the Ten Commandments were an important and necessary code for a people struggling to eke out an existence under harsh conditions. Some of them reflect universal truths that nearly all societies have honored. Their mere compilation was an achievement. Listing the Commandments together as a single code for behavior was a new step, but looked at individually, nothing about them is particularly unique. Ancient societies, like societies today, sought to curb undesirable behavior such as theft, murder, and lying. You might call it enlightened self-interest. If I agree not to steal your cows, it will make it more likely that no one will steal mine. No surprise there. As both a religious and legal code, the Ten Commandments reflect some commonsense prohibitions that all societies have honored; what makes them more than a list of rules, however, is that they go beyond that in attempt to regulate religious behavior as well. And it's here that we start to walk into a minefield.

This point is important. The Ten Commandments are not a mere civil code, like an ancient version of your town's rules and regulations. Because they are not, any argument that all U.S. law is based on the Ten Commandments must ultimately fail. In short, too many commandments deal with aspects of life that the U.S. government does not presume to control and in fact cannot control.

I'm not the first one to make these points. In light of Moore's lawsuit, parsing the Ten Commandments became a national pastime for some media commentators and religious leaders. Most recently, my friend Bill Press did it in an entertaining fashion in his book *How the Republicans Stole Christmas.* Press, a former seminarian, knows the Bible well enough to comment on it as an expert. For many others, the fight over Moore and his monolith tended to lead to one of two camps: Some of Moore's opponents asserted that the Commandments are little more than an ancient legal code of dubious value to the modern world. His supporters described them as the font of all moral and civic law.

The truth lies somewhere in between. The Commandments are a reflection of a society and time that did not recognize or value any distance between religion and government. In that sense, they are theocratic. Any discussion of the Commandments needs to begin here. They tell us about the collective mind-set of the society that produced them and its acceptance of state control of religion. This does not mean the Commandments are irrelevant to modern life, only that some of them must be looked at in proper context and viewed in light of a prescientific, pre-Enlightenment world in which government leaders did not hesitate to regulate the religious beliefs of their subjects. In this world, in fact, it was *expected* that government would regulate religious behavior.

Thus, the Commandments begin with a straightforward order for a reason: "I am the Lord thy God. You shall not have false gods before me." (As a Protestant minister, I am in this section using the Protestant version of the Commandments, since it's what I'm most familiar with. In my view, the fact that there are a number of different versions of the Commandments only complicates government's ability to display them.)

Why was God so concerned about competition from "false gods"? Remember, polytheism was the rule, not the exception, in ancient times. Judaism, as a monotheistic religion, needed a powerful opening statement to remind its adherents of why it was different. Thus, the opening commandment is a type of challenge to the faithful to break with past practices and embrace a one, true God.

Today the equation is flipped. Most religions are monotheistic. But polytheistic faiths still exist, and in recent years neopagan faiths have made something of a comeback. In any event, the government has no role to play in how many gods you choose to worship or whether you choose to worship at all. As Thomas Jefferson once observed, "It does me no injury for my neighbor to say there are twenty gods or no gods. It neither picks my pocket nor breaks my leg."

The Second Commandment warns against the making of graven images. In fact, it goes way beyond that, forbidding any likeness of *anything* that is "in heaven above, or that is in the earth beneath, or that is in the water under the earth." (Yikes! Better toss those nice paintings of pastoral landscapes in your living room.)

Once again we see ancient strictures reflected here. Pagan worship often involved the creation of statues or other images that were bowed down to and worshipped. (Remember the golden calf?) We know from the First Commandment that the Old Testament god is a jealous god. He wants no other deities before him. He also wants their images out of the picture.

Today you can fashion all of the god images you want. You can even bow down and worship a golden calf. This commandment has no reflection in modern law and has in fact become controversial. Roman Catholic churches, after all, retain images of Jesus, Mary, and the saints.

The difficulty most politicians have in convincing people of their sincerity when discussing religion is well illustrated by a little exchange I had on the FOX News Channel with U.S. representative Jack Kingston (R–Ga.) after he had successfully gotten the House of Representatives to pass a bill allowing all public buildings (including public schools) to post the Ten Commandments. He said it would be helpful in stopping school shootings like Columbine.

I told him that I'd like to discuss what he thought the contemporary meaning of the Commandments is. I quoted the first to illustrate that this was not a matter about which the government should take a position. I then asked him to explain what a teacher should say about the Second Commandment. His eyes turned downward, and he started talking about gun control (apparently confusing the Second Amendment with the Second Commandment). This was, of course, understandable since at that time Charlton Heston was known as both Moses from the *Ten Commandments* movie and the chief spokesman for the National Rifle Association.

The Third Commandment warns against taking the name of God in vain. It's a serious offense, and we are warned that "the Lord will not hold him guiltless he that takes his name in vain." Again, this is a rule particular to ancient times, when even the name of God was considered so sacred it was not to be uttered. Most people today interpret this commandment as a ban on swearing or blasphemy. I agree that swearing and blasphemy are usually crude and boorish behaviors. But they aren't illegal. In the United States, any effort to proscribe comments, novels, plays, editorial cartoons, poems, and so on that mock any or all religions would be a violation of the First Amendment's prohibition on the regulation of free speech and the press.

The Fourth Commandment admonishes us to remember the sabbath and keep it holy. Modern law contains a mere echo of this commandment in statutes that attempt to curb commerce on Sunday—so-called blue laws. By and large, these have fallen by the wayside in the face of the modern consumer state. An additional problem is what constitutes the sabbath. Most Americans say Sunday. Jews and sabbitarian Christians say Saturday.

The Fifth Commandment reads, "Honor thy mother and father." Generally, I would say this is a good idea—but again, law does not require it. Another problem with a broad rule like this is that it does not admit the need for exceptions. Must everyone honor his or her parents? What if they were bad parents? What if they neglected, beat, or abandoned you?

The Sixth Commandment states, "You shall not kill"—although some versions read "murder" (by no means a trifling difference). At last we have a commandment that is clearly reflected in the secular law. But even here we are not without problems. Again, the issue of exceptions is raised. Should you never kill? What about self-defense? What about war?

And while this commandment has been reflected in the law today, it by no means made its first appearance in the Ten Commandments. The state bans murder because it is an inherently evil act that destabilizes society. It was prohibited long before being carved onto the Ten Commandments.

The Seventh Commandment advises us not to commit adultery. Again, this is good policy. Cheating on your spouse is ethically wrong and can never be defended. But this is not a matter for civil authorities. Some states used to ban adultery, but most of the statutes have either fallen off the books or are no longer enforced. Adultery may be grounds for divorce, but it isn't likely to put anyone behind bars.

The Eighth Commandment tells us not to steal. Clearly, this commandment is reflected in our secular law—and with good reason. The concept of private property is an important right that cannot survive if a society turns its back on laws against theft. But, like the prohibition against killing, this rule predates the Ten Commandments.

The Ninth Commandment orders us to not "bear false witness" against neighbors. Let's be generous here and interpret "neighbor" as any fellow member of society. Basically, this commandment tells us not to lie. I agree; it's good policy to tell the truth. Is it illegal to lie? Perjury is illegal, but other forms of lying are not. And again we face the problems of exceptions: the fact that most people distinguish between "little white lies" and more serious forms of dishonesty is proof that a prohibition on all lying is seen as an overreach.

The tenth and final commandment warns us against coveting. We are told not to covet (desire) our neighbor's goods or spouse. Obviously, coveting is not illegal. Some would argue coveting is the basis of the modern consumer state. If your neighbor buys a new car, for example, you might be tempted to outdo him with a newer, bigger, shinier car. Is it wrong to lust after your neighbor's car, boat, house, or other goods? As a religious leader, I certainly have concerns about rampant materialism in American culture. I've counseled people to focus less on objects and more on spiritual matters. But I can't condemn people for merely wanting nice things. That's human nature. If there were literally a law against coveting your neighbor's new car, most of us would already be in the state pen.

Portions of the Bible, especially the Old Testament's legal codes, were written for a specific people living under a specific set of conditions during a pre-Enlightenment period. We would be foolish not to admit that. Does that mean the Ten Commandments have no value today? Of course they do—but we must face the history of this legal code squarely and acknowledge that it was designed for a simpler people accustomed to living under a religious state. The Ten Commandments make certain demands on the government that today we can no longer accept, mainly, that the state has a duty to enforce religious uniformity. I choose to worship only one god, but I would defend your right to worship five, ten, or none. My right to worship one and your right to worship ten stand or fall together.

Religious conservatives do a disservice to history when they claim that the Ten Commandments are the source of all human law. This claim ignores the rich tapestry and variety of sources that have informed the law over the centuries and misleads people about how the law evolved.

Pagan sources, for example, taught a variation of the Golden Rule long before that stricture ever appeared in the Bible. The universal nature of this rule tells me that it transcends specific religions and philosophies. It informed them all but belongs to none exclusively. Indeed, the Golden Rule is often described as an anchor for all faiths, and I know of no religion or ethical system today that does not honor it.

Rather than pretend that all of our law springs from a single source in the Old Testament, we would do better to provide people with a full account of the origins of the law. This can be done in a way that respects both the separation of church and state and historical accuracy.

Religious Right activists often assert that the Ten Commandments are displayed at the U.S. Supreme Court. This, they claim, justifies the placement of the Commandments in any other public space. However, they don't tell the whole story. The court's main chamber is decorated with a frieze running along the wall that depicts the evolution of the law over many centuries. Many lawgivers from different historical epochs are depicted. Moses is there, cradling two tablets, but he is hardly alone. Joining him are other historic lawgivers such as Solon, Hammurabi, Lycurgus, Mohammed, Augustus, Justinian, and Napoleon.

Lots of conservative pundits seem fuzzy about exactly what is on that wall, how it got there, and what it represents. Tucker Carlson, now a talk show host on MSNBC, once showed me a slide of this frieze during a televised debate and asked if I could name the bearded figure. It was Moses. I asked Carlson if he could read what was on the tablets. He laughed and said he didn't have his contact lenses in. My response was that even if he had, Carlson still would not have been able to read the tablets. They are in Hebrew. Moreover, only a few words are represented, nowhere near the entire text. This is a far cry from a carving of the entire Ten Commandments, in English, that confronted visitors to the Judicial Building in Montgomery. Moore's display was so obvious one judge noted that "one would need to be blind" not to know it was there and what it represented.

(Religious Right activists often also assert that a separate Supreme Court display of a single tablet containing the Roman numerals one through ten represents the Ten Commandments. According to the architectural sculptor who designed it, Adolph A. Weinman, the tablet really represents the Bill of Rights.)

A display like the one found at the Supreme Court is completely unlike Moore's. The U.S. Supreme Court display rejects the simplistic notion that all law springs from the Old Testament and gives a fuller and more meaningful account. Its purpose is to educate about the law, not indoctrinate about religion. Furthermore, it is artwork of genuine historical significance. It's miles removed from what Moore did in Alabama. At the courthouse in Montgomery, Moore stubbornly refused to permit other displays near his monument, because he was convinced that the Judeo-Christian god was the author of all law and sought a display that connected the law to a specific religious view. His goal was to endorse religion, using the power of the state. He cared not one whit about educating Alabamans about the source of the law. Moore's fundamental claim throughout the litigation was that as the highest judicial officer in the state, he had the right and indeed the responsibility to "acknowledge God."

In light of Moore's stunt, legislators in other communities tried to erect Ten Commandments displays or dusted off old ones that had been erected long ago but forgotten. Egged on by Religious Right groups, local officials and governors tripped over themselves to endorse the Ten Commandments. The Family Research Council, a Religious Right group based in Washington, D.C., announced a campaign called Hang Ten, designed to persuade government and education officials to display the Commandments. A number of cases were in the courts when the U.S. Supreme Court in 2004 agreed to hear two disputes involving the Ten Commandments on public land. The Court ruled in June of 2005 that a recently erected Ten Commandments display in a Kentucky county courthouse clearly endorsed religion and had to be removed. An older Austin, Texas, monument on a lawn that included other types of commemorative markers, the Court said, could stay.

The decisions were criticized in some quarters for being confusing, but read together they provide a coherent analysis about the context of these displays. Generally speaking, the Court will allow older displays that include other elements. But a Ten Commandments display slapped up last week in city hall to endorse religion will not survive.

Ironically, many of the older displays, it turns out, were put up for reasons that have precious little to do with religion. Granite Ten Commandments markers were erected in many communities during the 1950s by the Fraternal Order of the Eagles as part of a publicity stunt to promote the movie *The Ten Commandments,* the very epic in which Heston played Moses. So, though some activists see them as solemn reminders of our nation's heritage and undying respect for the Bible, they were mainly props (not unlike December of 2005, when movie promoters brought a giant King Kong to Times Square). In some cases, stars from the Cecil B. DeMille movie unveiled the monuments. It was largely about marketing a movie, not promoting faith.

Looking at these controversies today, I have to wonder what all of the fuss is about. Biblical codes like the Ten Commandments belong on church, synagogue, and temple lawns. Frankly, they look out of place in front of city hall. Putting them there makes about as much sense as sticking a tax accessor's office in the nave of a church.

Yet in recent years, we have seen numerous examples of local politicians grandstanding over these displays to the point of shamelessness. Moore is a perfect example. After his election as chief justice, he dragged his monument into the courthouse in the dead of night without consulting with his eight fellow justices. He knew the act would be controversial. He knew he would be sued. He must have considered the possibility of losing his case and costing Alabama taxpayers a substantial amount of money. Yet Moore did it anyway.

He did it even though he could have displayed the Ten Commandments in his private office, and no one would have complained. He did it even though he could have commissioned the creation of a truly educational display that included the Ten Commandments but also highlighted other sources of the law. He did it even though he knew he might lose his job.

Why did Moore do it, with so much at stake? Moore's supporters will tell you it's because he's a man of principle who is not afraid to stand up for what he believes in. I have never doubted the sincerity of Moore's religious beliefs, but I do believe it's possible he saw the fuss as a stepping-stone to higher office. Moore had been an obscure state judge laboring away in Etowah County, Alabama, when he first gained national headlines by displaying a hand-carved Ten Commandments plaque in his courtroom. Moore used the controversy generated over that issue to win his seat as chief justice on the

Alabama Supreme Court, an elected position. During the race, he promised to display the Ten Commandments at the state supreme court. The promise went over well with Alabama's religiously conservative voters.

After being kicked off the court by his colleagues for refusing to move the monument after a direct order from a federal judge, Moore's name was immediately proposed for higher office. Some fundamentalists even wanted him to run for president on the Constitution Party ticket. As I write these words, Moore is an announced candidate for governor of Alabama. Speculation is that he may have his eye on a U.S. Senate seat some day.

Moore's story plays well with the Religious Right. He portrayed himself as a victim of the secular, God-hating left, even though he brought his troubles on himself. After being removed from the court, Moore made the rounds of the Religious Right rubber-chicken circuit, where he was always received as a hero by adoring crowds. The obligatory book followed.

Fame, adulation, acclaim, and the possibility of higher office—that's what Moore gained from his Ten Commandments fight. Ten years ago, Moore was yet another state judge working in a forgotten corner of the state. Without something to set him apart, Moore would have likely remained there, his aspirations for higher office dashed. Instead, he rode his Ten Commandments monument to national fame and became a celebrity in the world of the Religious Right. Again, I have no doubt that he is a sincere devotee of the Ten Commandments; it's just that his devotion to the monument had the additional advantage of putting him in a position to gain more power. (I leave it to others to assess whether this was the power he "coveted" from the beginning.)

Moore's monument also experienced an unusual post-courtroom life. It was removed from storage and loaded on to a flatbed truck by a right-wing group called American Veterans Standing for God and

Country that took it on a nationwide tour, not coincidentally one that hit a lot of states like South Dakota, where Democratic candidates just happened to be facing tough reelection campaigns in 2004. Crowds of fundamentalists turned out to see and touch the monument. Watching them, I couldn't help but feel that what was dubbed "Roy's rock" by some journalists had become more important to these people than the actual Ten Commandments. They treated it like some holy relic from the Middle Ages, like a fragment of a saint's bone or a splinter from the true cross. Folks who lived during the Middle Ages can be excused for investing such objects with magical powers, given the low educational achievements of the age. What excuse do Moore's followers have?

Therein lies the problem. Too many of these battles over symbols, it seems, become excuses to elect someone somewhere to some political office. Politicians who cannot even name, let alone who are willing to follow, the Ten Commandments never hesitate to lecture the rest of us on their value. As a member of the clergy, I find that infuriating. Newt Gingrich was one of the biggest boosters of the Ten Commandments during the 1990s, frequently berating the federal courts for rulings that required government to refrain from promoting religion. Gingrich is also a serial adulterer who perfected a style of politics known as "win at any cost"—a campaign technique that has about as much in common with the Ten Commandments as a cup of sand does with the Rock of Gibraltar. Gingrich is the last person I'll accept lecturing me on the need for properly venerating religious codes. Gingrich has since published a book in which he encourages people to take a "religious tour" of Washington to see the many symbols of faith in and around government buildings. What he does not suggest is going to the chamber of the House of Representatives to look at the "In God We Trust" logo etched behind the speaker of the House's podium, where he often presided—just before he would adjourn the body and go off for adulterous liaisons with Callista Bisek, a congressional aide twenty-three years his junior, a woman he eventually left his second wife for and married.

Politicians can be expected to exploit the Ten Commandments; after all, they exploit everything else in the pursuit of power. But what excuse do private groups have for their pro–Ten Commandments efforts? Specifically, why are so many religious groups eager to link the Commandments or other religious symbols to the raw power of the state?

I see such crusades as seriously misguided. As a religious leader and a follower of the Christian faith, I'm supposed to insist that we meet the higher standards religion demands. In other words, I'm supposed to be promoting the Ten Commandments, not the mayor. Yet the mayor, often pressured by religious conservatives, keeps stepping on my turf. It's time he went back to his office and stuck to his job— balancing the city budget, overseeing municipal laws, and seeing that the streets are safe. Leave the promotion of faith to me and my coreligionists.

Yet some of my coreligionists are eager for the mayor's help. Why? They have big churches. They have lots of property, often occupying choice locations in town. They could put the Ten Commandments up in prominent places that they own, ensuring high visibility. After a lawsuit in Boise, Idaho, in which a federal judge ruled a Ten Commandments monument unconstitutional, the local Episcopal church across the street volunteered to take it and display it on its front lawn. It is now seen by many more people because it is on a busy street. From that location it sends the accurate message that these religious ideas are embraced at a religious institution. Some religious leaders accept arrangements like this, but others go to city hall instead.

It makes no sense. I have come to the conclusion, after watching dozens of these battles play out over the past twenty years, that what is going on here is a type of religious one-upmanship. Demands that city hall or the state capitol display the Ten Commandments or any other religious symbols are little more than one faith saying to others, "Mom likes me better than you."

What's the point? I am secure enough in my faith that I do not need, or want, the government's imprimatur or "blessing." Others seem to feel differently. Their constant efforts to display their symbols in conjunction with the state blare to the world, "Look, everyone! The government thinks my religion is cool!" It's a rare combination of spiritual immaturity and spiritual insecurity, and it wreaks havoc wherever it rears its head.

These displays are often nothing more than in-your-face statements to members of minority faiths about who's really the boss. Fundamentalists, dismayed over the fact that America has changed over the past seventy-five years and that the nation is now more religiously diverse than ever, seek to reclaim glory days they believe they once enjoyed by marrying their sacred symbols to state power. It's a grotesque and offensive ploy.

Although battles over the Ten Commandments have been the most visible arenas for governmental seizures of religious iconography lately, the issue does have other battlefronts.

For example, county and state official seals sometimes contain religious words or symbols. In general, courts have found seals with explicitly religious messages to violate the First Amendment. A famous case from Edmond, Oklahoma, for example, ended with a cross being removed from the city seal. I agree with these rulings. After all, even a street criminal being pushed into a squad car ought not to think he's being taken off to a religious inquisition at the county jail.

In a major case from Ohio, a federal appeals court upheld the use of the phrase "With God, All Things Are Possible" in the state seal. Although I see no reason for the Buckeye State to have an official position on the power of God, I also found the Religious Right's reaction to this ruling rather peculiar. Some were quoted noting that they had always thought the phrase would be sustained because it no longer conveyed a religious idea. What does this mean? It can't be good for the vitality of religious faith in America when the state's use of a religious motto renders the word *God* meaningless.

And then, of course, consider what happens every year in December. The Supreme Court and lower federal courts have ruled that local governments may display religious holiday symbols on public property—but there's a price. The sacred symbols must be part of a larger display that also includes secular elements so that the overall effect of the display does not endorse or promote religion.

I would run screaming from a deal like this. Pairing my sacred symbols with Rudolph the Red-Nosed Reindeer and Frosty the Snowman is as bad as hanging a Santa Claus poster from the pulpit of a church. Religious conservatives, who claim to value faith and take it so much more seriously than the rest of us, don't run from this idea—they embrace it. They have seized this Faustian bargain, only too happy to surrender their sacred symbols to the all-powerful machine of the consumer-driven Christmas. Thus, we see appalling mixes every year. Let me give you a sad example. In the early 1980s, the city of Pawtucket, Rhode Island, was sued because it had put up a Nativity scene along with a Santa Claus house, reindeer pulling Santa's sleigh, candy-striped poles, a Christmas tree, carolers, and figures representing a clown, an elephant, and a teddy bear. All of this was erected in a public park downtown in the hopes of attracting more shoppers. When the case reached the Supreme Court in 1984, a majority of justices voted to uphold this mix of the secular and the sacred.

Officials in the Reagan administration watched the case with interest because for many years the official December holiday display in an area behind the White House was devoid of manger scenes owing to fears of litigation. The Pawtucket case opened the door to a new kind of display.

At the time, I was working for the national office of the American Civil Liberties Union and was based in Washington. I was sent down to the Ellipse to watch the "new" display's unveiling and comment to the press. It was a very cold day, and I didn't want to dawdle. I headed right for the manger. There was a scene with plaster characters, including the baby Jesus, shepherds, wise men (who in the biblical account don't even show up at the same time as the shepherds; they come about a week later). The display, though, was surrounded by a fence. Incredibly, right next to it was another fence, in this case a necessary one, to contain a group of live reindeer, carefully labeled "Santa's Reindeer." What a ludicrous juxtaposition! It looked like a kind of "Christmas zoo" with caged critters, live and in plaster. It got a lot of press attention, and the next day the "baby Jesus fence" was lowered to appear less like a prison. What had Pawtucket wrought?

I have seen Nativity scenes that were truly beautiful and even moving—in churches and on church lawns. I've been known to stop my car and watch what are called "living Nativity scenes" as I pass through towns. By contrast, I've seen some of the tackiest-looking detritus adorning the lawns of city halls. A Nativity scene, no matter how well crafted or how well maintained, looks out of place and jarring on the cold marble steps of a government building. Placed on the lawn of a church, nestled among holiday greenery with a towering steeple in the background, it looks perfect. Why would we want to put it anywhere else?

Courts have also ruled that private groups may, with their own money and resources, display religious symbols on government property. Again the Religious Right, so eager to nuzzle up to the government, has been quick to exploit this loophole. But again there is a catch: all religious and political groups must be given access to that same space either at the same time or on a rotating basis. Thus, the sacred symbol beloved by so many becomes just another decoration that comes and goes. It may not even last through the holiday season;

after all, the Jaycees have the lawn next week. Let me clue the Religious Right in on something: on a church lawn, you can keep the Nativity scene up *as long as you like.*

Sometimes these symbol conflicts get quite messy. In Ottawa, Illinois, a few years ago, a federal judge allowed a public park to continue to display sixteen paintings depicting the life of Christ, holding that the facility was an open forum for the dissemination of ideas. An atheist group promptly petitioned for the right to erect a banner reading "Jesus Christ Is a Myth." Around the same time, Judd Gregg, now a U.S. senator but then governor of New Hampshire, threw a fit when a Pagan group demanded the right to display a sculpture on the grounds of the statehouse alongside a Nativity scene. A federal judge sided with the Pagans and their art, which consisted of a pyramid of stones flanked by four larger wire pyramids.

The city of Columbus, Ohio, sees regular battles over a cross erected by the Ku Klux Klan in Capitol Square. The Klan has a right to put it up because other groups use the space for religious and political displays.

Naturally when unpopular symbols like this are erected, people start complaining. Why do those people have a right to do this? they ask. Who said they could upset Christians with their banners and sculptures?

The answer is pretty obvious: the same First Amendment that gives a Christian group the right to erect a Nativity scene in a public park also extends that right to atheists, Pagans, and others. Religious Right–style Christians often argue that no one could be offended by a Christmas display. But they get offended by non-Christian ones. People get deeply offended precisely because religion (or its rejection) matters.

Display defenders often assert that their holiday is somehow incomplete without government recognition of it. I can only feel sorry for such people. No one in his right mind goes to city hall for an authentic Christmas experience. If you want the sense of community, love, and peace that the holiday is supposed to be about, you won't find it emanating from the deputy mayor's office. My guess is you will find it at home, surrounded by loved ones, or in a house of worship. Providing this sense of community is one of the things religious groups do best. To be frank, government is lousy at it.

Every year Religious Right groups escalate their whining about an alleged "war on Christmas" that supposedly exists in American government. They complain that advocates of separation of church and state use the First Amendment to attack this beloved holiday. In 2005 the Liberty Counsel, a legal group affiliated with the Reverend Jerry Falwell, actually called a press conference to moan about the assault on Christmas *two weeks before Halloween*. (You would think they would still be fighting the possible divisive effects of black cats and candy corn.)

The Religious Right's complaints are hard to take seriously in a country where department stores and malls start decorating for Christmas in early November, and radio stations play Christmas music as soon as the last Thanksgiving drumstick has been consumed. There seems to be no shortage of holiday spirit in public places throughout December. As I've already noted, government often gets in on the act with its barrage of Santas, sleighs, and snowmen alongside the crèches.

So what's the problem? I'd call it one of unrealistic expectations. Religious Right organizations want the government to celebrate Christmas as a religious holiday. That is not going to happen. It cannot happen. Christmas is already an official holiday mandated by federal law. The government is closed. Most people have the day off. That's as far as the government can go.

For better or for worse, Christmas has become a holiday with significant secular overtones, and it is on this territory that government must stay. Government often has an ulterior motive for pushing

Christmas. These days, Christmas has morphed into an orgy of commercial greed marked by commands to spend, spend, spend and buy, buy, buy. Local and state governments, always with an eye on the bottom line, feed that view and happily take the tax revenue that often follows. The business community doesn't seem to care if anyone even remembers that Christmas marks the birthday of Jesus Christ. From their perspective, that's actually an impediment, since religious divisions might scare off some holiday revelers and their credit cards.

Thus, for business and often governments it's all Frosty, Rudolph, and Santa all the time. Naturally, this bothers some religious people. I can see why. Yet their constant appeals to "keep Christ in Christmas" seem to fall on deaf ears. Their remedy is odd: instead of speaking louder, or more persuasively, they expect the government to fix things up—even though the government is the one entity that is prohibited from celebrating Christmas as a religious holiday and has absolutely no incentive to decouple Christmas from the business machine.

I've read the same polls you have. I've seen newspaper accounts of people who believe the Christmas holiday is too much—too much spending, too much eating, too much partying, too much everything. If you celebrate the holiday, you've undoubtedly felt that it can become overwhelming, that its religious component frequently seems to get buried under mounds of gift wrap.

But I must tell you a simple, if hard, truth: this did not happen by government edict. The culture made Christmas what it is. The culture can take it back. Segments of the religious community have been trying to do that for years. They issue the same pleas over and over. But every year, as the holiday rolls around, deck the halls with MasterCard becomes the dominant message. The religious community has failed to reclaim Christmas. I understand the frustration. I've raised two children and know the pressure of coming through on

Christmas morning. What I don't understand is blaming the failure of the religious community to rescue Christmas on the courts. The courts have nothing to do with the shape Christmas is in. No court has ever said that a truly private expression of the religious dimension of Christmas is a problem. The religious community would do better to aim at Big Business and the American culture that encourages overspending and debt, not an encounter with God, as the ultimate holiday experience.

Some of the complaints Religious Right groups lodge about Christmas verge on the ridiculous. During the 2004 and 2005 holiday seasons, Religious Right groups began carping about store clerks who wished customers "Happy Holidays" instead of "Merry Christmas." An entire Internet-based movement, the Committee to Save Merry Christmas, sprang up that promoted boycotts of stores whose staffs did not offer the religiously correct greeting. I actually believe volunteers went around to stores, noted how they were greeted, and reported back to central command. (While I was making an appearance on Michael Medved's radio show, a caller told me there was also a site with the motto "Every time someone says 'Happy Holidays,' an elf dies." At least the creators of that site have kept a sense of seasonal humor.)

Please. Some people simply have too much time on their hands. To be honest, I feel sorry for anyone whose holiday experience is defined by the type of greeting they get from a seasonal worker at Target. For those who can't figure out why clerks in these stores say "Happy Holidays" instead of "Merry Christmas," let me clue you in: *more than one holiday is celebrated at that time of year.*

When I was a kid, "Happy Holidays" was a way of expressing good thoughts for a merry Christmas and a happy new year in one convenient and short greeting or salutation. Since then, it has been expanded to encompass those who are celebrating non-Christian holidays at the end of the year. In any case, the clerks who offer such greetings are clearly striving not to offend; in fact, they are trying to be respectful. Not everyone celebrates Christmas, and "Happy Holidays" is a safe way of expressing good thoughts for you no matter what holiday you celebrate.

Do people really have nothing better to do than organize store boycotts on the basis of the greeting offered? The fact that this has become a major issue for the Religious Right shows the paucity of their vision and just how thin their "war on Christmas" really is. They desperately need better anecdotes. In late November 2005 I appeared on FOX News Channel's *The O'Reilly Factor* with Jerry Falwell to debate this issue. When I asked for evidence of the alleged war on Christmas, the best he could come up with was a case from a few years ago involving a public school that told a student to stop distributing candy canes wrapped in religious messages. Even the ACLU of Massachusetts supported the student.

Some war on Christmas. Maybe the school officials overreacted—although given the number of allergies that afflict children these days I can see why they might have wanted to curb reckless candy distribution. But let's assume for a moment the school officials did overreact. One quick phone call or letter to the school district's attorney would have resolved the matter. If this is the sum total of the Religious Right's war on Christmas—years-old anecdotes and unremitting whining about what the greeter at Wal-Mart says to you—I'd say the war is a figment of their imaginations. It was conjured up mainly to fill the coffers of Falwell's various organizations. (And believe me, Falwell and his ilk send out plenty of fund-raising letters about the issue.) It is strange, isn't it, how someone like Falwell, who pretends to be holier than thou and poses as the most serious Christian of our times, never hesitates to use the season of peace and love to bash his enemies and make a quick buck?

The self-styled saviors of Christmas have also embarked on a furious campaign to save a symbol that isn't even a Christian one—the decorated conifers called "Christmas trees." Absolutely nothing in the Christian Bible suggests there is religious significance in pine trees. There is a legend, with no historical evidence to support it, that Martin Luther decorated an evergreen as a spiritual act. The Puritans in America did not believe in celebrating Christmas, with or without trees.

Lately, the Reverend Jerry Falwell and his supporters have invested these trees with enormous theological influence. In late 2005 a bureaucrat in Boston sent out a press release announcing the arrival of a "holiday tree" to be lit on Boston Common. Falwell went ballistic and threatened to sic some of his alleged fifteen hundred Christian lawyers on the city. Boston mayor Thomas Menino said he had no plans to call the tree anything but a "Christmas" tree. But what would Falwell's lawyers have done if the mayor had called it a "holiday tree" or even a "tree of lights"? Did Falwell really believe he would get an "activist judge" to force a name change? That is ridiculous.

Frankly, I don't care what these decorated trees are called. However, when a government official does decide to use a more neutral term, more power to him or her. By doing so, he or she is merely being respectful of the diversity in our country, a positive value in my mind.

Genuine religious symbols have deep meaning for believers. In the days of the early, persecuted church, the fish became an underground symbol of support and sometimes safety for members. Religious symbols in modern-day America play a less dramatic role but still retain great power. Symbols mark a community of believers and provide instantly recognizable signs that often reverberate across the culture and speak even to members outside the community. I am not a Muslim, but I think of that faith whenever I see the symbol of a star and crescent moon.

Symbols, therefore, must be closely guarded by religious communities, lest they be co-opted by the government. Examples of this in history are legion. Crusaders hoisted the cross in their wars against Islam. Medieval crests and coats of arms frequently contained crosses, and kings whose behavior could never be called Christlike appropriated the symbol. Theocratic Muslim states today incorporate Muslim iconography on their flags.

The linkage of religion and government through symbols is far from benign. In fact, it tends to tar the church with the actions and attitude of the state. This is why government co-option of religious symbols often sparks a backlash not just from nonbelievers but from sincerely religious persons. They do not want to see the symbols they hold sacred linked to a government whose messages and policies they may not accept.

Few Americans today would support the notion of an officially Christian U.S. government—for some simply because there are just too many expressions of Christianity to make it practical. But what about generic expressions of religion? Can religion be employed in a general, watered-down way and linked to government in a manner few would find offensive? Some argue this is an acceptable answer to our battles over religion. Is it worth doing?

Examples of this approach are legion. Our coins and paper money carry the phrase "In God We Trust," and it doubles as a conational motto along with "E Pluribus Unum." The Pledge of Allegiance contains the phrase "under God." These practices do not date back to the founding period. They are much more recent than many people believe. I would argue they were done for specific political reasons, that is, in pursuit of certain national policy objectives that had little to do with religion. Although they will probably never receive a serious examination in the country, they ought to. It's long overdue. We need to ask what we as a nation gain from these practices and seriously question their value to the religious community.

A little history is useful. "In God We Trust" first found its way onto coinage during the time of the Civil War. A Pennsylvania minister, the Reverend Mark Richard Watkinson, became convinced that the bloody conflict was God's punishment on the nation for failing to recognize him in the Constitution. Backed by a powerful nineteenth-century conservative Protestant group called the National Reform Association, Watkinson wrote to Secretary of the Treasury Salmon P. Chase recommending that the words "God, liberty and law" be added to the coins. Chase agreed in principle but changed the motto to "In God We Trust." It first appeared on the newly minted two-cent piece.

The motto was used on coins until 1905 when President Theodore Roosevelt approved the design of new coins without the motto. But public reaction in favor of the motto was strong, and Roosevelt quickly reversed himself. In 1908 a law was passed mandating use of "In God We Trust" on all coins. It was also etched on paper money, but its use there was not mandated until 1957. It is sometimes still possible to find an old note without it.

"Under God" in the pledge has an even shorter lineage. The Pledge of Allegiance was drafted in 1892 by a Baptist minister named Francis Bellamy to mark the four hundredth anniversary of Columbus's voyage to the New World. Bellamy's original version contained no religious references, in large part because he was trying to get people to agree about some core principles, not divide them along religious lines. "Under God" was added by Congress in 1954, after prodding from the American Legion, which felt the phrase would be a blow to "atheistic communism." When he signed the legislation into law, President Dwight D. Eisenhower observed, "From this day forward, the millions of our school children will daily proclaim in every city, every village, and every rural schoolhouse, the dedication of our nation and our people to the Almighty." Two years later, Congress voted to make "In God We Trust" the national motto.

In all three cases, adoption of religious language was seen as a way to achieve certain policy goals—heal a divisive civil war or stand up to an unpopular political philosophy. Far from being part of our nation's heritage, they are examples of religion being employed to prop up what are viewed as desirable governmental political goals.

Since then, they have mutated into something even worse: they have been declared essentially meaningless. "In God We Trust" on the money has been challenged in court at least twice. In both cases, the federal courts declared use of the phrase "ceremonial" and held that it is not really religious. Phrases like this, courts have said, are merely examples of "ceremonial deism," and they lose their religious significance through constant use over time. Those courts are indeed on to something. Remember that those coins and bills are the same ones used to bribe public officials, to have that "just one last drink" before driving home, or to purchase illegal narcotics.

"Under God" in the pledge met the same fate in the courts, with one notable recent exception. California physician Michael Newdow convinced the U.S. Court of Appeals for the Ninth Circuit to rule against the use of "under God" in the pledge in public schools in 2003. The case then reached the Supreme Court, which dismissed it on the grounds that Newdow did not have full custody of a child in the school district. Having been in the courtroom that day, I have to say it was obvious the justices simply did not want to deal with this issue. Had they been forced to, I'm certain many would have tried to resurrect the "ceremonial deism" line and upheld the religious language of the pledge.

Some people, including a number of advocates of separation of church and state, see this as a trivial issue. I can understand why. A fleeting reference to God in the pledge and stamping religious mottos on the money *is* trivial. That's exactly the problem. Religion isn't supposed to be trivial. Religion is supposed to be meaningful.

In an effort to find some acceptable way to link religion and government, we have allowed the courts to adopt the legal fiction that religious affirmations and slogans aren't really religious. Worse than that, we have permitted the state to endorse the most bland, watered-down, and ultimately meaningless religious statements possible. I fail to see how any of this helps religion.

Religion has the power to change lives. I've seen it happen. It happens because religious people work hard to spread their faith and take the time to make a commitment to another human being. Over the years, I've had people tell me many stories about their involvement or reengagement with the church. Some of these accounts are quite dramatic. The people who tell these stories are serious, contemplative and reflective. They are describing something real that to them is extremely powerful. To date, I've never had anyone tell me they had a life-changing encounter with religion because they saw "In God We Trust" on a nickel—even on the new "Jefferson nickel," where the phrase is more prominently displayed than on earlier versions.

The ceremonial use of religion by the state is among the cheapest examples of empty spirituality available. As time passes, it descends to the level of mere ritual—something that must be done, but not ever thought about. Virtually every politician in America now ends his or her speeches with "God bless America." Do they say this because they truly want God to bless the nation or because it is expected, because no other closing is seen as acceptable? If it's the latter, and I believe it is, we are simply going through the motions.

Real spirituality is marked by an intense level of commitment and demands that are not always easy to meet. The best preachers in the pulpit challenge worshippers to push themselves. The founder of my faith never said his way would be easy. He warned his followers of rock-strewn paths, resistance, struggle, and persecution. He even advised them it would be easier to enter heaven if they gave up their worldly possessions.

Real spirituality makes demands on us—but it can also give back in spades. The sense of a real and powerful encounter with God in the context of worship with a community of like-minded believers is deeply meaningful and moving. The joy felt in the joint declaration to follow Christ and his edicts is, in my view at least, without parallel in human experience. All of that can be difficult to conjure up. It is a high standard, and sometimes we strive and fail. I am aware when leading worship that not everyone is able to reach the level of commitment and experience that I would like them to. That's not the point. The point is they strive to. There is great meaning and dignity in that very attempt. Symbolic religion and the use of sacred faith by government for purely ceremonial reasons doesn't even come close. It demands nothing of the adherent and gives the same back. It is empty and formulaic. Compared with what goes on in church, I find watered-down expressions of government-led generic "to whom it may concern" religiosity cold, sterile, and offensive.

Compare a Saturday or Sunday worship with a city "prayer breakfast" and you'll find a great deal more authentic faith and spirit in the former. The 2006 National Prayer Breakfast in Washington, D.C., was a hot ticket with plenty of lobbyists clamoring for an invite. (Ironically, many people were drawn to the event to hear not a preacher but a rock star—Bono of the Irish band U2.) There were plenty of open seats at the worship services I attended the week before and after.

In their defense, fundamentalists sometimes argue that generic spirituality can still be a unifying force among a community of believers. However, I am highly skeptical that such a thing as nonsectarian prayer even exists, and if it did I'm sure the prayer would not be worth uttering. Rather than lead people in nonsectarian prayer before government meetings, our leaders would do better to recommit themselves to the First Amendment's guarantee of religious liberty, so that everyone has the right to pray in whatever manner they see fit before the meeting. Your pastor does not lead nonsectarian prayers at church. Why burn to say them with a member of the city council during a government meeting?

Call me old-fashioned, or even conservative, but at the end of the day that's what I believe prayer and promotion of religion are for: to please God. So-called civil religion is all too often more about winning votes than worshipping God. It's also a way to claim divine sanction on the cheap. We can stamp "In God We Trust" on our coins from now until Judgment Day. If all we do is stamp it, and never attempt to live up to that standard—if indeed the mere placement of that slogan becomes a substitute for meeting that standard—we are wasting our time. We will be judged according to our actions toward our fellow man, not by what we had the temerity to etch on our money.

In the end, I believe the Religious Right, through its constant promotion of various forms of civil religion, has exchanged mere symbolism for substance, formulas for faith. Its claims to be protecting our religious heritage ring hollow when one looks at what it actually defends: a bland system of watered-down religiosity forever yoked to the government, a scheme where the rules are rigged so that the perceived needs of the state always reign supreme and religion is little more than a useful prop for policy objectives that may or may not coincide with the teachings of the founder of Christianity.

It's bad enough that the Religious Right enables and defends this type of meaningless religiosity. The offense is compounded by accusing those of us who unmask it for the faux spirituality that it is of being antifaith. That is appalling.

I did not enter the ministry and devote my life's work to defending religious liberty so that the country would always be safe for ceremonial deism. I do not defend our First Amendment so that a pastor can read a thirty-second nondenominational prayer before a meeting of the zoning board. Such things are not worth fighting for. I do my job not because I hate or fear faith, but because I love it. I never want to see it drained of power and significance by being tied to the state.

Oddly enough, that should put me in the company of the Religious Right. The fact that it does not is a damning indictment of them, not me. The leadership of the Religious Right long ago traded true spirituality for something else—for prepackaged, public consumption religion guaranteed to do nothing to advance the true mission of the church. What did they get in return? A Nativity scene flanked by elves on the town green for two weeks every year and bragging rights about God's magnificent appearance on tens and twenties.

No matter how I parse that, I can't see it as anything but a raw deal.

4

Faith-Based Initiatives
PAYING FOR PIETY

WHEN GEORGE W. BUSH WAS INAUGURATED as president in January 2001, he had a plan to roll out one major policy initiative each week. On week three he introduced something called the faith-based initiative.

For a week before and after, I spent most of my time on the telephone with reporters or in front of television cameras answering the same questions over and over again: "What exactly is a 'faith-based' initiative?" and "Are you concerned about it?"

I tried to boil down my answers to a simple point: This is government-funded religious outreach. And yes, I was definitely concerned. A few days after the initiative was announced, I told one reporter it was "the worst idea since they took King Kong off Skull Island and brought him to New York."

During the campaign, Bush had been vague about what this initiative would look like. Looked at in broad terms, he did not seem to be promoting anything too radical. Even Bush's opponent, Vice

President Al Gore, endorsed faith-based initiatives during the campaign. Gore's announcement stunned civil liberties advocates, but it was soon obvious what was going on: the effort was part of a strategy by Gore advisers to get God back in the Democratic column.

So here we are years later, and what's the problem?

The faith-based initiative, as conceived and executed by Bush and his supporters in the Religious Right, has turned out to be something far more problematic than simply a plan to funnel tax support to religious groups to underwrite their social service work. Instead, the initiative has taken on significant political overtones and is being used as a lure to win Bush more support from segments of the religious community, particularly African-American churches. At the same time, claims are being made about the initiative's potential and success rate that do not jibe with reality. Finally, the initiative is being used as a mechanism to significantly erode the church-state wall in America by challenging long-standing rules that govern the state's ability to fund services provided by religious groups.

At the end of the day, the faith-based initiative amounts to little more than a scheme by the federal government to put the poor on church steps one day and drop a bag of money there the next and pray they find one another. Those in need deserve better.

Before we go much further, I need to make one thing clear: the term *faith-based initiative* is a euphemism. Bush's advisers cooked it up during the 2000 campaign for explicitly political reasons. I do not care for it.

Despite the claims of the Religious Right, the United States is far from a "faith-phobic" country. Unlike many Western nations where the influence of religion is on the wane and attendance at church services has dropped, America's population retains a strong interest in all things spiritual; more than 90 percent of Americans say they do not doubt the existence of God, and about half of the pop-

ulation attends religious services regularly. Americans regularly attest
to the power of prayer and huge majorities say they believe faith is
important to their daily lives.

Americans recognize that religion has the potential to divide
people and spark conflict. This is why they are often reluctant to embrace schemes that mix church and state like a tossed salad. But the
idea of faith and religion as generic concepts are overwhelmingly re-
garded as positive by the people.

Enter the faith-based initiative. Calling it what it really is—
government-sponsored religion—would have alarmed too many
people. Thus, Bush's supporters devised a much more innocuous
term, one they knew would resonate deeply with some Americans
and sound utterly nonthreatening to most others.

The phrase was successfully pitched to the media and immediately adopted. We are now stuck with it. Complicating matters is that
the Bush administration uses the term *faith-based initiative* to apply to
just about any program that involves or has ever involved tax support
for a project undertaken by a religious organization. It's my belief
that by faith-based initiative, Bush and his backers mean something
very specific—and I'll define that shortly. By using the term to apply
to long-standing or existing programs, the Bush administration can
claim that its faith-based initiative really isn't anything extreme or
even a departure from current practices, when in fact it is.

It is true that the federal government as well as state and local
governments have been giving tax support for religious groups to
provide social services for many years. This practice is so common it
has become rather noncontroversial. Catholic Charities is a good
example. This organization often receives 75 percent of its budget or
more from government sources. Jewish, Lutheran, and other religious providers have also accepted government grants.

As state and federal governments become less committed to direct provision of many social services, they contract the work out. Religious groups, accustomed to providing direct aid services, were naturally interested in taking on the job.

If this type of funding has been happening for a long time, then why all the controversy over faith-based initiatives? The answer is that Bush wanted to discard many of the existing rules that governed this system and move toward a new and unprecedented era of government funding for specifically sectarian activities.

In the past, religious groups were essentially contracting with the government to provide a secular service. Catholic Charities did not run its government-funded programs as Catholic projects. People of many different faiths were hired to staff these initiatives, and the programs contained no religious content. The bottom line was to provide the needed service—be it shelters for the homeless, soup kitchens for the hungry, or job training for the unemployed. The services were offered to all in need without regard to religious belief or church membership. No one was pressured to take part in religion. Services were usually provided in a neutral setting, that is, not a house of worship. In some cases, religious organizations would take the additional step of creating an entirely separate nonprofit entity to administer government funds.

These rules generally worked well, but Bush insisted they be scrapped. He argued that requiring religious groups to downplay the religious content of their programs was a mistake. It was the religious impulse, Bush argued, that made the programs most effective.

In 2004, for example, the president went to a predominantly African-American church in New Orleans in observance of Martin Luther King's birthday and strongly implied that his initiative was designed to fund religion.

"Problems that face our society are oftentimes problems that, you know, require something greater than just a government program or a government counselor to solve," Bush said. "Intractable problems,

problems that seem impossible to solve, can be solved. There is the miracle of salvation that is real, that is tangible, that is available for all to see."

Continued Bush, "Miracles are possible in our society, one person at a time, but it requires a willingness to understand the origin of miracles. Miracles happen as a result of the love of the Almighty professed, by the way, taught, by the way, by religion from all walks of life, whether it be Christian, Jewish, Muslim, Hindu; people who've heard that universal call to love a neighbor just like you'd like to be loved yourself, and then surround someone who hurts with love."

At another point, Bush, noting that the Bethel African Methodist Episcopal Church has a child-care center, brandished a Bible, calling it the "handbook" for the faith-based operation. He added, "We ought to say, we want results, we welcome results, and we're willing to fund programs that are capable of delivering results. We want to fund programs that save Americans, one soul at a time."

Bush went on, "Faith-based programs are only effective because they do practice faith. It's important for our government to understand that."

I was struck especially by the phrase "one soul at a time." Until then, I had not been aware that the state of my soul was of any interest to the federal government. What an utterly inappropriate rationale for the initiative! Mr. Bush is not America's pastor, and the federal government is not a funding trough for salvation.

What's even stranger is that Bush's words conflicted with the media line his own supporters had been parroting for the past four years. One of the architects of the faith-based initiative, Stephen Goldsmith, the former mayor of Indianapolis, tried to make a sharp distinction between what could and could not be funded.

Appearing on CBS's *Face the Nation* with me, Goldsmith insisted that the faith-based initiative would "buy bread, not Bibles," a line he loved to repeat in the media. It was a clever phrase that overlooked the obvious: if the government spends more tax dollars for bread, it frees up more of a charity's private money for buying Bibles. There is an even bigger flaw, though. It is terribly difficult to segment a program so clearly that you can just turn off the spiritual spigot whenever a government dollar flies by and open it up again when the privately raised dollars arrive.

Further complicating matters, much of the discussion over the faith-based initiative has been marked by faulty assumptions. Here's one example: Bush repeatedly implied that the more religious a program was, the more effective it would be. He was simply playing into a common bias among the American people that since religion is good, everything religious groups do must be successful.

In fact, there was absolutely no evidence that the old system of religious groups providing social services in a secular manner was ineffective or inefficient. If anything, it was time-tested and had been operating smoothly for many years. Catholic Charities even had "economies of scale"; that is, the group was large enough to maintain a staff and facilities that could deal with all of a client's needs.

Bush's new approach, meanwhile, really was risky and unproven. Bush was essentially arguing for a massive shift in social service funding. He wanted to transfer tax dollars from longtime religious providers who were offering secular programs to the fundamentalist Christian groups that already are his political allies and African-American churches he hoped would become so. In the case of the former, Bush's theory seemed to be that because the fundamentalist groups included more religion in their programs, they would naturally do a better job. He also had a vision that local churches could provide more programs if they received government grants, when in fact many urban churches are barely able to pay for Sunday services as members move further into suburban congregations.

The president's "vision" lacked any objective data to back it up. At the same time, there is no evidence that these fundamentalist groups are willing or able to provide social services across the board. Their track record is at best spotty. There is an additional problem: fundamentalist groups are in no way willing to provide services in a secular manner.

These days, fundamentalists see secularism as their avowed enemy. This perspective is completely misguided. I see the secular state as the great champion of religious liberty. It's highly ironic that we wouldn't even have fundamentalist religions in America were it not for the fact that our secular state, by taking no positions on the truth or falsity of religions, allows the development of all kinds of new groups and religious structures.

Here is where Bush's theory of faith-based initiatives breaks down: he believes that the more religious a program is, the better it will succeed. Yet the more religious a program is, the less likely it is to qualify for government support. The state, after all, is not supposed to be in the business of funding explicitly religious (sectarian) programs. At least, that is what the majority of members of the U.S. Supreme Court believe.

Fundamentalist Christian groups frequently boast about how merely providing a social service is not enough. There must be religious proselytizing as well. This is not surprising, since theologically, fundamentalism is marked by a belief in the fallen state of humankind. Fundamentalists genuinely believe that problems such as alcoholism, chronic unemployment, and the inability to pay one's bills spring from a depraved condition brought about by a person's failure to be right with God.

I reject this theory of social ills, but I understand why to fundamentalists it makes perfect sense. They believe in the essential wickedness of people and in the existence of literal demonic forces that seek to undermine and trip us up at every stage. People who hold this worldview have no problem attributing human foibles to supernatural causes. Thus, to them, the root of all problems is a failure to worship

God in the proper manner. Once the person is "born again" or adopts the correct far right, fundamentalist religious beliefs, his or her problems will evaporate.

We could sum up the conflict between fundamentalist and non-fundamentalist views as this: Fundamentalists reject societal causes for people's ills. In fact, they often ridicule the very idea. To fundamentalists, people are poor, addicted to drugs, or homeless because they aren't in a proper relationship with God. If they get right with God (by adopting fundamentalist religious beliefs) their problems will be solved. It's that simple.

Thus, any faith-based initiative that leans heavily on fundamentalist Christian providers will end up, by default, including government funding and support of specific religious views. Fundamentalists do not believe that providing for someone's physical needs is enough. There must always be a religious conversion as well or the job remains half done. The conversion is their end goal. The providing of a bowl of soup, a bed on a cold night, or a job-counseling program is merely the attractive bait to bring the person to the door. Once inside, it's hard-sell evangelism all the way.

Not surprisingly, I have several problems with this approach. To begin with, I am appalled by any theology that refuses to recognize the societal causes of poverty and other ills. All too often, people fall through the social safety net from no fault of their own. A woman with children who is abandoned by her husband and left destitute has a bigger problem than having chosen to attend the wrong house of worship. A child who is neglected because his parents are drug addicts is not being punished by God for failing to pray enough.

Fundamentalists are free to believe such simplistic notions, but I resent having to pay for them. Government at all levels should avoid propping up any religious view with tax aid. Yet that is exactly what the Bush faith-based initiative does. It takes tax money from mainline groups willing to provide secular relief and aid and shifts it to hard-core fundamentalists whose main goal is furthering their hellfire-and-damnation scenarios and winning new converts.

My second problem with the faith-based approach of the Bush administration is that it puts vulnerable people in an extremely difficult situation. Most people, even those skeptical of organized religion, have no problem approaching a religious provider for secular services. It is commonly known that these religious groups just want to help. They have no ulterior motive and aren't in the business of pressuring anyone to adopt new or different beliefs. But the fundamentalists do have an ulterior motive: to convince those in need that they are wicked sinners who must immediately adopt rigid forms of ultraconservative Christianity if they are to have any hope of improving their situation. The government simply has no business paying for this.

The choice for those in need becomes either putting up with this hard-sell evangelism or going without the service. We should not put people in a situation like this. It is fundamentally wrong. It is an affront to a person's sense of dignity and self-worth. If an individual is homeless, hungry, addicted to drugs, or has some other serious problem and truly wants help, that person deserves to get that help. End of discussion. His or her religious beliefs should never even come into play. To the government, they should be completely irrelevant. The question should not even be asked.

Under Bush's faith-based initiative, the question is not only asked, but so much hinges on the answer. Time and again, Bush has visited fundamentalist Christian groups and lauded them as models for his initiative because they change people's souls. Speaking at a Dallas church in the fall of 2003, Bush remarked, "People need to know a higher power that is bigger than their problems. What the faith-based programs say, time after time, is that miracles are possible." In another case, Bush picked up a Bible from someone in the front row during a church visit to promote faith-based initiatives, calling it a "good go-by."

So now the government is going into the business of promoting miracles and Bible study? Pardon my lack of enthusiasm.

Bush, a recovered alcoholic, talks constantly about religion's ability to change people's lives and behaviors. When Bush employs this language, he is invariably talking about fundamentalist forms of Christianity. The idea of a sudden, life-changing encounter with religion that leads to dramatic shifts in a person's life is nothing new. Remember, it happened to Saint Paul on the road to Damascus. But fundamentalists have adopted this experience in the modern era and all too often act as if anyone who has not had this dramatic conversion is not a genuine Christian. When Bush talks like this, he is essentially employing code language that resonates among fundamentalists, but he is not even describing the spiritual experience most Americans have had.

Like everyone, I've heard accounts by people who really do change at least some of their destructive behaviors after adopting fundamentalist religious beliefs. Such anecdotes have great power to convey ideas and stir up emotions, but they do not stand as empirical data. Fundamentalist groups claim great success in getting people to drop behaviors like alcohol abuse, drug use, and criminal activity. They have yet to present any objective data backing up these claims.

That doesn't mean they haven't tried. In 2003 the group Prison Fellowship, run by ex-Watergate felon Charles Colson, released a study indicating that prison inmates who had gone through its Inner-Change program in Texas, which is steeped in fundamentalism, had a lower rate of recidivism, returning to prison less often than members of a control group.

The media eagerly picked up on the study and reported it as a great success for faith-based initiatives. But it wasn't that at all. The study simply did not hold up under scrutiny. Two months after it was released in June of 2003, Mark A. R. Kleiman, University of California–Los Angeles professor of public policy, debunked it. Kleiman noted that Prison Fellowship started out with 177 inmates. Along the way, 102 of them were kicked out of the program or left for various reasons. That left InnerChange with only success stories. Naturally they did better than the control group.

When Kleiman added all 177 inmates back into the study, he found that InnerChange inmates actually did slightly worse on recidivism than the control group. Observed Kleiman in *Slate* magazine, "That result ought to discourage InnerChange's advocates, but it doesn't because they have just ignored the failure of the failures and focused on the success of the successes."

An in-depth study of the faith-based approach in Bush's home state uncovered numerous problems. As governor of Texas, Bush had appointed a task force to find ways to implement the initiative. State agencies were ordered to work with religious groups, and government oversight was reduced or dropped entirely. The scheme was supposed to provide better services to those in need. The Texas Freedom Network's Samantha Smoot told reporters during an October 2002 press conference, "Evidence points instead to a system that is unregulated, prone to favoritism and commingling of funds, and even dangerous to the very people it is supposed to serve."

Americans United for Separation of Church and State filed a federal lawsuit in Iowa to block taxpayer funding of InnerChange there. Again, impressive-sounding claims were made about the remarkable changes that would occur in inmates' lives. The evidence was lacking.

Our attorneys did find that the program was saturated with fundamentalist Christianity. Other religions were mocked and disparaged. Prison inmates—men who have served hard time behind bars, mind you—were taught fundamentalist social policy as if it were straight from the Bible, including the notion that men should run households.

The program was rife with controversial claims. Gay inmates were told that homosexuality is an "abomination" and that they could change their sexual orientation through prayer.

Despite these problems, inmates in the program received significant perks—more calls to family members on the outside, access to a computer lab, cells with private bathrooms, and so on. Participation in the program also made it much more likely that an inmate would receive parole. All of these desirable benefits were available only to those inmates willing to embrace fundamentalist Christianity.

In 2002 researchers at the University of Pennsylvania's Penn Center for Research on Religion and Urban Civil Society did a meta-analysis of twenty-five previous studies examining the effectiveness of faith-based groups. The study found that there is no empirical data backing up the frequent claim that religious groups provide social services more effectively than secular groups.

The report noted that qualities such as "sound financial management and quality of staff were far more important than religious affiliation in predicting a program's success."

Noted the study's authors, "Champions of [faith-based organizations] regularly cite near perfect success rates of programs for drug addicts, prisoners, at-risk youth, and other populations. But closer examination of these accounts of extremely high success rates tend to reveal mere simple summary statistics based on in-house data often compiled by the religious organizations and ministries themselves. What is needed, above all, is accurate and unbiased information that can serve as the basis for an enlightened public discussion."

I love the optimism of those working in academia. Unfortunately, an "enlightened public discussion" is the last thing advocates of the faith-based initiative want. Consider the quote from the report about the importance of "quality of staff" in these programs. What this means is that staff members must be properly trained to do the job. A drug and alcohol addiction counselor, for example, should be certified and properly trained in the nature of addiction to be truly effective.

Unfortunately, proper training is not the main criteria fundamentalist groups look at when hiring staff for their social programs; religious belief is. Many fundamentalist groups maintain statements of faith and insist that all employees hew to these doctrinal points. Adherence to dogma becomes more important than an ability to do the job. Thus, a qualified person can be excluded for failing to hold the "right" religious beliefs.

In August 2002 a Methodist home for troubled children in Decatur, Georgia, agreed to interview Alan Yorker, a psychotherapist, for a staff position. Yorker had the necessary qualifications, but his interview was abruptly terminated when a staff member learned that he is Jewish. He was told he would not even have been called to an interview if he had a more "Jewish-sounding" name.

(The same facility fired a counselor, Aimee Bellmore, who had received outstanding performance evaluations, after it learned she is gay. Bellmore's case raises an important point that is often overlooked. Religiously based hiring discrimination extends not just to an individual's church affiliation but other factors as well. Bellmore might have belonged to the Methodist Church. That was irrelevant. The home fired her for being a lesbian.)

If this trend continues, publicly funded faith-based organizations will be able to fire single moms, people in interfaith marriages, anyone who publicly dissents from a church tenet, and so on. People aren't just being fired because they belong to the "wrong" church. They are being fired for who they are and how they live. Indeed, in virtually every case where a privately funded entity makes such a religious judgment, its right to do so is upheld.

Fundamentalists' insistence of elevating adherence to rigid theology over secular qualifications is especially dangerous in areas like drug and alcohol addiction. Fundamentalist groups often claim high rates of success in this area—but offer no objective data to back up those claims. They offer plenty of anecdotes that have great emotional appeal, but, again, anecdotes are not data. In fact, many of these programs championed by fundamentalists reject the medical model of addiction—the belief that alcoholism is a disease, for example—and instead insist that abusing drugs or alcohol is evidence of a personal failure that can be corrected through intensive Bible study or an embrace of fundamentalist Christianity. The faith-based initiative would heap generous amounts of tax money on these organizations despite their shaky, nonscientific approach and their blatant use of religious discrimination in hiring staff.

Bush and his supporters frame this issue, the ability of religious entities to hire and fire at will, as a constitutional right. Religious groups, we are told, have a right to hire their own staff members. When it comes to purely religious functions, I completely agree. Roman Catholic churches do not ordain women, and it would be absurd and unconstitutional to try to force a Catholic church to interview, much less hire, a woman candidate for the priesthood. Many conservative denominations will not ordain or hire gays. This is their right, even though I find the theology behind such decisions incoherent and repugnant.

But this right should not extend to publicly funded programs that are supposedly offered in the public good. When taxpayer money is turned over to religious groups to underwrite social services, that action is supposedly taken to benefit society at large. Helping drug addicts get clean is a social good that benefits us all. Providing shelter for the homeless springs from our shared sense of care and concern for one another. When religious groups voluntarily decide to seek taxpayer support for these programs, they must forfeit their right to discriminate on religious grounds because they are now acting on behalf of the state. We would not permit the government to discriminate in this manner; why should we allow it from people acting as agents of the state and indeed funded by the state? Once they accept tax aid, religious groups start pursuing a goal that must go beyond narrow parochial interests. They must adopt the values of the larger society, one of which is nondiscrimination.

In recent years the House of Representatives has passed several social service bills that allow religious groups to accept tax money under the faith-based initiative yet still base hiring on narrow religious criteria. This is appalling and nonsensical. These organizations are supposed to be providing services to the larger society in a secular manner. Why do they need to discriminate on religious grounds? They aren't providing sectarian programs!

On a practical level, does anyone seriously believe that a Buddhist or freethinker ladles out stew in a soup kitchen differently from his or her Pentecostal or Catholic counterpart? Do Methodists fold sheets in a homeless shelter according to a different pattern than do Presbyterians or Mormons?

Not surprisingly, the answer is intertwined with politics. The Bush administration wants its fundamentalist political allies to believe they have a legal right to accept tax aid and still run public programs rife with sectarian dogma. They have no such right. Bush and his allies in Congress and the fundamentalist religious community know exactly what they want and talk about it openly. In the fall of 2002, U.S. representative Mark Souder (R–Ind.), a frequent booster of the Bush approach, remarked that Bush's goal is to help "overtly Christian organizations pick people up, change their character, convert them regardless of what religion they are and change their lives." This is a curious goal for any government to pursue.

I picked up a law degree through night classes at Georgetown University. I am acutely aware of the importance of America's civil rights laws. Since the days of Harry S. Truman, government policy has prohibited making grants or contracts with groups that discriminate in hiring on the basis of certain criteria, including race and religion. This is a perfectly sensible corollary to the fact that the government itself cannot hire or fire on those bases.

In the Bush administration, things have changed. In every set of regulations issued to implement this program, and in an executive order signed by the president, there is clear language that claims to permit a federal grant recipient group that is a religious organization to hire persons solely on the basis of their religious beliefs.

This means that a Roman Catholic provider can refuse to hire, or fire at will, a pregnant and unmarried woman; it effectively permits a fundamentalist Christian church to put the statement "No Jews or Muslims need apply" on the top of its employment application form. Bush claims this is designed to protect the integrity of the religious "identity" of the organization. Indeed, under the 1964 Civil Rights Act, private religious groups can make such employment decisions with privately obtained funds. In 1964, of course, no one contemplated churches becoming, even in part, taxpayer-funded entities.

When public funds enter the equation, both the constitutional and moral calculi change. It is flatly wrong to create a system in which you can be taxed to help pay for a job you cannot obtain, even if you are eminently qualified for the position.

This approach of sanctioning religious discrimination in public programs has spread into areas where it simply makes no sense. The House of Representatives, for example, voted in 2004 to allow Head Start programs to be able to discriminate in the selection of teachers and even volunteers on the basis of religion. Head Start is a popular program for low-income children and their families designed to give youngsters a leg up before school starts. It is an academic program and has nothing to do with religion. Although Head Start centers sometimes lease spaces in churches, the program is legally nonsectarian. It may not include religious worship, because Head Start is an

extension of public education and serves families from many different faith backgrounds.

Why on earth should Head Start programs be allowed to discriminate on religion when hiring? To say it again, *the program has no religious content*. The only criteria for hiring someone should be that
person's qualifications to teach young children and help prepare
them for kindergarten. Imagine that you are a Muslim and your child
goes to a program where other parents are allowed to come in and
read their child's favorite book to the class. When you sign up, you
are told that Muslim parents are not welcome. What kind of a message of bigotry does this send to the children?

The insistence that even a program like Head Start must be allowed to hire and fire on the basis of religion is further proof that the
entire faith-based approach is little more than a sop to the president's
fundamentalist allies. Examples like the one I just gave were explained to the House of Representatives, but members voted to
place the discriminatory provisions in anyway, over orders from the
White House not to "compromise" this principle.

For too many faith-based providers, promoting a sectarian message is job one—even if that message conflicts with the larger goals
and needs of society. Consider sex education for young people.
Many Americans might be surprised to learn that many sex education programs are now largely faith based. Federal law bans any discussion of artificial contraceptives in federally funded sex ed programs.
Health educators with integrity won't offer such instruction because
it is incomplete. Thus, conservative religious groups have stepped in
to fill the void.

Poll after poll has shown that a solid majority of Americans favor
comprehensive sex education for teenagers. Americans want sex education to stress the importance of abstinence but also discuss forms
of birth control. Federal funding can go only to programs that are

"abstinence based," which has been interpreted to mean no talk about birth control.

Fundamentalist Protestant and orthodox Roman Catholic groups are getting most of the federal money for sex education. What they are offering America's teens is a smorgasbord of religious dogma mixed with fear-based claims about the awful things that happen to sexually active teens. Most teenagers see right through this. The appallingly high U.S. teen pregnancy rate is proof that the faith-based approach isn't working.

Legally, religious groups are not supposed to put dogma in their publicly funded programs—but many do anyway. In 2005 the Department of Health and Human Services defunded a Pennsylvania group called the Silver Ring Thing whose abstinence program was rife with fundamentalist dogma. Department staffers acted as if their diligence and oversight had led to the uncovering of the abuses. In fact, the only reason the department was even looking at the Silver Ring Thing is that the American Civil Liberties Union of Pennsylvania had filed a lawsuit over the group's activities. Had the ACLU not forced the issue, the Silver Ring Thing would have undoubtedly gone right on using tax funds to promote fundamentalism.

Americans United has also found versions of AIDS prevention programs and grant proposals that originally carried with them a request that recipients be faith based or at least willing to "partner" with faith-based groups.

Federal grants to groups like the Silver Ring Thing, which had no track record of effectiveness and whose approach runs counter to what polls show most Americans want, are clearly designed to placate Bush's far right religious base. Most Americans support comprehensive sex education, but the Religious Right does not. Federal support for the Silver Ring Thing and groups like it becomes a way for the administration to show its solidarity with conservative Christians and claim to be making a difference on an issue that concerns them.

But Religious Right–style Christians are not the only faith community the faith-based initiative is designed to attract. There is also a significant component aimed at African Americans. Blacks tend to vote for the Democratic Party. In recent years, Republican strategists have been looking for issues to peel off enough African-American votes to shift the political balance in America. They have highlighted social issues such as abortion and gay rights. But more quietly, behind the scenes, the faith-based initiative is being used as well to woo black clergy into the arms of the GOP.

In April 2001 the White House hosted the first of many forums on the initiative for black clergy. The political dimension escaped no one. One anonymous aide told the *New York Times,* "The Republicans said that the Democrats had traditionally done a good job reaching out to the African-American community and this was their effort to do a better job."

Since then, Bush's White House Office of Faith-Based and Community Initiatives has frequently sponsored events for African-American clergy in inner-city neighborhoods. These events are portrayed as seminars, and the message is far from subtle: there is a lot of federal money available.

Of course, few get a share if they are unwilling to play ball with the administration. The vote buying has become obvious. One African-American Philadelphia minister and former Philadelphia Eagles football star, Herbert Lusk, was awarded $1 million in federal grants after endorsing Bush on behalf of his whole church while being piped via satellite into the Republican National Convention in 2000. Since the convention was held in the "City of Brotherly Love" that summer, Lusk could have simply taken a taxi for his appearance. Obviously, the convention planners thought it better imagery to have the church pulpit on the giant video screens being seen by delegates and at-home television viewers. Other black pastors are led to believe they can receive similar largess if they'll climb on the GOP bandwagon. In St. Louis, the Reverend Sun Myung Moon, founder of the controversial Unification Church, even doled out gold watches to fellow clergy during a so-called faith-based pep rally.

James Towey, until recently the head of the White House faith-based office, denies there is a political dimension to the initiative. Unfortunately for Towey, there is and he's up to his neck in it. In 2002 and 2004 Towey made a series of campaign appearances alongside Republican congressional and gubernatorial candidates whom polls showed were locked in tight races. In 2004 Towey and his staff just happened to pop up in swing states putting on seminars telling pastors how to get their slice of the faith-based pie. Are we supposed to believe it was just a coincidence that Towey and his staff just happened to appear in states or districts with close races—every time?

The last straw was seeing the *Miami Herald* report that Towey watched the 2004 election returns with the family of Governor Jeb Bush in Florida. Towey had promoted Jeb Bush's candidacy and was there to see his victory from the front parlor.

In fact, the faith-based initiative has had a strong political dimension from its first day. The first director of the White House's faith-based office, John J. DiIulio, was an academic who never really fit in with the Bush administration's slash-and-burn style of politics. After he left the position, DiIulio gave a revealing interview with *Esquire* magazine in late 2002. DiIulio seemed frustrated over his tenure in the White House, telling *Esquire,* "What you've got is everything—and I mean everything—being run by the political arm. It's the reign of the Mayberry Machiavellis."

DiIulio criticized presidential advisers like Karl Rove "who consistently talked and acted as if the height of political sophistication consisted in reducing every issue to its simplest black-and-white terms for public consumption, then steering legislative initiatives or policy proposals as far right as possible."

A storm of criticism erupted, and DiIulio was pressured to retract some of his remarks. However, some of his criticisms were echoed in February 2005 by David Kuo, a former staffer in the faith-based office. Kuo denied there was an explicit political agenda behind the initiative but conceded that some GOP strategists were intrigued by black pastors' interest in the plan.

Kuo quickly became disillusioned and wrote a scathing article for the respected and popular Web site beliefnet.com, in which he attacked the initiative as mainly window dressing. "Conservative Christian donors, faith leaders, and opinion makers grew to see the initiative as an embodiment of the president's own faith," wrote Kuo. "Democratic opposition was understood as an attack on his personal faith. And since this community's most powerful leaders—men like James Dobson of Focus on the Family—weren't anti-poverty leaders, they didn't care about money. The Faith-Based Office was the cross around the White House's neck showing the president's own faith orientation. That was sufficient." In other words, what worked and who really needed it was largely irrelevant.

While I believe there was a little more to the initiative than that, Kuo's perspective as an insider is valuable. He also seems to have missed one piece of the puzzle: I believe the faith-based initiative was designed primarily to placate the Religious Right by eroding the church-state wall. The fact that it has also been used to make inroads in black and Hispanic religious communities, which are often strapped for cash, by holding out the possibility of government funding is gravy as far as the Republican Party is concerned. The approach over time morphed into an effort to please as many religious leaders as possible to shore up the GOP base and reach out for new support. These explicitly political goals only underscore that the initiative, despite Bush's lofty rhetoric, isn't really about helping people in need.

TV preacher Pat Robertson, normally a reliable Bush ally, was skeptical of the faith-based initiative when it was first unveiled. There's an old saying that even a broken clock is right twice a day, and Robertson actually managed to raise some relevant objections. Robertson was worried that the faith-based initiative would entangle churches in government red tape, telling his *700 Club* audience on February 20, 2001, "[F]ederal rules will envelop these organizations, they'll begin to be nurtured, if I can use that term, on federal money, and then they can't get off of it. It'll be like a narcotic; they can't then free themselves later on." Robertson called the initiative "a real Pandora's box."

But then a funny thing happened: About a year and a half later, a Robertson-affiliated charity called Operation Blessing received a $1.5 million grant under the faith-based initiative. Robertson has not uttered one more word of protest since. His about-face led conservative commentator Cal Thomas to quip, "Robertson was right to warn of a 'Pandora's box.' But he has now opened that box and is taking the money."

Also, consider this: Robertson has asserted that Hindus worship demons. He has called Muslims insane and once opined that Presbyterians, among others, reflect the "spirit of the Antichrist." Under the terms of the faith-based contract, Operation Blessing is obliged to contract out with other groups. Quick, which three aren't likely to get a subgrant?

At the same time, a Florida minister named Bishop Harold Calvin Ray was awarded $2.1 million in faith-based money for a project he calls the National Center for Faith Based Initiative. Ray had been an early and ardent supporter of Bush and his faith-based plan. I debated him on the FOX News Channel and other venues; in the green room I could hardly get past his entourage or have time for any leisurely chat because he was busy discussing a land purchase on his cell phone. By the summer of 2001, Ray had taken to complaining in the media that not enough was being done. He promptly clammed up once his check was cut.

Grants like this look like payola, and for good reason—they *are*

payola. No other factor can explain a $1.5 million grant to a "char-
ity" owned by Robertson, a "charity" with such a checkered past
that it was investigated by Virginia officials after newspaper reports
surfaced that Robertson was using Operation Blessing airplanes to
ferry diamond mining equipment in and out of Zaire (now Congo),
where Robertson had business operations. A lot of children in
America go to bed hungry every night. Surely $1.5 million would
have alleviated the sufferings of at least some of them. Bush chose
instead to give the money to an already well-funded television
preacher who is widely acknowledged as a giant embarrassment to
the Christian community. That single act did more to discredit the
faith-based initiative than perhaps every other strike against it.

Amazingly, faith-based funding may even go toward construction
costs. In regulations promulgated by the Department of Housing and
Urban Development, there is a section that indicates that funds can
actually be used for the construction of additions to churches and
other religious buildings to the extent that the activity in those
buildings is secular.

So, if the annex is used 20 percent of the time for a job-training
program, 20 percent of the bricks and roofing tiles can be purchased
with tax dollars. I'm sorry, but in America we don't use public funds
to build temples, mosques, churches, or synagogues. Moreover, in
1971, the Supreme Court made clear that if church-related colleges
get building grants, they cannot use them for dual use (that is, religious and secular) and could even be required to sign a contract that
any building would be used for secular purposes "in perpetuity." If
you can't build a classroom, you certainly can't build a new wing on
a cathedral. And indeed, what level of entanglement between church
and state would be necessary to monitor the percentage of activity
that is religious? Perhaps the government was planning to divert
some of its spy cameras that routinely catch people speeding through
red lights to church social halls.

Evidence continues to mount against the faith-based initiative. It is used as a sop to the Religious Right and in a blatantly political manner to win new support in communities that do not normally back the GOP. Faith-based funding has been used to silence critics. Claims are made about the approach and its effectiveness that do not square with reality. The initiative threatens to strangle the independence of America's houses of worship by making them dependent on state money. The approach violates the separation of church and state by forcing all taxpayers to support the religious views of a few.

I haven't even touched on the issue of religious favoritism. Bush and his supporters claim that any religious group willing to help can qualify for funding—but then make it clear that certain groups need not bother. Appearing on John McLaughlin's *One on One* program on February 2, 2001, Stephen Goldsmith was asked if Wiccan groups could get faith-based money. He replied, "The government is trying to furnish health care, trying to furnish shelter, it's trying to furnish food. For me, I don't think Wiccans would meet the standard of kind of being humane providers of domestic violence shelters."

Perhaps Goldsmith was unduly influenced by *Hansel and Gretel* as a child. Obviously, Americans as individuals can and do have all kinds of personal biases against people of particular religious persuasions; the federal government cannot, however. To have an approved religion list developed by the executive branch is repugnant. (I should also point out that, in my travels around the country, I've met plenty of Wiccans. None were inhumane. Goldsmith's views seem more informed by his personal prejudices than reality.)

On top of all of this, there's a kicker: the faith-based initiative doesn't do what it's supposed to do—help those in need. In 2003, a shelter for homeless veterans in Northampton, Massachusetts, lost a third of its funding after the money was diverted to faith-based groups. The shelter had a long history of providing services to veterans. The faith-based groups did not. How did this policy change help those in need? Indeed, the funding the shelter lost was sent to faith-based facilities in North Carolina and Utah. Time after time, in appearances with Towey, I would ask, "Will you be supplying maps so that disabled vets will be able to walk from Massachusetts to Utah before next winter's storms hit in New England?"

Ironically, the Massachusetts shelter later got the federal money back. It hired a chaplain and claimed to be faith-based too. It's absurd that groups with a track record of success should have to jump through hoops like this. When the government is looking for contractors to help the less fortunate, it should ask two questions: Is this group effective? Is it willing to help everyone in need without imposing religion on anyone and abide by the Constitution?

The Bush administration's refusal to even consider, let alone ask, questions like these is rapidly bringing us to a point where religious affiliation becomes the only thing that matters. This is ironic, as Religious Right boosters of the faith-based initiative frequently assert that all they want is a level playing field. They just want, they say, the same right to apply for and receive government grants as secular groups.

They have had that for years. What they want is preferential treatment—and they're getting it. Far from being uneven, the playing field is increasingly tilted toward conservative religious groups. We need to be honest here. The Bush administration has no incentive to dole out government funds to churches or denominations that oppose many of his policies. It's no surprise, therefore, that most of the faith-based money is going to theologically conservative groups.

No one seems to be asking the question of how this affects people on the ground. The Bush administration has insisted all along that those in need will always have secular alternatives. This is absurd on its face. Residents of New York City might have a range of providers to choose from. Someone living in rural North Dakota is likely to have far fewer. If the nearest secular provider is some distance away, a poor person lacking private transportation or access to public transportation isn't going to be able to access it. The rule instead should be that all providers offer secular services—even if the provider is a church. Groups that want to offer explicitly religious programs retain that option, using their own money.

This last point is worth fleshing out a little because we as a nation seem to be rushing headlong toward government-funded, fundamentalist-oriented social services for no good reason. Traditionally, religious groups have provided various services to the community on their own dime. When those programs are privately funded, they can be as religious as the sponsoring church wants them to be.

As a minister, I've never felt the need to hit someone over the head with my faith. It always seemed counterproductive. I've been involved with churches that have sponsored social services ministries over the years. Our operating theory has usually been focused on deeds over words. If we believe the Bible commands us to care for the poor—and clearly it does—we must fulfill that obligation through joint action and let that action speak for our faith. There is no need to pressure someone to attend a prayer service, watch a video about Jesus, or come to church on Sunday.

Jesus did not use food or the promise of a bed as a lure for the hungry and the homeless. He provided for the physical needs of those in pain, knowing that these actions were more powerful than any sermon. The church provides for those in need not because those people are viewed as big targets who can be sucked into the apparatus of the church. It provides for those in need because it is the right thing to do.

Too many leaders of the Religious Right have lost sight of this fact. They offer soup kitchens and homeless shelters for the same reason they offer singles' clubs and child care: to attract more converts. But these programs are not the same and should not be seen as equivalent. Jesus did not tell us to run dating clubs. He did command us to care for the least among us.

Are people in the pews being challenged to do that today? Often they are not, and it's ironic that the faith-based initiative, hailed as the great promoter of religion by its backers, makes the job of engaging people in the pews even harder.

I have witnessed truly remarkable things in churches. I've seen people dig deeper in their pockets and raid their purses for spare change because a pastor challenged them to provide for those in need. I've watched people volunteer countless hours serving soup, sorting through old clothes, and collecting canned goods for food pantries. It's not glamorous work, and no one gets paid a dime to do it. Many times no one even thanks them. They do it anyway. Why? They believe God expects no less.

Persuading people to go the extra mile, to dig deeper and sacrifice time, money, and material goods, is a unique talent claimed by many religious leaders. When they are successful, two goals are met. First, the immediate needs of the food pantry, homeless shelter, or whatever are fulfilled. But equally important, the congregants are drawn more deeply into the lives of their church. They gave the extra money. They donated time. They can look with pride on what they, as a community, accomplished.

What happens when the federal government or the state comes in with a huge grant? Why should congregants dig deeper and go the extra mile if the government is standing by with a check? What's more fulfilling and personally satisfying to a congregation—energizing everyone to work side by side to raise money, build an addition, and open and stock a food pantry or having the church secretary fill out and mail a grant application to the Department of Health and Human Services?

People often ask me, when I'm out giving a speech, why religion is on the decline in many other Western nations. I really do believe it is because the churches in those countries got too close to the state. As religious groups got more and more of their needs met by government sources, the people in pews grew alienated. Why should they give more on Sunday if they already paid taxes to support religion? Didn't they already give at the office? Gradually the sense of alienation grew. If all people are ever asked to do is join in ritual and recite creeds over and over, if they are not drawn more fully into the life of a congregation, they will soon see little need to keep showing up on Sunday morning. So they begin to stay home.

Many of them probably also began to perceive the church as little more than housebroken and compliant. Houses of worship in America have a reputation for challenging the government and its policies. Will they still do that when they are dependent on state subsidies for their very livelihood? How credible is a religious leader who on Monday blasts a government policy and on Tuesday accepts a large check from that same government? The actions of Pat Robertson and Bishop Ray are sadly pathetic examples of how prophetic words of criticism diminish or disappear when the government has funded the church's public address system.

Throughout my long involvement with churches, I've always abided by a simple rule: a pastor must listen to his congregation. If the church members sitting in the pews are reluctant to pay for a social service program the pastor desires, that's probably a sign of something. The congregation is trying to send a message, and the message isn't "Go ask the government to pay for that." The message is "We are not yet comfortable with this approach" or "You have failed to inspire us to follow your vision." Either way, the pastor has some work to do—and it's not filling out a grant application.

The Bush administration would like religious leaders to believe unlimited amounts of faith-based money are theirs for the taking. In fact, administration officials have conceded that the faith-based initiative involves no new money.

There are better alternatives. I'm a big fan of interfaith initiatives. If several small or medium-sized churches pool their resources, they can achieve more than they would acting individually and avoid unnecessary duplication of services. These projects also build interfaith cooperation and promote understanding among denominations. We need more of that in times like these. Ironically, the Bush faith-based initiative does just the opposite: it actively pits religious groups against one another and against providers in the secular community for a shrinking slice of the social service funding pie.

Houses of worship also need to remember that Americans are an exceedingly generous people. Confronted with devastating back-to-back hurricanes in the Gulf Coast in 2005, Americans did not yawn and change the channel. They reached for their checkbooks. They sorted through closets for used clothing to donate. They ferried food down to soup kitchens. Some even took in storm evacuees or helped resettle them with furniture, toys, and dollars.

Americans put aside their partisan differences to help and did not listen to those who shamefully tried to use the hurricane to divide us. Speaking on FOX News Channel's *Hannity & Colmes* program, right-wing bomb thrower Ann Coulter asserted that "Barry Lynn's church" probably didn't help hurricane victims. Coulter should have made a few phone calls first to avoid being embarrassed. My denomination, the United Church of Christ, had already donated millions to the relief effort at the time Coulter said that.

No one had to tell Americans to do these things. They started doing them immediately, as soon as they saw the scope of the destruction. They would have continued doing them even if the Federal Emergency Management Agency's response had not been inept. Americans did those things because we are fundamentally a good and decent people who want to help those in need.

Billions of dollars move annually through houses of worship. Billions more in donated goods and services follow. Countless volunteer hours are offered. The money, time, and energy are there. Religion has a role to play in helping those in need. So does the government.

Do I believe the state has an obligation to be active in this area? Absolutely. Ditto for religion. Indeed, the more religious institutions that exercise their First Amendment rights by existing, the more funds go to the poor and needy here and around the globe.

The faith-based initiative takes two approaches that work so well together on parallel tracks and forces them into an unnecessary and dangerous head-on collision. My guess is the state will emerge from that encounter with a few dents. The church, by contrast, could be totaled.

This stand wins me no friends in the Bush administration. On December 9, 2004, Towey attacked me during a conference in Washington, D.C., when he vowed to fight "secular extremists" who are blocking the initiative. He asserted we're merely trying to raise money through scare tactics. "Barry Lynn should send the president a dozen roses for all the fund-raising help this has given him," Towey groused.

The sad thing is, I knew James Towey before he went to work for the White House. As he's quick to tell you, he once worked for Mother Teresa. I believe there was a time when Jim really wanted to help the poor. His commitment to the less fortunate was real.

But Jim, like a lot of people who come to Washington, got seduced by political power. How else can you explain his decision to work for an administration that constantly cuts taxes for the wealthiest Americans while slashing spending on social programs aimed at the neediest among us? What else could account for his decision to put aside his vowed nonpartisanship and campaign on behalf of the most reactionary candidates, men and women who have never cared one iota for the poor and whose policies have widened the gulf between the rich and the poor to an extent not seen since the era of the robber barons?

Towey is not the only one. I've seen it happen to ministers too. And that is the final tragedy of the faith-based initiative. It takes people who may at one time have really wanted to help the less fortunate and turns them into players, schemers looking for their next inside-the-Beltway contract or federal procurement. What else could explain churches diverting money from their social service budgets to hire grant-writing consultants?

Pat Robertson was right. Tax money *is* addictive. And the pursuit of it threatens to take the religious community to some strange places. One of them is an odd land where clergy take their solace not from the words of Jesus but from the maxims of the occupant of the White House. In this place, it seems, passages from the Bible become less important than grant proposals listed in the *Federal Register.*

Towey may believe I am a "secular extremist." I see it differently. When I oppose the faith-based initiative, I fight not to oppose the church. Far from it. I fight to preserve the integrity of its very soul.

5

Religion and Politics

FINDING THE RIGHT BALANCE

I HAD BEEN WORKING for Americans United for Separation of Church and State for just a few days and was still packing up things from a job in Hanover, New Hampshire, when my wife handed me an ad from *USA Today* that nearly made me spill my coffee.

It was October 1992, and the presidential election was less than a month away. The ad in question was headlined "Christian Beware: Do Not Put the Economy Ahead of the Ten Commandments." It went on to attack then Arkansas governor Bill Clinton for his stands on social issues and concluded with this question: "How then can we vote for Bill Clinton?" Specifically, it included positions that Clinton took on various social issues and then challenged them with scriptural references that allegedly denoted that Clinton stood for the "sinful" position. It ended authoritatively with yet another biblical "proof text" that voting for a "sinner" made you one as well.

At the bottom of the ad, in tiny type, was a line stating that it had been paid for by the Church at Pierce Creek in Vestal, New York. It solicited tax-deductible contributions to pay for similar ads in other newspapers.

I was floored. *USA Today* is the nation's largest-circulation daily. A full-page ad there probably cost a little less than the $100,000 one will set you back today—but I doubt much less. Clearly this little church had wanted to make a big splash. I decided right then and there Americans United would help it along.

Federal tax law bars all nonprofit groups that hold the 501(c)(3) designation from endorsing or opposing candidates for public office. That is the tax category of more or less every house of worship in America. This ad clearly expressed opposition to Clinton. It flatly instructed people not to vote for him. A church placed it just before the election, with the obvious aim of affecting the outcome of the race. This church then had the temerity to solicit tax-deductible donations to place more ads like it!

Americans United wrote to the Internal Revenue Service, enclosed a copy of the ad, and requested an investigation. It took more than two years for our efforts to bear fruit, but in 1995 we learned that the Church at Pierce Creek had lost its tax-exempt status. This was the first time in history a house of worship was stripped of its tax exemption solely for its partisan politicking.

The church's pastor, Daniel Little, was defiant throughout the process. Speaking on a now-defunct cable network in April 1995, Little insisted he had not bothered to consult with an attorney before placing the ad, remarking, "Why should we consult attorneys? We have the word of God . . . Principle sometimes takes precedent over silly laws."

For the pastor of a small church, Little seemed awfully full of bluster. Something was going on here. A little investigating soon revealed that the church was the home congregation of strident antiabortion protestor and founder of Operation Rescue Randall Terry—and what's more, this little church in an out-of-the-way area had lined up big legal guns to help press its case against the IRS: TV preacher Pat Robertson's legal eagles were coming to town. The Robertson group, the American Center for Law and Justice, promptly sued the IRS, alleging the church's free speech and free exercise of religion rights had been violated.

What exactly was going on at the Church at Pierce Creek? Looking back on the case ten years later, I think it was all carefully choreographed. Religious Right activists wanted to test the law banning partisan endorsements. My hunch is that some Religious Right fat cat gave this church the money for the ad, knowing it would spark action by the IRS. Presto—instant test case!

It almost worked, but there was one little problem: Instead of winning a ruling declaring the IRS regulations unconstitutional, the Religious Right and Robertson's attorneys were handed a stinging defeat. The trial court and then a federal appeals court ruled unanimously in *Church at Pierce Creek v. Richardson* that the federal tax agency has a legal right to place conditions on the receipt of tax-exempt status and upheld the "no politicking" rule.

The Religious Right is well skilled at making the best of a bad situation, and it did so here. National right-wing organizations used the federal court ruling to cry that houses of worship are being "muzzled." Free speech, they claimed, had been trampled on. Predictably, they persuaded a member of Congress, in this case Representative Walter B. Jones of North Carolina, to introduce legislation repealing the IRS language. Jones's bill has not passed—and in fact it failed handily the one time it received a vote in the House—but the Religious Right has continued to use the church politicking issue to raise funds and spur activism.

As a pastor myself, I find this activity misguided and even dangerous. My job in the pulpit is to try to bring my congregants closer to an encounter with God. Certainly a pastor may discuss issues dealing with social justice and contemporary controversies. Many pastors, for example, believed that God was greatly offended by the treatment of African Americans prior to the civil rights era. A religious leader has no obligation to be silent in the face of such injustice—but candidate endorsements are not part of the job description.

And of course I concede that this cuts both ways politically. My denomination supports a woman's right to obtain a legal abortion and opposes efforts to deny gay people their civil and legal rights. I back these stands. Plenty of religious leaders disagree with me, however, and frequently speak out from the pulpit to express an opposing view. This is their right. Issue-based advocacy in churches is absolutely permitted. No federal laws bar it or even put significant limits on it.

But this does not mean it is ever in a pastor's job description to act as a political boss. I like the aroma of incense in a sanctuary, but I can do without smelling cigar smoke wafting up from the basement where political deals are being hatched by the board of deacons. They don't teach you how to hand down a list of endorsements in the seminary and for good reason. Instructing people on how to vote simply is not part of the job. It is an arrogant abuse of power that very often divides congregations and isolates certain members in the pews. That is the opposite of what a pastor seeks to achieve.

But again, none of this means a house of worship cannot address a political, moral, or social issue. This point is worth looking at in some depth, because the Religious Right has deliberately tried to mislead the American public about federal tax law and what it says. They do this in an effort to rally people in support of changing the law to allow church-based politicking.

As usual, the Religious Right is dead wrong when its leaders claim that pastors' mouths are being sealed with metaphorical duct tape. Religious leaders, houses of worship, and denominations speak out on political issues all of the time. If you doubt this, simply open up a newspaper. You will see examples of ministers, priests, rabbis, and other men and women of the cloth speaking out on any number of issues.

Conservative churches cannot seriously claim to be gagged. Their clerics frequently assail legal abortion and the expansion of gay rights, among other issues. Most recently, conservative churches spearheaded successful efforts in many states to add amendments to state constitutions banning same-sex marriage. They organize in churches to back referendum questions. They hold rallies in churches to condemn the federal courts and have actively promoted the last two Supreme Court nominees, John Roberts and Samuel A. Alito, at big gatherings called Justice Sundays.

There is no shortage of church-based activism on a range of issues. Houses of worship have rallied around issues like legal abortion, gun control, affordable housing, taxation, welfare reform, and other issues. In fact, I'm hard-pressed to think of any significant issue where religious leaders have not spoken out.

Much of this activity takes place at the local level and never captures national headlines. A church, for example, might address a municipal zoning law or downtown redevelopment plan. Church leaders might address the city council on the need for affordable housing or back an increase in the minimum wage. A pastor might oppose a proposed citywide gay rights ordinance. This kind of thing happens all of the time in communities all over America. It is so commonplace it is no longer considered controversial, nor should it be.

The Religious Right says our pastors are muzzled. Yet members of the clergy walk the halls of Congress alongside lobbyists for secular concerns, pressing their views and often being warmly received. You see them in the senators' dining room. I've been there myself. They do the same in the state capitals. Religious voices, in fact, are often among the most welcome in the public square. Having worked on Capitol Hill for a number of years, both as a lobbyist and an observer of the scene, I can attest to this firsthand. A lobbyist representing big business or a defense contractor is usually assumed to be a hardball operator looking to line someone's pocket or seal some type of high-powered political deal that could involve millions in taxpayer dollars. Religious lobbyists are not looked upon with such suspicion and are often offered a type of deference by virtue of their tie to faith.

Conservative Christians have formed national organizations that have great sway over our political system. Radio counselor James Dobson's Focus on the Family has an aligned group in Washington, the Family Research Council, which has an annual budget of about $10 million. Highly placed members of Congress regularly address this group, and its president, Tony Perkins, is warmly received in hundreds of congressional offices and at the White House. Religious Right groups meet regularly in a type of "holy war council" to share ideas and plot strategy. Collectively, their organizations bring in hundreds of millions a year. Yet we are to believe they have no influence?

In recent years, Dobson has decided to expand his political operations. He formed a more overt political group, Focus on the Family Action, with a different type of tax-exempt status. The organization raised $9 million in its first six months of existence. Dobson has also been offering candidates endorsements as a private citizen, not as the head of Focus, which he legally may do. Dobson's intervention in a 2004 Senate race in South Dakota is widely seen as contributing to the defeat of former senator Tom Daschle. Dobson has since issued thinly veiled threats to other Democratic senators who represent conservative "red" states. Some kowtow to him, worrying they may end up like Daschle. Again, in light of this, how can Dobson and Perkins seriously argue that they are muzzled? In reality, they have the type of political access that many secular lobbyists can only dream about.

In their effort to mislead the people, Dobson and other Religious Right leaders usually fail to note that the IRS ban on partisan activity applies to all 501(c)(3) organizations, not just houses of worship. It's not a special prohibition on religion. Scientific, literary, educational, public policy, and other types of organizations must abide by these rules. Most have no problem doing so. Why can't the houses of worship?

Furthermore, the IRS is not hyperdiligent in applying this rule to religious organizations, and there has been nothing like a crackdown on houses of worship. If anything, the IRS looked the other way for a long time while churches violated the rule. Consider that the Church at Pierce Creek was the first church ever to lose its tax-exempt status since the IRS adopted the "no politicking" rule in the 1950s. Houses of worship are not being subject to special scrutiny in any way.

And make no mistake, many houses of worship have gone way over the line in this area. They aren't functioning in a "gray zone"; they are flat-out endorsing or opposing candidates. This problem afflicts both conservative and liberal churches. I've seen virtual campaign rallies taking place in some churches. I've seen candidates shill shamelessly for votes while standing in pulpits. I've seen pastors pass out or place in the pews alleged "voter guides" that were so slanted in favor of one candidate that they obviously qualified as campaign material. All of this is unlawful and should have been stopped long ago.

It's not enough to shift the blame to candidates. A candidate's job is to get elected. He or she may choose to run close to the edge of the law to reach that goal. A house of worship, especially a huge megachurch with thousands of members, represents an irresistible target to some who aspire to public office. One pulpit appearance or endorsement from a pastor can reach thousands in a few minutes. Yet pastors must be careful. They have an important obligation to learn the law and stick to it. Not all candidate appearances in church violate the Internal Revenue Code, but an event that has all the trappings of a campaign rally the Sunday before the election clearly does. It invites IRS scrutiny. On the other hand, inviting all candidates for an office to the church social hall for a discussion of positions (even if all don't come) is perfectly permissible public education. So is voter registration, when it is done without regard to party affiliation.

In 1996 Americans United decided to take a harder look at this issue. We formalized a special project—called Project Fair Play—to educate religious leaders and the American public about the provisions of the Internal Revenue Code. The project has two components: the dissemination of educational materials that explain IRS provisions to church leaders every election year and a mechanism through which Americans United reports blatant violations to the IRS.

Since 1996 our organization has submitted fifty-six complaints to the IRS. I want to outline some of them now, just to provide a sense of the scope and scale of the problem. These are not gray areas or situations loaded with ambiguity. They are examples of houses of worship and other religious ministries that I believe were blatantly violating federal tax law.

March 1996: Second Baptist Church of Houston established a special project to encourage members to attend the local GOP precinct convention and essentially take control of it by electing certain individuals, mostly church members, to local committees. (This church was later subjected to a three-year IRS audit.)

November 1996: A Buddhist temple in California hosted a fundraising event on behalf of then vice president Al Gore.

July 1997: The pastor of an Edmond, Oklahoma, church used the church bulletin to endorse a slate of specific candidates in a city council race. The church was involved in a zoning dispute at the time, and the candidates, the pastor told parishioners, held views favorable to the church.

February 2000: During Sunday services, former congressman Floyd Flake, then pastor of a New York City church, invited Al Gore to speak to the congregation. He then pointed to Gore and said, "I don't do endorsements from across the pulpit because I never know who's out there watching the types of laws governing separation of church and state. But I will say to you this morning and you read it well: This should be the next president of the United States." (Flake told the *Wall Street Journal* he was investigated by the IRS, conceded he had broken the law, and signed an agreement not to do it again.)

March 2004: An Austin church allowed a Republican Party political action committee to hold a fund-raiser in its church. Candidates appealed for votes and collected money.

July 2004: The Reverend Jerry Falwell issued an e-mail to supporters nationwide urging them to reelect President George W. Bush. Wrote Falwell, "For conservative people of faith, voting for principle this year means voting for the re-election of George W. Bush. The alternative, in my mind, is simply unthinkable." The e-mail was sent under the auspices of Falwell's tax-exempt ministry and posted on his Web site.

August 2004: A Miami church hosted a rally for the Democratic Party, featuring speeches by party officials and appearances by local candidates and former presidential candidate Al Sharpton.

November 2004: A church in Bellwood, Pennsylvania, ran an ad in the local newspaper announcing it would provide transportation to the polls for voters—but only if they agreed to vote for President George W. Bush.

Note that these events were not educational forums. They were not open to all candidates, nor did they seek to acquaint voters with all of the candidates and their positions. These events were something else. They were designed to advance specific candidates and certain political parties. They constitute direct intervention in partisan campaigns, the very thing the IRS statute does not permit.

You will note that I haven't reported on the outcome of all of these conflicts. This is because federal privacy laws prohibit the dissemination of information about the result of investigations like these, absent federal rulings or court action. As the originator of the complaint, Americans United is no more entitled to this information than the man behind me in line at Starbucks.

The IRS does not interpret its statutes simply to bar pastors from issuing pulpit endorsements or using church coffers to advance candidates. The standard states that *intervention* in a partisan campaign is unlawful. Every election year, the IRS produces special publications designed to help religious leaders understand the law and what constitutes unlawful intervention. The IRS always places special emphasis on voter guides or material produced by outside organizations.

For a number of years, the Christian Coalition roamed the country, seeking to place what it claimed were "fair and balanced" (even before there was a FOX News Channel) voter guides in the foyers or even pews of churches. The problem is, the guides were anything but evenhanded. They were precisely the opposite. Christian Coalition voter guides were about as subtle as a sharp stick in your eye. Anyone could tell, even by glancing at the guides, which candidate the coalition favored. (It was almost always the Republican—surprise! I recall that a Democratic U.S. House member from Mississippi got coalition approval once. He immediately switched parties and became a Republican.) The coalition employed a number of sleazy tricks and dishonest tactics to produce the guides. It based its guides, which might cover five or six issues, on answers it got from candidates after querying them on sometimes as many as one hundred issues. With a huge range to choose from, the coalition found it easy to make candidates appear to be sharply different, when in fact they sometimes were not. In some cases, the guides were flatly erroneous, but when the errors were pointed out, it was too late—the guides had already been distributed.

Many candidates never bothered to fill out the questionnaire. Knowing they would never get a fair shake from the coalition, many Democratic candidates simply tossed the questionnaires. One of the coalition's favorite tactics was to make it appear that the candidate had filled out the questionnaire anyway. Group leaders would give the candidate's responses to perhaps three or four issues on the guide and then list "no response" for the rest. This created the impression that the candidate had answered some questions but ignored others. Where did the coalition get the answers it did put down? It claimed to get them from public sources, but often they were simply based on assumptions about cookie-cutter Democratic positions. Not surprisingly, candidates who refused to play ball with the coalition were not favorably portrayed.

The coalition managed to get this material distributed in churches for many years, despite the clear bias of the guides and despite the fact that the coalition was an explicitly political group closely tied to the Republican Party. I once held a press conference in the lobby of a hotel where the Christian Coalition was meeting and asserted, "The Christian Coalition is no longer an appendage to the Republican Party; the Republican Party is an appendage of the Christian Coalition."

The coalition operated as a 501(c)(4) organization. Legally it could produce voter guides. The coalition would tell pastors that its guides were legal. That was true, up to a point. They were legal for a 501(c)(4) group to produce, but they were not legal for 501(c)(3) groups to distribute. Robertson's coalition did lose its tax exemption retroactively for one year's activities, but the Bush administration seemed reluctant to spend much time on the matter.

The issue has become less relevant in recent years since the Christian Coalition has all but collapsed because of tax problems, loss of effective leadership, and a race discrimination lawsuit brought by employees. But other organizations still produce voter guides and often try to pass them on to church leaders. Much of this material is nothing more than thinly disguised campaign material designed to portray one office seeker as the next candidate for sainthood and his opponent as a good fit for the House of Horrors Wax Museum at a rundown carnival. Pastors must be extremely wary of these overtures.

Ironically, there is so much houses of worship can do legally in the political arena that skirting the law should never even be an issue. I've already noted that churches can host educational forums where all candidates are invited to share their views and answer questions. During the primary season, when many candidates may be running, these events can be very valuable and serve as a community-wide resource.

A church can register voters—in all parties. A pastor can stress the importance of voting and offer sermons on the civic good of being politically engaged. Houses of worship can offer transportation to the polls and engage in other activities to spur turnout. In some parts of the country, churches are even used as polling places. I would always prefer that government facilities be used first, but if churches are pressed into this duty, they must abide by state and local laws governing sign placement and leafleting on behalf of candidates, and pastors must not interfere with anyone's right to vote.

A pastor, as a private citizen, can work on a political campaign. A pastor can even endorse a candidate—again, as a private citizen. The endorsement should be offered at a neutral location, not from the pulpit. If the endorsement is in the form of a letter, it should be on the pastor's personal stationery, not church letterhead. A pastor can donate his own money to a candidate. He may never donate church funds.

While all of these activities are legal, some might still spark controversy. As a religious leader, I make it a policy never to endorse or oppose any candidate for public office, even though I have the right to do so as a private citizen. Over the years, I have occasionally been asked to provide these endorsements. I have always refused. This has not stopped people like Jerry Falwell, for example, from accusing me of being an "operative" for Democrats like Al Gore. Interestingly, during the 2000 campaign, the only time I spoke to Gore was after I spotted him leaving a movie theater after a screening of *The Perfect Storm*. Gore was not likely to want my help: Americans United was repeatedly critical of some of the church-state positions of Gore's running mate, U.S. senator Joseph I. Lieberman.

I simply don't hand out political endorsements. My thinking is this: Even a church with a reputation for being politically conservative or politically liberal has dissenters and members who feel differently. The last thing I want to do is alienate those folks. The job of a spiritual leader is to bring people together, not drive them apart. The introduction of partisan politics into the church does divide people. In church, we come together in a spirit of communion and fellowship to commune with God. God is not a Republican; God is not a Democrat. God does not care if a Senate or House bill passes or fails. God does not endorse candidates. He does not "ordain" anyone to run. Anyone who claims to be running in God's name or with God's sanction is likely to be dangerous. God has more important things to do than be concerned about who represents District 5 in the state legislature.

Many parishioners are offended by pulpit endorsements. If my pastor ever offered one, even if I liked the candidate he backed, I would get up and walk out. I don't attend church services to be told who to vote for. My fellow congregants are adults. They read the papers and follow the news. They have their own hierarchy of issues. Some are concerned about poverty, homelessness, and education. Others see fair taxation and economic matters as their major concerns. It is not for me or any other religious leader to tell them that they are wrong or to insist that my hierarchy of issues is more important and thus must be substituted for theirs.

In May 2005 the pastor of a Baptist church in Waynesville, North Carolina, drew national headlines after he expelled several members of his congregation. Their crime? They had voted for U.S. senator John F. Kerry in 2004. Pastor Chan Chandler insisted he had been

within his rights to deny those folks membership—and he was correct up to a point. Pastors have the right to set the parameters for
church membership. But many members of Chandler's congregation
decided they did not care for his decision to link church membership
to political affiliation. Many left the church. Among them were several Republicans. They had not voted for Kerry but could not tolerate a pastor who refused to respect political differences. Eventually,
Chandler had to resign from the pastorate.

Chandler had obviously made his political views known, but at
what cost? His church was splintered, and he lost his job. I have to
wonder how partisan politics can be so important to a religious
leader that it leads him to drive wedges into his congregation instead
of finding ways to bring them together.

Chandler's situation was an extreme example. But in my travels
around the country, I've encountered many people who tell me they
are simply tired of politics emanating from the pulpit. They don't
mind a sermon based on a political issue every now and then, but it's
clear some pastors have become obsessed and rarely discuss anything
else. Every now and then I tune in to the Reverend Jerry Falwell on
television. While Falwell is always careful to toss in a few Bible
verses, most of his sermons are just political rants. If he's not running
down gays, he's attacking feminists or blasting public schools. This
grows old very quickly. When I watch Falwell, whose services take
place in a megachurch that looks more like a sports stadium than a
house of God, I have to wonder why anyone would seek to communicate with the Almighty in such a place and through such a media-
tor. The services are obviously staged for maximum television appeal,
and they are usually more about Falwell than they are about Jesus.
The constant carping on politics only adds another layer the wor-
shipper must penetrate before God can be reached.

Pulpit-based politicking of specific candidates is also arrogant. Do
some pastors really believe their congregants are so dense they can't

make political decisions for themselves? Religious Right advocates, in a pathetic attempt to draft Dr. Martin Luther King into their cause, sometimes assert that thanks to the IRS, King would not have been able to tell churchgoers in Alabama not to vote for Theophilus "Bull" Connor during the civil rights struggle.

Connor served as public safety commissioner of Birmingham, an elected slot, during much of the civil rights era. In that position, he was notorious for ordering police to unleash attack dogs and use water cannons on nonviolent protestors. His name today is synonymous with hard-core racial segregation and the reckless use of force. Connor's tactics made national headlines, and clips of the attacks he orchestrated were carried on the evening news. Everyone in Birmingham certainly knew about them. Does anyone seriously think African Americans might have been tempted to vote for Connor unless King told them not to? It's insulting for any religious leader to assume that his congregants are too stupid to know what to do unless taken by the hand and led into the voting booth.

It's especially ironic to see the Religious Right try to claim King as an ally in its misguided crusade. In fact, John Lewis, a King associate and now a member of Congress, has stated on numerous occasions that King never endorsed a candidate for public office. He did not have to. King stood up to Connor's brutality and, through nonviolent means, exposed its ugly face to the world. That tactic was far more effective than a pulpit-based partisan campaign against Connor, which merely would have expended energy saying things anyone who was paying even the slightest bit of attention already knew or, sadly, had experienced firsthand.

King realized that deciding whom to vote for was not the problem facing blacks in the Jim Crow South. The problem was winning the right to vote at all. Once this obstacle was overcome, church members were quite capable of making a rational decision without being handed a list of endorsements from their pastors.

The civil rights movement is, in fact, an example of how religion can be integrated into a political movement in a way that expands, and does not decrease, human freedom. Some of King's staunchest allies were secular Jews from northern states who came to the South to right what they saw as a great moral wrong—the disenfranchisement of an entire class of people based on the color of their skin.

These people, and others like them, came not just because the Torah or some other holy book commanded them to. They came because they saw fellow members of the human race being denied their rights, assaulted, and imprisoned, and they decided to set that right. King's personal lawyer, Stanley Levison, was a nonobservant Jew usually identified as an atheist. King used to gently tease Levison, saying, "You believe in God, Stan. You just don't know it."

Key to the movement was that it welcomed observant Jews, nonobservant Jews, nonbelievers, Catholics, Protestants, and those of other faiths. The push for civil rights acknowledged that participants brought different motivations to the struggle yet validated everyone. Many secular Jews, for example, could point to a long tradition of social activism stretching back many generations. Southern blacks, accustomed to mobilizing in churches, framed the struggle in explicitly religious terms. Yet no nonbeliever was ever excluded for failing to embrace the religious rationale championed by some.

The fight for civil rights, therefore, was an issues-based struggle, partly anchored in houses of worship but welcoming of the nonreligious, which did not hinge on getting certain people elected to high office. Its goal was to change the hearts and minds of the people by highlighting the great injustice of Jim Crow segregation and denial of voting rights to African Americans. The religious leaders taking part led by moral example and relied on persuasion, nonviolent activism, and the force of example to make their points. They did not simply hitch their entire movement to a certain candidate, help that person get elected, and wait to reap the benefits.

Religious Right groups frequently compare their theocratic goals to the civil rights struggle. Nothing could be more offensive. Modern-day battles over curtailing legal abortion and gay rights are the antithesis of the fight to win civil rights. They are designed to curtail human rights, not expand them. Today's Religious Right anchors its activity in a handful of ultraconservative denominations. They do not seek and do not have secular counterparts. They see no point in changing hearts and minds, insisting they can get what they want via the ballot box. Thus, so much of what the Religious Right tries to accomplish is tied to a certain candidate or candidates.

Time and again the Religious Right has made the same mistake. They believe if they can just elect the right people or put the Republicans in charge of Congress, all they want will be delivered to them on a silver platter. The problem is, politics simply does not work this way. Too many conflicting dynamics come into play. Elected officials must satisfy more than one constituency. Politics, by its very nature, is about the art of compromise. The Religious Right, which bases its policy goals on absolutes supposedly derived from the Bible, sees compromise as surrender.

This mind-set leads too many conservative religious leaders to believe that pulpit-based politicking is justifiable. This is essentially an "ends justifies the means" argument. They come to believe that if a political goal that is desperately wanted is not implemented because there is resistance to it among the population, bending federal tax law by endorsing or opposing candidates is acceptable. The goal must be accomplished, never mind the cost.

There is a final reason why pulpit-based politicking is such a bad idea: it puts religious leaders in the position of knowingly violating the law. Pastors are supposed to model a high standard of behavior and ethics. While there may be some occasions on which knowingly violating an unjust law is acceptable, this is not one of them. Pastors in the South who willfully defied Jim Crow laws during the civil rights era were, by dramatic example, showing the nation the need for change. Pastors who violate the law and issue partisan endorsements today are not free speech heroes. They are simply selling their souls for a perceived political gain—one they most likely won't even receive.

The men and women in the pews are not fooled. Public opinion polls have consistently shown strong opposition to pulpit-based politicking. A poll released by the Pew Research Center for the People and the Press on August 30, 2005, found that 63 percent of respondents said it is never right for clergy to discuss candidates and issues from the pulpit. Even 56 percent of self-identified evangelicals opposed pulpit-based politicking. The average churchgoer, it seems, does not feel a burning need to take a minister's advice with them into the privacy of the voting booth.

Some people who know of my work on free speech issues for the American Civil Liberties Union are surprised that I oppose efforts to permit endorsements from the pulpit. There are several reasons why I take this stand.

First, tax exemptions are not "rights" accorded to any particular kind of organizations, including religious ones. Nothing in federal law or the Constitution mandates that religious bodies (which do, after all, receive many great services) be tax exempt. Therefore, it is permissible to condition this valuable benefit on something. Here, the extraordinary amount of money saved by churches for this privilege—they don't even have to apply to get it—far outweighs the "cost" of simply agreeing not to get involved in partisan politics and let your church become a cog in someone's political machine. A few religious bodies don't accept the benefit, or the burden, of tax exemption. They opt to pay taxes instead and say what they want.

Second, legislative proposals to allow pulpit politicking are unfair. They have focused only on houses of worship, not secular charities and nonprofits. U.S. representative Walter B. Jones doesn't seem to think tax-exempt medical groups or an environmental organization or even my own 501(c)(3) group, Americans United, are "muzzled" in any way. Or is it possible that he wouldn't want all those other groups being allowed to speak up for or against candidates? Jones once candidly admitted, prior to the 2004 election, that he wanted to permit large churches in North Carolina to help elect his friend, Richard Burr, to the Senate. Jones's bill did not pass, but Burr won anyway. Nevertheless, Jones certainly expressed exactly why he wants his legislation enacted!

Frankly, I like the fact that there are a wide range of groups that do the job of public education, advocacy, and charitable work that do not feel pressured into candidate endorsements. Believe me, if all tax-exempt groups could endorse candidates, the candidates would be searching for political help there before the ink was dry on the bill.

Before leaving this topic, I want to talk about some broader issues, including the extent to which religion can influence the law.

I noted in the opening chapter that American law is not based on the Bible, the Ten Commandments, or any other religious text. Our Constitution is secular and includes no references to Christianity or even God for that matter.

Because our Constitution establishes a secular republic, religion and religious texts cannot be the source of our laws. Laws must have a secular rationale. The Religious Right does not accept this principle. It is at the core of their beef with America. They quite simply reject the idea of secularism, and they use it to signify some amoral, libertine perspective on life.

The Religious Right has twisted secularism to mean something it is not. Secularism means simply nonreligious, not antireligious. A secular state is neutral on theological questions. It allows its citizens to hash out religious questions in private arenas but remains neutral itself. Of course we want the government to be secular, because the alternative is some kind of religious state. Most religious people accept a secular government for this reason. Religious Right groups, by contrast, would like for laws to be based on their particular religious understandings.

I've had some curious exchanges with Pat Robertson over religious understandings as the basis of law. One day on his *700 Club,* Robertson was bemoaning why the U.S. State Department was helping to draft a constitution for Afghanistan that was based in part on sharia, or Islamic law. He even called for separation of church and state in Afghanistan!

Pat Robertson demanding separation of church and state! Had I wandered into a parallel universe? I wrote Robertson a quick note, telling him I agreed with him and that I assumed he would also now want to keep a clear separation of church and state in the U.S. Constitution. I even enclosed an Americans United membership form. A few weeks later, I ran into Robertson at an event and told him I was absolutely serious in backing his comments. I have yet to receive his membership form.

It's fun to needle Robertson, but it's also crucial to remember why he is wrong. However, he's not the only one out there who is wrong on this issue. Some progressive evangelicals repeat many of Robertson's errors when trying to find a biblical justification for their own policies.

Best-selling author Jim Wallis's book *God's Politics* says repeatedly that God is not a Democrat or Republican. That's good. Wallis cares about the poor and is an opponent of heavy-handed uses of the military to resolve global conflicts. Again, I can agree.

I part company with Wallis over core issues, however. His book came out at a most unfortunate time—right after the 2004 election. I read the book as a misguided attack on both secular values and groups that seek to base U.S. public policy on something other than the interpretation of their favorite holy scripture. The Christian Bible is important to both Wallis and me, but as I have said, it does not hold a special place of authority in the sphere of American government. Wallis has accused Americans United and the Anti-Defamation League of generating "a cry of alarm . . . in response to anyone who has the audacity to be religious in public." Where did he get this nonsense? I am troubled only by certain ways politicians publicize or promote religion.

I mentioned being troubled by some of Senator Lieberman's comments during the 2000 presidential campaign. Lieberman's speech accepting the nomination as the Democrats' vice presidential candidate was laced with scriptural references and comments about his deeply felt religious beliefs. He seemed to think this facet of his life was an important matter of introduction to the American people, since he was not then a national figure. I was sitting in a CNN studio waiting to comment on his speech, and I took a wait-and-see attitude, figuring that the entire thing would not be a sermon. But as Lieberman's religious rhetoric escalated, I felt he was frequently crossing a line best left uncrossed by a politician. I interpreted his comments as an assertion that religious people are more moral than nonreligious ones, a sweeping generalization that is inaccurate in fact and pandering in purpose.

Wallis seems to endorse this effort to escalate the "God talk arms race," when to me it only feels like the most base pandering. President Bush, in both of his campaigns, stressed his devout faith. I do not doubt that it is genuine, but I wonder why he believes it is so relevant. Too often, efforts to justify a policy on religious grounds only serve as a distraction. For example, when the president brought in a group of handpicked religious leaders to support the invasion of Iraq as a "just war" right after Pope John Paul II had condemned it as otherwise, I observed that perhaps Mr. Bush should have spent more time on intelligence gathering than theological butt covering.

Frankly, I want to hear a lot less about where candidates worship and more about how they'll govern. I look forward to a presidential debate when it is acceptable to hear one of three answers to inquiries about a candidate's faith: "I am a Christian/Jew/Muslim/Buddhist/ Hindu/other," "My faith is so personal I do not want to discuss it," or "I derive my principles from reason and have no spiritual beliefs."

I am not holding my breath for this to happen any time soon. However, I am comfortable asserting that each of the above should be an acceptable answer in the United States. Obviously, Americans are free to vote for a candidate solely on the basis of religious belief, just as they can vote for the taller candidate or the one with the bigger shoe size, but I wish they wouldn't.

I would also be quite happy for candidates to mimic John F. Kennedy, who said in a famous 1960 speech, "I believe in an America where the separation of church and state is absolute—where no Catholic prelate would tell the president, should he be Catholic, how to act . . . I believe in a president whose religious views are his own private affair, neither imposed by him upon the nation or imposed by the nation upon him as a condition to holding that office."

Values are found not in the constant repetition of the mantra "religion is good" but in specific policy objectives. Wallis has led many Democrats to believe their party is perceived as having a values deficit, and he seems to believe that more God talk will do the trick. Why not instead remind Americans of what the party's real values are—a commitment to civil rights, civil liberties, and economic justice, for starters?

Now, unfortunately, in no small measure because of the "help" Wallis has given them and their communications staffs in widely publicized meetings on Capitol Hill, many Democrats are confusing the assertion of values with the quotation of the scriptures. Wallis is only half right when he argues, "The Democratic Party should move much more deliberately . . . to use moral and religious language and to argue for social reform."

Nancy Pelosi, House minority leader, is a devout Roman Catholic, who, I am told, goes to mass almost every day. In past congresses, she did not speak much of her faith. Now she is known to quote scripture on the House floor, once even observing that the Bible "tells us to minister to the needs of God's creation is an act of worship." If I heard this from a pulpit, I'd say amen. When I hear it on the House floor, I have to wonder why.

Does God think we should drill for oil in the remote Alaskan wilderness? I doubt he has a position, yet Lieberman seems to think differently. He quoted scriptures in arguing against drilling in the Arctic National Wildlife Refuge, remarking, "For me, all this began in the beginning with the Bible and with the instruction that God gave to Adam and Eve that they should both work and guard the Garden of Eden, which is to say they should not only develop and cultivate it, but also protect it."

Again, it was a great sermon. On the floor of the Senate, it was less than useful for the simple reason that it's all too easy for a conservative to find a Bible passage exhorting us to make the most of what God has given us and we're left with yet another Bible-quoting smack down.

What I want to avoid are exactly these kinds of scripture-quoting wars in government. I do not want to see the debate over capital punishment boil down to advocates asserting "an eye for an eye and a tooth for a tooth" while the other side talks about Jesus stopping the death by stoning of the woman accused of adultery by insisting that only "he that is without sin shall cast the first stone."

Scriptural affirmation for secular law is what one strives for in a theocracy; commonly shared community values based on the Constitution's framework for justice is what we ought to seek in a democracy.

Let me be as clear as possible about this: *religious texts are a poor basis for government because religious texts are notoriously open to varying interpretations.* Jerry Falwell and the Reverend Jesse Jackson both read the same Bible, yet both have come to radically different conclusions on interpreting it. Falwell claims to take the Bible literally, yet even a cursory glance at his views shows that he is guilty of picking and choosing among the scriptures, seeking support for whatever policy goal he has in mind.

To my mind, Falwell has put the cart before the horse. He settled on his political views, then scoured the Bible to back them up. He did not allow the Bible to lead him to adopt certain views on social issues. This is a common tactic. Anyone can play this game because the Bible is a huge, sprawling work written over many centuries by numerous authors who were responding to unique sets of cultural challenges. Thus, the Bible can be used to buttress just about any position, even ludicrous ones. The Southern aristocracy found support for slavery and the separation of the races in the Bible during the Civil War. Their Northern counterparts read the same book and reached the opposite conclusion.

Both liberals and conservatives are fond of a practice called "proof texting," that is, wrenching passages from the Bible and using them to support a certain political point of view. On poverty, for example, conservatives can point to Old Testament passages warning that everyone must work or face starvation. Liberals can quote Jesus, who frequently spoke of the needs of the poor and offered specific remedies: if you are wealthy, give your money away to help the less fortunate.

What is Congress or a state legislature to do—convene a panel of Bible scholars to decide which side has the better proof texting and then base laws on that? Nothing could be more dangerous than for the state to attempt to adjudicate theological debates over interpreting the Bible. The state does not have to. The fact is, the Bible was never intended to be a blueprint for modern government. It may surprise you to hear a minister say that, but it's true. The Bible is many things, but it was never meant to be a guide for political action in the twenty-first century. It is also not a science textbook or even a history of the end of the world.

The fact that many religious leaders are guilty of selective inter-pretation and application of the Bible cannot simply be overlooked. It is damning to the fundamentalists' argument. Fundamentalists say the Bible is inerrant and thus can serve as a manual for political ac-tion. They love to quote Leviticus 18:22, which forbids homosexual acts. Great. Are they also willing to abide by Leviticus 7:25–27, which warns against eating blood and fat? If so, they'll have to give up juicy steaks. Will they follow Leviticus 19:19, which forbids the wearing of clothes made of mixed fibers? Leviticus 19:27 orders men not to clip the hair on their temples or beards. I am aware of Orthodox Jews who follow this law—but why doesn't Jerry Falwell? (I know some "Christian Reconstructionists" who do try to abide by all of these arcane rules. It is a small group.) Even more problem-atic for literalists, Jesus is quoted in the New Testament noting that he had come not to change one word of the law.

Falwell might as well be waving a copy of *Moby-Dick*. As I've said, the Bible is not the basis of our government or legal system. The Constitution is. The Constitution is not based on, nor was it inspired by, the Bible. The Bible contains no examples of republican govern-ment. The Bible does not call for a separation of powers. The Bible features autocratic kings, not democratically elected presidents. The Bible speaks of all power being invested in a mercurial deity who de-mands submission to complex rules of behavior. It sanctions slavery and the subjugation of women. Our Constitution begins with the words "We the People." It once sanctioned slavery and tolerated the subjugation of women. The genius of our Constitution is that it, unlike the Bible, can be changed to allow for new circumstances and ideas.

Finally, we must confront our own cultural biases. Many Ameri-cans believe the Bible inspired American law not because it did but because most Americans are familiar with the Bible. Culturally speaking, the United States is a Christian nation. Most Americans belong to Christian denominations, and the various forms of Christianity are the dominant religion. Since the Bible and Christianity played such an important role in American history and public life, it is only natural that some people would assume that the law springs from these sources or ought to be anchored in them. It did not and cannot be. Despite the cultural landscape of America, the Bible is no more a law book or a model for U.S. governance than is the Koran or the Upanishads.

Laws, as I stated earlier, must have a secular rationale. This is not just my opinion but a finding of the U.S. Supreme Court. In a famous 1971 case, *Lemon v. Kurtzman,* the Court devised a three-part test to be used for determining when a law violates church-state separation. The first prong says a law is unconstitutional if it "lacks a secular legislative purpose." While some court members have criticized the test, it has never been overturned.

Over the years, I have been amused to see some legislators scramble desperately to come up with a sham "secular legislative purpose" to excuse laws that clearly meddle in religion. Thus, we are told that laws fostering formal prayer in public schools aren't really about religion at all; they are merely intended to give the kids a minute or two to clear their heads and prepare for the day's business. Statutes promoting the biblical story of creation in science classes are awkwardly divorced from the Bible. Government displays of religious symbols are merely meant to honor heritage, not promote religion. A poster with the phrase "In God We Trust" is acceptable to hang on public school walls, some courts have said, because it has lost its religious significance! (When the word *God* loses its religious meaning, God is on a seriously disjoined trajectory.)

Courts usually see through these shams. But the fact that lawmakers feel compelled to make them is sad. A law that lacks a secular legislative purpose is basically an attempt to write a specific theological understanding into our nation's governing codes. That such laws are still put forth in 2006 is an embarrassment. It also demonstrates the Religious Right's ongoing hostility to a core value of our system of government: the need for secular laws.

The issue of gay rights is a good example. Over the years, I've heard numerous preachers and pundits fulminate against gays. They've advocated various legislative proposals: that gays be denied the right to adopt children, that they be forbidden to teach in public schools, that communities be forced to repeal statutes banning discrimination against gays.

I've probed and prodded the religious and political leaders who make these pronouncements. I've debated them. I've dialogued with them. Sometimes I've simply yelled at them. What is it about gays, I want to know, that has them so worked up?

I still don't have the answer. It's obvious some of these people just don't like gays. But rather than put that prejudice front and center, they try to dress up their homophobia in something more respectable. We are told that gay people represent some threat to the existing order. Their very existence undermines our republic, we're led to believe. They are portrayed as a nefarious force that seeks, for some reason, to erode all moral authority.

Buried underneath all of these assertions is usually some type of appeal to religion. When you finally peel back layer after layer of prejudice, what remains is something like this: "But the Bible/the Koran/the pope/the Reverend Sun Myung Moon/Pastor Bob says homosexuality is wrong!"

Not good enough. The pope, Reverend Moon, Pastor Bob, et al. may indeed say this and sincerely believe it. But if not one of them can put forth an argument for denying gays their civil rights that rests on a secular rationale—and I have yet to hear one that holds any water—they must lose. Fears and prejudices, usually based on a close reading of ancient holy books, are not a good enough excuse for a policy of state-sponsored discrimination.

People sometimes call or write Americans United with information about a religious leader speaking out on a political issue. They seem to believe that's a violation of the separation of church and state. We always set them straight. It's not a violation. There are lawful ways for religion and politics to interact.

There are also unlawful or just plain unwise ways. The IRS and the courts will have their say with the former. America's congregants seem to be pretty skilled at dealing with the latter.

6

Sex and Sensibility
THE RELIGIOUS RIGHT'S WAR
ON OUR PRIVATE LIVES

O F ALL THE THINGS I do to defend the separation of church and state and oppose the Religious Right's effort to impose its narrow version of religion on all of us, nothing disturbs its leaders more than my advocacy of women's reproductive freedom and gay and lesbian rights.

As a Christian minister, I believe women have an absolute right to determine their own reproductive fate. I believe the right to have children or refrain from having them is a basic human freedom women all over the world should share. To make this meaningful, of course, requires access to affordable, reliable, and safe forms of artificial birth control and legal abortion.

Young people, I believe, should be taught about sex in an open and honest manner. They need to understand how the human reproductive system works. They need training about human relationships. They need accurate information to dispel myths and misinformation they may have picked up from television or friends on a playground blacktop. (Indeed, these days it is difficult to figure out which is the worst source.) In other words, they must be taught, in an age-appropriate way, comprehensive sex education that includes a frank explanation of birth control.

Young people also need to be taught that some people are gay, that this is their own business, and that all individuals deserve to be treated with respect. No public school should tolerate any form of harassment, whether it is based on race, sex, or sexual orientation.

I say these things not in spite of being a Christian minister. I say them because I am a Christian minister. I believe God made us so different for a reason. He does not celebrate or tolerate hatred based on those differences.

God also does not celebrate ignorance. Our bodies do the things they do for a reason. We are to teach our young people the facts about the sexual dimension of human existence without shame or guilt. The Religious Right, which obsesses over sex to an unhealthy degree, substitutes fear for knowledge and then wonders why so many young people are confused.

My advocacy of these views and my refusal to join the Religious Right's puritanical moral crusades infuriates people like Jerry Falwell and Pat Robertson, who loudly proclaim that I must not really be a religious person. The Bible, aside from some of the codes found in the Book of Leviticus, is certainly not filled with proscriptions on sexual conduct. When Jesus found a group of people ready to stone a woman accused of adultery—a penalty authorized by law at the time—he said, "Let he who is without sin cast the first stone." The crowd dispersed. Jesus appropriately told the woman to "sin no more," but he did not say that her sin was worse than the unlisted sins of the would-be "law enforcers."

Ironically, my views in this area are still rather conservative. I don't think young people should have sex because they are not emotionally ready for the experience or the consequences. But, as a strategy to prevent teen sex, ignorance leaves much to be desired. Education helps young people make informed decisions. It is always the better option.

I came to these positions over the course of my life, from assessing situations in the real world, not right-wing fantasies. As a young seminary graduate, I cotaught a human sexuality course for juniors and seniors at a Catholic high school in conservative South Boston. I told students that they could anonymously put any questions in a shoe box during the week and we would answer them every Friday. Some of these students were already engaged to be married, yet many of the questions were simple and basic inquiries about the reproductive process. Others, though, were written by young people who were almost certainly petrified to hear the answers. This was one of the few racially integrated schools in the city, public or private, and once a young woman asked, "I'm white and if I sleep with a black man but don't get pregnant by him could I still have a black baby with a white husband?" There wasn't a lot of snickering about such questions. Too many in the class didn't have a clue as to what the answer was.

My activism in this area comes from good sources. My mother, when she was in her eighties, told me she had once been picked up by the police in one hardscrabble anthracite coal town in eastern Pennsylvania and driven to the edge of the city and told never to come back. I was a little surprised and asked what on earth she had done. Her response: "One of my girlfriends, her mother, and I were passing out birth control information door to door."

My mother was not trying to be a radical. She simply saw the devastation brought to this region by extreme poverty and limited economic choices. She knew that many women, if they could, would choose to have fewer children. But an oppressive partnership of church and state made that impossible.

It sounds jarring to many today to hear there was a time when artificial contraceptives were opposed as vociferously as abortion is today. What's really jarring is that this time was not so long ago. The Supreme Court's *Griswold v. Connecticut* case, in which the Court struck down Connecticut's ban on artificial birth control for married couples, was handed down in 1965. The case was not about a dead-letter law that no one enforced. It came about after Estelle Griswold, executive director of the Planned Parenthood League of Connecticut, and Dr. C. Lee Buxton, a physician and professor at the Yale School of Medicine, decided to test the law by opening a birth control clinic and openly distibuting artificial contraceptives. The clinic was located in New Haven, and not long after it opened, Griswold and Buxton were arrested and put on trial. Both were found guilty and fined $100.

Forty years later, it seems incredible that this could have happened. Yet even today there are Religious Right activists who argue that *Griswold* was wrongly decided. Some extreme fundamentalists and orthodox Roman Catholics argue that artificial forms of birth control interfere with God's plan to determine how many children a woman will have.

Nor is this an issue that is no longer relevant. Many fundamentalists attack certain forms of birth control—intrauterine devices (IUDs) and Norplant are examples—as being "abortifacients" that cause a failure of a fertilized egg to implant in the uterine wall. As I was writing this book, a spate of stories hit the news media about pharmacists refusing to fill birth control prescriptions, stepping between a doctor's medical judgment and a woman's moral choice. In one instance, a pharmacist filled the prescription, but the clerk at the register refused to ring up the purchase, citing religious objections. Religious Right activists are seeking legislative action in several states to permit this intrusion and supporting a federal bill called the Workplace Religious Freedom Act, which they hope will achieve the same goal. Some states even considered passing laws to protect these pharmacists.

Some people don't think of issues like legal abortion, access to birth control, and protecting the rights of gay people as having much to do with the separation of church and state. In fact, there is a close relationship. Opposition to all three issues almost always stems from ultraconservative religious groups. As a friend of mine who is active in protecting reproductive rights once observed, "When extremists are blocking women's clinics on Saturday mornings, they are waving the Bible, not the Constitution."

My premise is pretty simple: if this nation had a real respect for the constitutional principle of separation of church and state, the law would enshrine the absolute right of women and men to make moral choices on issues of reproduction and human sexuality without the interference of the government at any level.

Regrettably, that principle is not revered, but reviled, in the quarters of some of the most powerful forces in and out of government today. We are subject to tremendous challenges to the right to reproductive choice and women's health policy precisely because these potent religious groups hold extraordinary sway at this time in our history. If syndicated columnist (and self-professed atheist) Nat Hentoff were the only antichoice voice in the country, there would be no antichoice movement. But that's far from the case. The reality is, when a woman's right to choose is challenged, or when the rights of a gay person are threatened, it is nearly always at the behest of someone with a Bible in hand, claiming divine truth for his or her particular position on the matter.

Interestingly, an entire antichoice movement has grown up around an issue that isn't even mentioned in the Bible. There are no direct references to abortion in either the Old or New Testaments. What is there seems to cut against the fundamentalist point of view. The Book of Genesis mentions that under Jewish law, the penalty is far greater if you kill a woman than if you hurt her in a way that causes a miscarriage. Obviously, if abortion had literally been viewed as murder, the penalty would have been identical.

Bible literalists, therefore, have a big problem. But not to worry, they are nothing if not creative. The Bible is a long work with many passages open to various interpretations. To buttress their opposition to legal abortion, fundamentalists often cite a few lines from the Book of Jeremiah, in which God asserts, "Before I formed you in the womb, I knew you." This supposedly implies a full-blown right to "personhood" for fetuses.

Yet it's just as easy to argue that passages like this simply reflect the idea that God is the creative force of the universe, the source of everything according to biblical tradition. If that's all these passages mean, they are not about the politics of abortion, despite fervent attempts to press them into that service. This is, however, just the kind of interpretational license that led the equivalent of the Religious Right 150 years ago to condemn Dr. James Young Simpson of Scotland for using chloroform during childbirth to reduce pain because his critics asserted that it violated the biblical tenet that children should be brought forth in pain. We have not come very far.

So, here is the antichoice movement claiming a moral high ground even though the ground is based on nothing but shifting interpretational sand. Even the earliest Christian church, the progenitors of Roman Catholicism today, did not view all abortions as a crime. Indeed, many of the early church fathers—and I emphasize that gender—did not believe that abortion raised any substantial moral questions until the point of ensoulment, which scholars often indicated was thirty days after the conception of a male child and sixty days after conception of a female one. (Apparently, even they recognized men needed a head start to stay even with women.)

As a historical summary, then, the idea of fundamentalist Protestant or Catholic doctrine indicating that abortion is murder is a theological accretion, not something derived from the imperative of scripture. But even if the Bible screamed loud and clear that all abortions should be banned, even if it denounced condoms by name, even if the fundamentalists are correct that the Book of Leviticus's condemnation of homosexuality is still relevant today, it would not matter as a legal question for this simple reason: *American law is not based on the Bible.*

Although Americans United for Separation of Church and State is not primarily a reproductive rights organization, I would have to be blind not to have noticed over the years that the enemies of reproductive choice are also enemies of church–state separation. There is precious little difference between them.

It's also true that the Religious Right tends to lump advocates of church–state separation, reproductive freedom, and gay rights into the same vast liberal conspiracy. Its leaders don't think much of it. They particularly don't think much of women. To fail to recognize this patriarchical premise is to miss what is so dangerous about the Religious Right's viewpoint.

Pat Robertson once offered the opinion that he would not take feminism seriously until there was a chess grand master who was female. Actually, at the time Robertson made that comment, there was already a female chess grand master. Several more have qualified since. To my knowledge, Robertson is still not checking out Gloria Steinem books from the library.

Jerry Falwell, in praising the Promise Keepers movement, where weepy men promise to reassert their God-given right to lead the family and ask for forgiveness for letting women get into positions of authority in the first place, once said, "It appears that America's anti-Biblical feminist movement is at last dying, thank God, and is possibly being replaced by a Christ-centered men's movement."

In other words, Religious Right leaders are of the opinion that women are clearly an inferior class of humanity. This is, of course, one of the reasons the Religious Right believes state legislatures and Congress, still dominated by men, are better at making decisions about reproductive choice than individual women are. They seem to believe that women are just not smart enough or moral enough to reach the right decision.

I know better. One of the most exhilarating two minutes of my professional life was when I had the privilege of speaking to over one million women, men, and children at the March for Women's Lives on April 25, 2004. The speaker before me was Senator Hillary Clinton (D-N.Y.), so you might say my positioning left me with a hard act to follow. Nevertheless, the crowd was extremely receptive, particularly on two points. First, I noted that President George W. Bush's new budget cut aid to children, cut women's health care, and cut education programs but still contained money for a manned mission to Mars. My response: "Look, we're all prochoice. Let him go!" On a more serious note, I said, "At this moment, this ground is sacred space, where every child is a wanted child, and all of us respect the moral decision-making power of every woman here."

Although the concept of women's rights in America stretches back to the suffragettes of the late nineteenth century, it is the more modern manifestation of the movement that so terrifies the Religious Right. I emphasize the word *modern*. Writing in the journal *Christian Ethics Today*, scholar Timothy L. Boschen defined fundamentalism as "a religious movement that seeks to militantly defend orthodoxy against the incursions of modernity." Nowhere is this more apparent than in the battle over what the Religious Right gleefully calls culture war issues—and that the rest of us might consider modern controversies—reproductive freedom, sex education, and gay rights.

In the United States one could add that fundamentalists often seek to defend their orthodoxy against the promise and vision of the Constitution as well. Regrettably, the unholy mix of fundamentalism with government power is all too visible in potent expressions throughout the country and in Washington, D.C.

I don't want to belabor the Bush administration's antichoice record, but a few highlights are worth noting. As his first major executive act, Bush reimposed the international "gag rule" preventing U.S.-based recipients of population program funds from performing or even discussing the availability of abortions even with privately obtained funds. In this instance, he assumed all money was fungible and interchangeable—something he rejects in the previously discussed faith-based initiative. What this means is that he signed a death sentence for women whose names we will probably never know, all over the globe, by making it much more difficult to obtain necessary medical information.

Bush appointed John Ashcroft to be his first attorney general, a man who had as a senator sponsored the most radical antichoice constitutional amendment in American history. Ashcroft's proposal declared life to begin at the "moment of fertilization," which was to have as its intended effect allowing states to once again criminalize the use even of commonly used birth control devices including the pill, the IUD, and Norplant because all of them are considered "abortion-inducing" by the farthest fringes of the antichoice movement.

Bush made a decision to sharply curtail stem cell research under the belief that fetal stem cells are "persons" but then reluctantly concurred with the idea that existing lines (which he must have known contain many nonviable ones) should not merely be discarded. Debates on stem cell research in Congress often sounded more like medieval religious discourse than a twenty-first-century science-based analysis.

Against this backdrop, we have seen a steady erosion of the right to choose, a chipping away at the foundation under the hope that eventually the entire edifice of reproductive privacy will collapse. Our federal courts are clogged with cases dealing with parental consent laws, criminal penalties for assisting minors to obtain legal out-of-state abortions, state bans on so-called postviability abortions that allege to establish for all pregnancies an arbitrary moment of "viability," "fetal harm" bills, and battles over the misnamed "partial birth abortion" ban. Congress passed a bill in 2005 that made it two separate federal crimes to kill a pregnant woman on federal land. It was called the Unborn Victims of Violence Act. Obviously, there are few such crimes—and murder on any land, federal or nonfederal, is still murder, a capital crime. The point was to assert that a fetus has a separate existence (even if it existed only a few days or hours) and was thus a separate, legally recognizable "person" under the Constitution.

Thanks to the Religious Right, we seem fated to be kept locked in a perpetual cycle of battles over reproductive rights. One action that might lower the number of abortions, legal or otherwise, is better and more affordable access to birth control and improved sex education for young people. Regrettably, but predictably, the Religious Right opposes both.

Facing one of the highest teenage pregnancy rates in the Western world, the Republican-controlled Congress in the mid-1990s pushed through an amendment to the "welfare reform" bill making millions available for sex education classes in public schools and other forums—as long as those classes are "abstinence-based" and contain no useful information about artificial birth control, of course. Bush likes the plan so much he expanded it, despite the fact that there is absolutely no scientific evidence that it works to significantly delay sexual activity. Even worse, it now appears that when young people who learn only about abstinence do become sexually active, they engage in riskier sexual practices than their peers precisely because they are ignorant of how to use contraceptives properly.

The state of American sex education in public schools is now nothing short of a first-class scandal. What information about birth control is given is most often counterproductive. Condoms often break, young people are told; they aren't reliable.

Since we the taxpayers have now spent over $500 million on this abstinence-only education, U.S. representative Henry Waxman (D-Calif.) in 2004 decided to have researchers actually review the content of the programs we are paying for. The conclusions were alarming. Eleven of the thirteen funded programs contained significant errors and distortions. One program taught that a pregnancy occurs one out of every seven times a couple uses a condom. If that were true, the birth rate in the United States would be so high the continent would probably sink.

The *Washington Post* reported on December 2, 2004, "Many American youngsters participating in federally funded abstinence-only programs have been taught over the past three years that abortion can lead to sterility and suicide, that half the gay male teenagers in the United States have tested positive for the AIDS virus, and that touching a person's genitals 'can result in pregnancy,' a congressional staff analysis has found."

The *Post* reported that "several million children ages 9 to 18 have participated in the more than 100 federal abstinence programs since the efforts began in 1999." The programs Waxman reviewed are used by sixty-nine organizations in twenty-five states.

Under pressure from the Religious Right, sexuality information is being censored all over the country, often by the government itself. In local schools, some of the activities being criticized, and often eliminated, are nearly unbelievable. In Lynchburg, Virginia, Falwell's hometown, the school board refused to approve a textbook unless a drawing of a vagina was blacked out. This action supposedly promoted abstinence, although no one has ever been able to explain how.

In Franklin County, North Carolina, three chapters of a ninth-grade health text were literally cut out because they dealt with disapproved topics like AIDS, sexually transmitted diseases, and contraception. A teacher in Belton, Montana, was temporarily suspended for answering a student-initiated question about oral sex.

Making sure children know enough to make critical judgments is exactly what the Religious Right is afraid of. Its leaders and activists are afraid of information. Do they really think that if you never know about a condom you won't think about sex until your wedding night?

Under federal law these days, states can receive federal money only to support programs that have as their "exclusive purpose, teaching the social, psychological, and health gains to be realized by abstaining from sexual activity." The statute actually contains the following statement of what must be taught: "that a mutually faithful monogamous relationship in the context of marriage is the expected standard of human sexual activity." It is interesting to note that this standard is so strict that men like longtime House member Henry Hyde, who had an extramarital affair he termed a "youthful" indiscretion, even though it occurred at age forty-one, and former Speaker of the House Newt Gingrich, who lambasted President Bill Clinton for his sexual activities while carrying on an adulterous affair with a staff member, could not meet it. (As a footnote, I should add they both supported the measure.)

What sort of activities is this money funding? One grantee is Choosing the Best, Inc., of Marietta, Georgia, which received over a half-million dollars. Choosing the Best provides a fear-based approach to abstinence-only sexual education, associating feelings of guilt and shame with sex. Choosing the Best's curriculum was written by Bruce Cook, who has previously served as a National Director for Campus Crusade for Christ, a fundamentalist Christian group.

Shame is highlighted in one exercise concerning the spread of sexually transmitted diseases. Boys and girls are invited to chew cheese-flavored snacks and then sip some water, after which they are to spit the resulting "bodily fluids" into a cup. After a game in which the fluids are combined with those of other students, ultimately all cups are poured into a pitcher labeled "multiple partners" sitting adjacent to a pitcher of fresh water labeled "pure fluids." In the final segment, each boy and girl is asked to fill a cup labeled either "future

husband" or "future wife" with the contents from one of the pitch-
ers. I have heard young people describe this exercise as "gross"; I
have never heard anyone describe it as "helpful."

Another group, the Pennsylvania-based Silver Ring Thing, was
accused of saturating its program with fundamentalist Christian
dogma. Program participants were given $12 silver rings to wear as
symbols of their pledge to remain abstinent until marriage. The *Pitts-
burgh Post-Gazette* on May 18, 2005, described the program like this:
"During presentations, organizers quote Bible passages on stage; students who wear the ring make a vow to remain abstinent, which the
group calls a covenant before God; for follow-up, the students are
encouraged to get the Silver Ring Thing Bible, which is full of
Christian messages, and there's no secular equivalent . . ."

The Department of Health and Human Services finally shut off
money to the group—but only after the American Civil Liberties
Union filed a lawsuit. A Louisiana abstinence program was also cut off
from federal money after a federal lawsuit in 2002. In that case, the
ACLU found evidence that one funded group hosted a religious re-
vival. Another used its money to buy inscribed Bibles for participants.

We are letting religious beliefs guide what should be secular
education—and doing our young people a great disservice in the
process. But it is even more complicated, and worse. States that got
any of the aforementioned "abstinence" funds had to come up with
state matching funds. To do that, many states actually diverted resources to abstinence-only programs—funding that formerly had
gone to much more useful comprehensive sex education programs.

Ironically, when it comes to other topics you'd think the Right
was downright pro–free speech absolutist. When they discuss evolution, you hear a constant babble about the need for "balance" in the
treatment of the alleged controversy over human origins—even
though evolution is not seriously contested by mainstream science.
Yet a "balanced treatment" of sex education, one that stresses the

importance of abstinence but notes that there is such a thing as a condom in the world, is unthinkable. You hear no comments to the effect of "Lay it all on the table and let the children decide."

The sad thing is, American teenagers can see right through the games adults play in this arena. Our popular culture is sex saturated. Teens routinely watch programs like *The OC* and see salacious music videos. Most of them probably even know there is such a thing as "sex" and that people do not routinely die from it. In a perfect world, sex would always be a morally responsible act between committed individuals. That is not what children see, however, and a majority of teens seem determined to experiment. We can help teens protect themselves and ward off unwanted pregnancy or we can continue to live in the fantasyland of the Religious Right and have one of the highest teen pregnancy rates in the world. That is our choice.

As I mentioned earlier, the Religious Right's goals in this area go way beyond ending legal abortion and denying information to teens. In a little-noticed speech in 1997, Robertson explained to a banquet audience that the real problem the Supreme Court had was not its reasoning in *Roe v. Wade.* He said the major error had occurred eight years earlier when the Court issued its ruling in *Griswold.* The Religious Right wants the power to oversee our sexual and reproductive lives, period.

Movement activists do not stop there. To Religious Right fundamentalists, abortion is only one "life" issue. There is another that, although less talked about, is literally relevant to every single American—unless someone out there has found a way to live forever.

In early 2005 the Religious Right turned a little-known, decades-long tragedy into its latest sideshow. The case involved Terri Schiavo, a Florida woman in a "persistent vegetative state" whose husband had to battle Congress, the White House, and the court system to disconnect her feeding tube. In many ways, the case represented the flip side of the abortion issue. Just as the Religious Right would like to determine when life begins, they also want the power to say when it ends.

There has been a lot of discussion in recent years about "physician-assisted suicide" and right-to-die issues. Oregon has a law, approved by the voters, that allows a physician to prescribe a fatal dose of drugs for a terminally ill patient under tight controls. The law has been invoked only 208 times since it went into effect in 1997 and has been used mostly by those suffering from terminal forms of cancer. This aspect of the debate has captured the headlines, but as the Schiavo case proved, a more common scenario faces American families every day.

We will all grow old and die. Death is not often a sudden thing that is quick and painless. Many people linger. Some die slowly of degenerative diseases. Others lose consciousness but remain alive, hooked to machines.

This can happen to any of us at any time. Mrs. Schiavo was only twenty-seven years old when she collapsed and lapsed into a persistent vegetative state. The hard truth is, anyone reading this could be in a car accident tomorrow or be struck by a truck crossing the street and end up like Mrs. Schiavo.

If that happens, who will make the determination of what is to become of you? Many Americans have living wills or advance directives that spell out what is to happen to them if they become incapacitated. Some people want every possible measure taken to keep them alive. Others eschew such extraordinary measures.

But not all Americans think to prepare such explicit instructions. Thus, when a tragedy strikes or a person becomes incapacitated simply owing to old age, family members may be flying blind. At some point, a decision will have to be made about what sort of measures are to be taken on behalf of an ailing individual who has no chance of recovery. Who should make that decision?

Most Americans would say family members should make it, in consultation with medical professionals. In fact, that is the law in most states, including Florida. Michael Schiavo, Terri's husband, was her legal guardian and expected to use what he knew of her wishes to give her peace. He had to fight interference from powerful national Religious Right groups that did not know him or know his wife. These groups knew Mrs. Schiavo's parents did not approve of Michael Schiavo's decision to remove her feeding tube. That was all they needed to turn the entire situation into an appalling circus.

I never expected to get involved in the final stage of this case. But eventually the rhetoric got so out of hand that I felt compelled to weigh in. In March 2005 then House majority leader Tom DeLay called his congressional colleagues back from vacation to pass legislation to reverse what seemed to be the Florida court system's final pronouncement on the matter: Michael Schiavo could remove the tube.

The congressional bill was an attempt to require a new start to the legal proceedings in a federal court district in Florida, what is called a *de novo* review of all the issues that had already been reviewed by over twenty state and federal courts during the previous tragic eight years of Mrs. Schiavo's life. The bill, however, specified that none of the earlier evidence on her medical condition, her wishes about life-sustaining treatment, or the qualifications of her husband as her guardian were to be considered.

Hours after the bill passed early on a Sunday morning, I was listening to a remarkable tape recording of DeLay speaking the previous Friday to the Family Research Council in Washington, D.C. During this session, DeLay made breathtaking comparisons between his political fortunes and the Schiavo case. He bemoaned "personal attacks" against him and other conservative leaders and said the Schiavo case would highlight those attacks.

"One thing that God has brought to us is Terri Schiavo, to help elevate the visibility of what is going on in America," DeLay told the crowd. "This is exactly the issue that is going on in America, of attacks against the conservative movement, against me and against many others." DeLay added that "the other side" was leading the attack, with a goal "to defeat the conservative movement."

At the time, DeLay was under fire for allegedly funneling illegal corporate contributions into Texas state government races, an action he was later indicted for. He seemed to be linking the forces that sought to end his political career with those that wanted to end Schiavo's life. DeLay went on to promise action to change the tax code to allow partisan politicking in church pulpits. There was no doubt that he was hoping the Family Research Council would do some hard-nosed politicking for him as his ethics troubles exploded.

Reporter David Kirkpatrick of the *New York Times* was keenly interested in the tape of this speech that we obtained. Since I was credited with releasing the tape, I had to deal with a spate of calls from television and cable networks. I was a little reluctant to appear on some of these shows because there were just a few points I wanted to discuss, and I worried the discussions might spiral out of control. Most of the "talking heads" discussing this case seemed to have miraculously earned medical degrees and also developed the psychic power of long-distance diagnosis. (Among them was Senate majority leader Bill Frist, a heart surgeon, who a few nights earlier had "diagnosed" Schiavo via videotape and insisted her condition was not hopeless.)

When I did appear on these shows, I made a few key points. First, I wanted people to understand that the same Religious Right activists who were pushing the Schiavo case were also bound and determined to control almost every other aspect of the lives of Americans. In their "pro-family" fervor, they wanted to control their families and everyone else's as well. They wanted to make decisions for all of us from the moment of conception until the moment of death—and now they were prepared to tell you when that moment could occur.

Second, there was more than a little blatant hypocrisy in the idea of taking the quintessential matters of family law and guardianship and forcing them into the federal courts. These were precisely the same lawmakers who were, in the same session of Congress, attempting to remove jurisdiction of all federal courts, up to and including the Supreme Court, over a variety of controversial social issues—including same-sex marriage, recitation of the Pledge of Allegiance in public schools, and government-sponsored Ten Commandments displays—a move legal scholars call "court stripping."

It was obvious that the Religious Right's effort to stop what they called activist judges was purely a "results-oriented" effort. If they don't like the result of a federal court decision, they want to shift the subject of the decision to the state courts; since the state courts in Florida reached decisions the Religious Right did not like in the Schiavo case, they wanted to "federalize" the legal debate on that topic. By the end of the Schiavo fiasco, which thanks to the Religious Right's interference had to drag on for several weeks, people like Tom DeLay did not know who to hate more: the Florida judges or the very conservative federal appeals court judges who put the final nail into DeLay's cynical strategy. One of them, Stanley F. Birch Jr. of the U.S. Court of Appeals for the Eleventh Circuit, chastised Congress directly, writing, "When the fervor of political passions moves the executive and legislative branches to act in a way inimical to basic constitutional principles, it is the duty of the judiciary to intervene" and "In resolving the Schiavo controversy, it is my judgment that, despite sincere and altruistic motivation, the legislative and executive branches of our government have acted in a manner demonstrably at odds with our Founding Fathers' blueprint for the governance of a free people—our Constitution."

Birch, by the way, was placed on the federal court by President George H. W. Bush.

What kept getting lost was that somebody must be allowed to make a final decision. I was very comfortable with a reasonable number of appeals, but when all is said and done, there must be finality for there to be justice in our courts.

Most Americans will never seek to get an abortion. However, we are all going to die someday. When that day comes, who do you want to make the decisions on your behalf—your spouse, children, and loved ones or the leader of some Religious Right group in Washington?

If the Religious Right has its way, advance directives and living wills would be meaningless. Some oppose them openly right now. "Pro-life" groups talk about the "right to life" extending until "natural death." The problem is, they define natural death in a most curious way. To me, there is little "natural" about being hooked up to a plethora of machines in a hospital bed. Yet right-to-life groups were more than happy to allow Terri Schiavo to exist attached to a feeding tube for any number of years, even though she had no chance of ever recovering. (An autopsy performed after her death showed that her brain had atrophied to half the normal size.)

It's true that at the end of the day, Michael Schiavo did prevail. But at what price? Yes, Schiavo was able to disconnect his wife's feeding tube. Consider what he had to go through before he could take that step. Religious Right leaders defamed and attacked Michael Schiavo. A lawyer for Schiavo's parents, giving a speech to a Religious Right gathering in Washington during the imbroglio, accused Schiavo of attempting to murder his wife for insurance money. The attorney also insisted that Terri Schiavo was animated and lively and could have been rehabilitated with the proper treatment. There was absolutely no evidence for any of these claims.

The attorney was not the only one making those claims. Right-wing religious leaders said Schiavo had not cared for his wife properly and denied her treatment that might have reversed her condition. None of this was true, but that did not matter to the Religious Right. They needed lies and defamation to make their case, so lies and defamation carried the day. By the time she died, Terri Schiavo's fate had long since stopped being of interest to the Religious Right. She had become yet another symbol, another piece of kindling to toss on the flames of the raging culture war. It must have been infuriating for many of those who loved her to watch the Religious Right's cynical manipulation of the case. No one should have to go through that. I'm sure Michael Schiavo is not a saint because none of us are, but consider what he had to go through: having to sit through the agony of allowing members of Terri's family to visit her each day (legally, he didn't have to) and then listen to them go before television cameras, often flanked by some Religious Right "advisers," only to make the vilest possible accusations against him. To my mind, Michael Schiavo showed a lot more restraint and class than all of the Religious Right leaders I've had to deal with over the years.

Controlling Americans' reproductive lives and their end-of-life decisions is not enough for the Religious Right. Increasingly, the movement wants control over the most intimate aspects of our private lives as well.

Consider human sexuality, an area where the Religious Right remains firmly rooted in the Middle Ages. The Religious Right's steadfast opposition to abortion and its insistence that teenagers be denied comprehensive sex education stem, I believe, from the same root belief that human sexual activity is somehow evil and dirty. This has been a problem in some Christian churches from the very beginning. Eve's tempting of Adam in the garden is often given a sexual dimension. Until the fall, Adam and Eve did not even know the shame of their own nakedness. After their exclusion, Eve received a sex-related punishment for her actions: pain during childbirth.

The image of women as the sexual tempters of men haunted the Christian church for many millennia. Fundamentalist Christians are hardly alone in almost fearing the sexual power of women. In hardline Muslim nations, women are seen as so dangerous to men that they are required to shroud their bodies in long black robes and may not leave the house unescorted by a male relative. In these countries, sex-related offenses are among the worst crimes one can commit. Adultery and fornication are punishable by death.

In the United States only an extreme fundamentalist faction called Christian Reconstructionists still advocates for executing adulterers and fornicators. While today's Religious Right argues frequently that there is too much emphasis on sex in American culture—a point I have no trouble conceding—its leaders tend to emphasize not the sexual misdeeds of married people or unmarried men and women. (In moments of acute frustration, I have sometimes said, "Well, at least those right-wing powerhouses like former congressman Bob Barr and former House Speaker Newt Gingrich *are* profamily. In fact, they are so profamily that they each have had three of them already.") Instead, they focus almost exclusively on gay men and lesbians.

The Religious Right's constant attacks on gay people are, in my opinion, among its most appalling activities and will stand as its most unfortunate legacy. One could easily make the case that American families are facing serious threats—none of which can be laid at the feet of gays. Half of all marriages end in divorce, and every year millions of children are left shuttling between mothers and fathers who have called it quits. This is not to suggest that divorce is never an appropriate option, but the hard truth is that divorce sparks fallout. Divorce seriously affects family finances. In some cases, it can leave women impoverished. Very rarely do Religious Right leaders ever talk about divorce or outline strategies for helping couples maintain healthy and fulfilling marriages so that divorce will be less common. I once asked Operation Rescue founder Randall Terry how he can be so unforgiving about abortion and gays and yet have gone through a divorce himself (clearly a biblical prohibition). He actually replied, "Well, we are all human." Rather than deal with the uncomfortable questions raised by this issue, Religious Right leaders focus all of their energies on crude homophobia.

Why does the Religious Right do this? I doubt it is because gays are breaking up huge numbers of straight marriages every year. Nevertheless, this is actually one of the principal arguments the Religious Right uses against the idea of recognizing same-sex marriages or even civil unions. Every year, plenty of marriages crash because of infidelity. In most cases, the offending partner is engaged in an affair with someone of the opposite, not same, gender.

Illegitimacy rates are disturbingly high in some parts of the country. Some women have children by more than one man without marrying any of them or expecting any assistance in nurturing these children or paying for their support. Statistically speaking, few of the men fathering those children and then not caring for them are gay.

Is it gay people's fault that so many Americans, male and female, are so obsessed with advancement at work that they neglect their children? Are gay people to blame when a straight couple's marriage becomes boring and predictable, and they decide to divorce instead of working on it? How did gay people bring about a culture where many families don't even eat a meal together, where children sit in their rooms plugged into video games and iPods instead of interacting with one another?

Religious Right leaders see a gay conspiracy everywhere. They are not, it seems, willing to admit that the fault for fractured American families may lie in the American way of life—all consumption all the time, isolating forms of personal technology, and an insistence on work schedules that emphasize duty to the firm and long hours behind a desk over a commitment to family—rather than nefarious attacks by gays.

Some Religious Right claims border on the absurd. Ever since Falwell "outed" Tinky Winky the purple Teletubby in 1999, Religious Right leaders have shown a disturbing and unhealthy obsession over the sex lives of cartoon characters. They are actually trying to persuade Americans that these characters are somehow being used to advance the so-called gay agenda.

Like many people, I'm unclear on what this gay agenda really is. Most gay people I know simply want to live their lives in peace and be left alone. Some of them want the legal right to marry. Some want to adopt children. They want to be able to care for their partners in the case of illness. These seem to be rather profamily goals.

Do gay people want acceptance by the larger culture? Of course they do. Everyone wants that. I find it hard to believe, however, that gay groups would seek this acceptance through strange venues and elaborate conspiracies, as the Religious Right seems to believe.

Consider this: Focus on the Family leader James Dobson accused SpongeBob SquarePants of being a dupe for the gay rights movement in 2005 after the popular cartoon character appeared alongside other animated figures in a video promoting tolerance. Ironically, the video didn't even mention gay rights. A few lines about toleration of gays appeared on a Web site put together by the video's creator. That was enough to make Dobson and American Family Association founder Donald Wildmon go ballistic. Observed a Dobson spokesman, "We see the video as an insidious means by which the organization is manipulating and potentially brainwashing kids. It is a classic bait and switch."

Dobson and Wildmon never actually accused SpongeBob of being gay. But their central contention—when animated sponges start hanging around with other cartoon characters, biblically incorrect impulses can result—was equally absurd. It's even more absurd that others in the Religious Right claim to have SpongeBob's sexuality pegged. The issue of SpongeBob's sexual orientation was first raised by Alan Sears of the Alliance Defense Fund, a Religious Right legal group, in his 2003 book *The Homosexual Agenda: Exposing the Principal Threat to Religious Freedom Today*. In the tome, Sears speculates that

SpongeBob is probably gay, helpfully pointing out that his best friend, Patrick, is a pink starfish. (What more do you need?)

At times I find it hard to believe this is not all a bad dream. The Religious Right is actually concerned about the sexual orientation of a cartoon character that does not exist, and they want people to know this. They write things about it; they discuss it openly. Now for a reality check: we are talking about *cartoon characters* here. Let's be clear: Leaders of national Religious Right groups that raise millions every year can't be bothered to help their supporters keep their own marriages intact, even though several polls have shown that Bible Belt states have higher divorce rates than other regions of the country. (The states with the highest divorce rates, according to the U.S. Census Bureau, are Arkansas, Alabama, Florida, Kentucky, Idaho, Mississippi, Tennessee, and West Virginia. The state with the lowest divorce rate? Liberal Massachusetts!) Instead, leaders of Religious Right groups spend time obsessing over the sexual proclivities of cartoon figures that *don't actually exist*. (And I'm the one called out of the mainstream by Religious Right activists?)

Sears, I should point out, appears to have the useful skill of being able to ferret out the gay agenda just about anywhere. In his book, he soberly informs readers that the wacky 1959 film *Some Like It Hot,* in which Tony Curtis and Jack Lemmon portray musicians who dress as women to hide from mobsters, promotes cross-dressing.

Even the kiddie movie *Shrek 2* came under attack by the Traditional Values Coalition, which claimed the film promoted cross-dressing. The group issued a bulletin warning of a "she-male" bartender voiced by talk-show host Larry King, noted Pinocchio's habit of wearing women's underwear, and pointed out that the film contains a wolf dressed in Grandma's clothing. The TVC was appalled that instead of condemning this deviant behavior, Shrek and his talking donkey sidekick casually associated with these seedy characters.

All of this might be funny if these claims weren't being used to persuade millions of Americans to hate their neighbors, coworkers, and in some cases their own children strictly on the basis of sexual orientation. And *hate* is the right word. I'm not letting the Religious Right off the hook here with any of its "love the sinner, hate the sin" malarkey. A lot of members of the Religious Right hate both. Over the years, I've attended Religious Right meetings, read its publications and fund-raising letters, and watched its videos and DVDs. When it comes to dealing with gay Americans, I see precious little love of anything.

But let's not get lost in the ridiculous because the reality is worse: Christian Reconstructionists, the most extreme wing of the Religious Right who advocate "biblical law" in America, say the Bible does not just outlaw homosexual acts but demands executing anyone who takes part in them. A book by Religious Right author George Grant titled *Legislating Immorality* laments the fact that legal codes calling for the death penalty for gay people have been abandoned. Despite this harsh language, the tome has been sold by both the Christian Coalition and TV preacher D. James Kennedy's Coral Ridge Ministries. Grant speaks regularly at events sponsored by the Alliance Defense Fund, an umbrella legal group created by prominent Religious Right leaders (Kennedy, Dobson, and Wildmon among them).

TV preacher Pat Robertson has compared gay people to Nazis. Addressing the audience on his *700 Club* on March 7, 1990, Robertson called homosexuality "antisocial" and a "pathology." He went on to say, "Many of those people involved with Adolf Hitler were Satanists, many of them were homosexuals. The two things seem to go together."

I've also noticed this curious feature: Religious Right leaders tend to obsess primarily over the activities of gay *men*. One of the

Religious Right's favorite tactics for spreading homophobia is to film gay pride and other events and showcase clips of men in provocative or sexually suggestive outfits. In Religious Right propaganda, gay men are frequently depicted as voracious sexual predators; even children aren't safe from them. Gay men, as the Religious Right tells it, seek to recruit among young boys.

The use of the term *recruit* is curious. It is an article of faith among the Religious Right that one can choose to be gay just as one can choose to join the Kiwanis Club or Toastmasters. The assertion is at odds with modern scientific understanding, which increasingly points to a genetic determinant for homosexuality. The Religious Right, never a movement concerned with scientific literacy, simply discards all of this research.

In recent years, Religious Right groups have spent a good amount of time, energy, and money fighting efforts to legalize same-sex marriage. Such marriages are legal in only one state, Massachusetts, although some other states and localities recognize domestic partnership arrangements.

Prodded by the Religious Right, a number of states have adopted constitutional amendments barring same-sex marriage. Religious Right organizations frequently pressure Congress to do the same. The Republican-led House and Senate don't seem too eager to do so, although they occasionally trot the issue out during an election year or when mounting scandals give the need for a distraction.

Some of these amendments go beyond barring same-sex marriage; they forbid the state from extending any of the benefits of marriage to same-sex couples. It's discouraging to see such discrimination enshrined in any foundational governing document. On a practical level, language like this merely means that a gay couple that has been together for twenty-five years has additional hoops to jump through in order to obtain some of the same legal rights Britney

Spears did the moment she said "I do" when marrying her first husband in Las Vegas—an old friend whom she dumped days later before having the marriage annulled.

With the help of a clever attorney, gay couples can usually craft legal agreements allowing them to own homes in common and create living wills bestowing power of attorney on each other. They can open joint banking accounts and merge finances in other ways. The Religious Right has not succeeded in denying gay Americans these rather mundane rights—yet.

I see no reason why same-sex couples should have to go through all of this. More important, it must be noted there are some rights no attorney can bestow upon same-sex couples. A gay man or woman has no legal right to visit a sick partner in the hospital. If family members oppose the visit, the partner can be excluded. A husband or a wife receives survivor benefits—a portion of a pension or Social Security benefits—when his or her spouse dies. The surviving member of a gay couple gets nothing. In some states, it is difficult, if not impossible, for gay couples to adopt children. In Alabama, former Supreme Court chief justice Roy Moore, best known for his stint as the "Ten Commandments judge," not only denied a lesbian couple custody of a child one of the women had from a previous marriage but went on to opine in his decision that homosexuality "violates both natural and revealed law," thus making it, in his own words, a "detestable and an abominable sin." (For good measure, Moore quoted from both Genesis and Leviticus.) Sin, of course, is not a legal concept. Moore went on in this loathsome opinion to call homosexuality "an evil disfavored under the law," "an inherent evil," a "detestable and an abominable sin," and "an act so heinous that it defies one's ability to describe it." He insisted that Alabama legislators could use drastic remedies to stop gays, writing, "The State carries the power of the sword, that is, the power to prohibit conduct with physical penalties, such as confinement and even execution. It must use that power to prevent the subversion of children toward this lifestyle, to not encourage a criminal lifestyle."

You read that right. Yes, this apparently meant, in Moore's view, that couples like the one that brought this particular case could be executed.

Occasionally, Religious Right groups argue that state recognition of same-sex unions or other forms of gay rights would infringe on the rights of houses of worship. It's a wholly unpersuasive assertion. Every house of worship in America has the right to determine its own parameters for would-be married couples. The Roman Catholic Church doesn't have to marry non-Catholic couples. A church can apply other conditions as well. Catholics who live together before marriage can be required to separate as a condition of receiving a church wedding. A church can refuse to marry an interfaith couple. It can require couples to undergo premarital counseling. It can make couples promise to raise children in the faith. These conditions are absolutely protected under the First Amendment. Any couple that tried to force a church to perform their marriage ceremony would lose in court and lose badly. This is simply one more scare-tactic argument the Religious Right raises against same-sex marriage. It is preposterous.

Indeed, it is the effort to curtail same-sex marriage through a constitutional amendment that does a disservice to real religious freedom. The Federal Marriage Amendment would "constitutionalize" the definition of marriage as the relationship of one man and one woman. It would say to Unitarian ministers, ministers like myself in the United Church of Christ, and Reform rabbis, "Even though you have ecclesiastical authority to perform same-gender marriage rituals, we the state will not recognize those." That preference for state "blessing" of only certain marriage rituals seems clearly to violate the idea of equal treatment of all faith traditions in America.

That leaves the Religious Right with one final argument, its constant fallback position: an appeal to the Bible, this time to the Book of Leviticus. Leviticus 20:13 does indeed condemn men lying with men, calling it an "abomination." Many conservatives interpret this as a broadside against homosexuality.

Let's assume it is. To be consistent, we should follow the other rules of life Leviticus lays down for us. Here are some other things Leviticus forbids: eating lobsters, clams, crabs, or oysters; trimming one's beard or sideburns; eating pork products; touching the skin of a pig; getting tattoos; wearing clothes of mixed fibers; and the hybrid breeding of livestock.

If Leviticus is the law, a lot of us are violating it every day. Biblical scholars have gone through all sorts of contortions to explain these passages and put them in their proper historical context. As a method of attempting to defuse incipient homophobia based on the Bible, I suppose the exercise has its uses. From a legal perspective it is irrelevant because, as I have explained several times in this book, American law is not and cannot be based on holy books. As a minister, I care what the Book of Leviticus says. (I also care what the Book of Revelation says, but I wouldn't base my life on its rich imagery.) As a lawyer, Leviticus or any other biblical book is irrelevant to me in a courtroom. No one in America should go to prison for engaging in gay sex any more than they should for enjoying a BLT sandwich after spending the day getting tattoos and cross-breeding livestock.

Deep down, I really don't believe most Americans want the most personal decisions of their lives, those dealing with reproduction, sexual relations, and death, to be made by TV preachers or those who follow them. Americans have always valued personal moral autonomy in these matters. The problem is that too many people refuse to believe the Religious Right represents a serious threat to their interests in these areas. Most gay and lesbian people, who have already felt the wrath of the Religious Right, know better. Americans whose children are being denied decent sex education in public schools should too. So should anyone who values reproductive rights or the right to make end-of-life decisions, or anyone who understands the need for freedom to make personal choices about the most intimate areas of our lives free from unwanted interference from religious zealots.

7

Religiously Motivated Censorship
ATTACKS ON THE FREEDOM
TO READ AND LEARN

WHEN THE FIRST MOVIE based on the Harry Potter book series was released, I went out to see it right away.

It's not that I'm an especially big fan of J. K. Rowling's series. In fact, I haven't read any of the books. But I made sure to see the first Harry Potter movie, and all of the subsequent sequels, simply because the Religious Right did not want me to. (They are genuinely fun, as it turns out.)

As Pottermania grew during the run-up to the release of the first film, I found it hard to believe some of the things being said about these books. My children are grown, but you would have to be living in a cave on a remote South Sea island not to have heard about the impact of the Potter books. Sales were phenomenal. Teachers and librarians reported kids who had never before expressed much interest in reading devouring the books and asking for more. Reports filtered in of ten-year-olds locking themselves in their rooms and reading seven-hundred-page tomes in one sitting.

Kids were reading books. We all want kids to read books. So there was no problem, right?

Wrong. The Religious Right had plenty of problems with the Potter series. Across the country, their foot soldiers worked night and day to attack the books and discourage public schools and libraries from promoting or even stocking them. The series, according to the Religious Right, was a plot to dupe children into the occult—and maybe even more.

In Alamogordo, New Mexico, a fundamentalist pastor named Jack Brock led a mass burning of Potter books on December 30, 2001. Brock told supporters the books "encourage our youth to learn more about witches, warlocks and sorcerers, and those things are an abomination to God and to me." For good measure, Brock also heaved a copy of the collected works of William Shakespeare on to the bonfire. (Perhaps the three witches in *Macbeth* sent him over the edge.)

In Lewiston, Maine, another fundamentalist pastor, the Reverend Doug Taylor, wanted to burn the Potter books publicly, but the local fire department nixed the idea. Taylor ended up attacking a Potter book with a pair of scissors. While a group of local kids looked on, probably wondering why this man was allowed to have sharp objects, Taylor remarked, "Some of you young people should take a look at where you're going. Hell is a very bad place."

According to the American Library Association (ALA), the Potter series now holds the distinction of being the seventh most commonly censored book in America. As the anti-Potter hysteria built throughout 2000, I kept waiting for the Religious Right big guns to weigh in. They did not disappoint me.

TV preacher Pat Robertson's *700 Club* on December 5, 2001, aired an interview with Caryl Matrisciana, a self-styled "expert" on the occult. Matrisciana, whose husband, Pat, made a good living producing anti–Bill and Hillary Clinton videotapes containing all manner of made-up, scurrilous charges throughout the 1990s, warned viewers that Rowling is into "the religions of Celtic, druidic, Satanic, Wiccan, and pagan roots and written them into her fiction books for children."

After the interview, a stern-faced Robertson faced the camera and growled, "Now, ladies and gentlemen, we have been talking about God lifting his anointing and his mantle from the United States of America. And if you read in Deuteronomy or Leviticus, actually, the eighteenth chapter, there's certain things that he says that is going to cause the Lord, or the land, to vomit you out. At the head of the list is witchcraft . . . Now we're welcoming this and teaching our children. And what we're doing is asking for the wrath of God to come on this country . . . And if there's ever a time we need God's blessing it's now. We don't need to be bringing in heathen, pagan practices to the United States of America."

So, according to Robertson, Harry Potter books might lead God to turn his back on our nation! Quite a powerful series, particularly since it is written by a woman who grew up in England and now lives in Scotland. For a time, Robertson's Christian Broadcasting Network was obsessed with the Potter books. The CBN Web site ran an entire series of articles attacking the books.

Religious Right groups are notorious for groupthink. Lemming-like, they all quickly hopped on board the anti-Potter train. "Is Harry Potter a Harmless Fantasy or a Wicca Training Program?" blared one press release issued by the Reverend Louis P. Sheldon's Traditional Values Coalition. Sheldon normally sticks to bashing gays and labored hard to link the Potter series to homosexuality. The end result was rather weak.

"While the themes in Harry Potter books do not expressly advocate homosexuality or abortion, these are the philosophical beliefs deeply embedded in Wicca," Sheldon wrote. "The child who is seduced into Wicca witchcraft through Harry Potter books will eventually be introduced to these other concepts." Once, feeling feisty, I asked the Reverend Sheldon if he thought Ms. Rowling might be preparing a volume called *Harry Potter and the Morning-After Pill.*

TV preacher D. James Kennedy of Coral Ridge Ministries in Florida didn't want to be left out. In an October 2001 broadcast, Kennedy interviewed Richard Abanes, a self-proclaimed "expert on the occult" and author of the anti-Potter tome *Harry Potter and the Bible.*

Appearing on Kennedy's *Truths That Transform* radio show, Abanes asserted that as a result of the Potter books, Wiccan groups in England were being flooded with new members. The leading Wiccan group in the United Kingdom, Abanes told Kennedy, has had to hire a youth minister.

Series author Rowling, Abanes asserted, "has had a fascination with the occult and witchcraft and wizardry ever since she was a little girl. And so, her creativity, her talent, when she wrote something, that came out on the page. I'm not sure she actually meant to draw kids into the occult, but that's indeed what's already happening, especially in England."

Abanes provided no evidence that interest in the occult was skyrocketing in England. In fact, there isn't any. Most Britons these days say they are skeptical of organized religion, and "none" has become the country's favorite religious preference. Britons also seem to enjoy having fun with pollsters who query about religious affiliation. An increasing number of people in the United Kingdom claim to be practicing the religion of "Jedi Knights."

And of course Jerry Falwell had to chime in. His *National Liberty Journal* noted that "there does appear to be a legitimate reason to be cautious in regard to Harry Potter" and went on to assert, "Even if the author's intent is anything but evil, the attractive presentation of witchcraft and wizardry both ultimately godless pursuits may desensitize children to important spiritual issues."

When I read this type of over-the-top hysteria about a children's book series, I can only wonder what planet these Religious Right leaders have been living on. Have they never read children's literature before? Witchcraft and other magical themes are a constant in what publishers call kidlit. Witches, fairies, dragons, and other mythical beasts have a long lineage in stories aimed at young readers. Witches are a staple in the Grimms' fairy tales, which are hundreds of years old and remain popular today. In the Grimm Brothers' tales, as in the Potter books today, good triumphs over evil in the end. Such stories usually end up teaching simple moral lessons that youngsters can readily understand.

I would not want anyone to think that fairy tales are themselves utterly immune from Religious Right criticism. During the late 1980s and early 1990s, a number of public school districts using a popular reading series called "Impressions" were repeatedly attacked over claims that some of the stories promoted witchcraft. There were some lawsuits, none of which were successful. (Incredibly, one story that mentioned a witch riding a broom was actually attacked as encouraging masturbation.)

I don't claim to be an expert at analyzing literature, but even I can see that Rowling's books are following a simple, often-used formula that appeals to young readers—and, based on the number of grown-ups I see reading the Potter series in airports and on the D.C. subway, plenty of adults as well: As a young boy, the orphan Harry is picked on by his obnoxious cousin Dudley and mistreated by his aunt and uncle who force him to live in a cramped alcove beneath the stairs. When Harry finds out he is a wizard, he is taken away from his dreary home life and becomes a type of celebrity at Hogwarts, the school for aspiring witches. At the school, Harry overcomes various obstacles while learning special powers that enable him to triumph over his enemies.

Harry is an orphan because a powerful wizard named Voldemort killed his parents. Throughout the series, Harry skirmishes with

Voldemort's agents. I have no doubt that the final book will feature a cataclysmic showdown between Harry and Voldemort—and that Harry, who represents good, will triumph. This is a children's tale, after all. Good must triumph over evil. Hansel and Gretel do outwit the witch in the end, after all.

Rowling herself does not see the series as an introduction to the occult. She has called the assertions that her books seek to lure youngsters into the occult "absurd." In one interview she observed, "I have met thousands of children now, and not even one time has a child come up to me and said, 'Ms. Rowling, I'm so glad I've read these books because now I want to be a witch.'"

I have no doubt that many children do fantasize about having Harry Potter–like powers. They were doing this before the Potter series was ever written and will be doing it long after the books are forgotten. Rowling did not invent the idea of witches, warlocks, and magic powers. Even one of her central themes, that of a training school for witches-to-be, is not original. In 1974, Jill Murphy published *The Worst Witch,* a kidlit novel about girls training to be witches at Miss Cackle's Academy for Witches. Several sequels followed. While Murphy's series never became as popular as Rowling's books, the tomes have remained in print over the years and were even dramatized on HBO. Somehow, Christianity managed to survive the 1970s.

Yet even some clerics who ought to know better keep beating on books like this. Cardinal Josef Ratzinger, before he became Pope Benedict XVI, endorsed a book criticizing Rowling's series. Benedict wrote that the Potter books "erode Christianity in the soul" of young people.

In a March 7, 2003, letter to Gabriele Kuby, a German Roman Catholic sociologist who authored a book criticizing Rowling's tomes, Benedict-then-Ratzinger wrote, "It is good that you are throwing light on Harry Potter, because these are subtle seductions that work imperceptibly, and because of that deeply, and erode Christianity in the soul before it can even grow properly." Benedict later gave Kuby permission to cite his letter in promoting her book.

In her book, *Harry Potter: Good or Evil,* Kuby asserted that the Potter novels blur the boundaries between good and evil, making it hard for young readers to distinguish between the two. She also asserted that the books glorify the world of witches and magicians at the expense of the human world.

Spare us this nonsense. It is simply impossible to think the Potter series confuses good and evil. Harry represents all that is good, pure, and decent. Voldemort is dark, evil, and sinister. Harry triumphs. End of story. Was that so difficult? This is a children's book we're talking about; unlike a complex adult work of fiction, where characters' motives may be obscure and people are often portrayed as having a mixture of good and bad qualities and evil can triumph in the end, kidlit usually oversimplifies things for the sake of plot and a coherent, comforting moral lesson.

The fact is, witches, giants, ogres, elves, trolls, unicorns, talking animals, and other magical creatures populate children's literature for a reason: kids love these types of characters—and they like them to be just a bit scary but with good winning out in the end. Have Rowling's critics never read a book by Roald Dahl? In Dahl's *Witches,* a band of evil female sorcerers meets in a type of convention and conjures up a plan to turn England's children into mice. A little boy foils the plot. Another Dahl book, *The BFG,* features a buffoonish giant who pledges to stop eating children after a little girl reforms him.

Religious groups have been down this road before and ended up looking silly in the end. L. Frank Baum's *The Wonderful Wizard of Oz* was a frequent target for censorship after it was published in 1900. Would-be censors were sure the book was unwholesome for children. Oz, after all, is a land where magic is very much alive, and no one seems to go to church. (Plus, in the books that followed the first

Oz tome, Baum makes it clear that Oz is governed by a type of benevolent socialism.)

You may remember a popular film called *The Sixth Sense.* It is about a little boy who keeps saying, "I see dead people." I know what I'm about to say is a spoiler, but it's an old movie: it turns out he actually *is* seeing dead people and that his main adult friend and supporter throughout the film, played by actor Bruce Willis, is dead himself. Aside from the literalism of the Religious Right, one of their other problems is that they see things that are *not* there.

The American Life League once sent out a press release condemning images in Disney's animated feature *The Lion King.* The group claimed that in one scene, in which the leader of the lions is roaring while standing on a cliff, a cloud formation floating by spells out the word *sex.* The group seemed to believe this was some kind of subliminal advertising for sexual promiscuity. With better than 20/20 (corrected) vision, I still can't see it. Then again, I couldn't see the penis-shaped coral in Disney's *Little Mermaid* either, another right-wing standby.

When all is said and done, this is my biggest beef with would-be censors: they would deny children and adults access to some wonderful books and stories on the most frivolous of grounds. We have not just a right but a duty to resist such nonsense. Technically "censorship" only occurs when a government body makes the decision to remove or restrict access to a film, book, or other material. Often the Religious Right seeks to use government powers, legislators, or the courts to do just that.

Consider this: In 1986, a group of parents in Hawkins County, Tennessee, attempted to ban several books from the local public schools. The books on the list allegedly promoted "secular humanism" and witchcraft. Lead plaintiff Vicki Frost really had problems with *The Wonderful Wizard of Oz.* The book, she said, depicted some witches as good when in fact witches are always bad.

Witches are always bad? Listening to Frost, one would conclude that such things as witches actually exist. I am aware that some followers of modern-day forms of Wicca call themselves "witches," but Frost was talking about the classic witch of children's literature—the kind with the warty nose, the pointy black hat, the flying broomstick, and so on. In other words, Frost seemed to really believe that some people can summon dark forces and gain magical powers of an evil nature. Such figures cannot be "good" or "bad" in the real world because *they don't exist in the real world.* Society should respond to those who hold neuroses like Frost did with sympathy, but we are not obligated to give in to them. The courts did not give in to her either.

Courts seem well aware of the efforts of religious interest groups to curtail access to materials in school curricula and libraries. Indeed, a landmark school censorship case reached the Supreme Court in 1982, *Board of Education, Island Trees Union Free School District No. 26 v. Pico.* In this case, school officials sought to remove several titles from a high school library over the objections of a parents committee. Challenged titles included Kurt Vonnegut's *Slaughterhouse-Five; Soul on Ice* by Eldridge Cleaver; and *Best Short Stories of Negro Writers,* edited by Langston Hughes. School board members called the books "anti-American," "anti-Christian," and "just plain filthy." The Court rejected the censorship plan.

In 1993 the school board in Olathe, Kansas, removed a teen novel, *Annie on My Mind,* from the school library because it deals with homosexuality. Parents who objected to the censorship sued, and a federal court ordered the book reinstated. Federal judge Thomas Van Bebber wrote that school board members may not ban books "based on their personal social, political and moral views."

I'm sure many in the Religious Right would disagree with me on some of these points, especially my refusal to believe that some books promote witchcraft. In California a group of students at a Christian high school sued the state, asserting that they were being denied access to state-owned colleges because they attended religious schools. State higher education officials pointed out that some of these youngsters had been educated with a curriculum that was just plain strange, noting that one Christian publisher put out a history textbook asserting that there really were witches in Salem at the time of the famous trials. I'd rather not debate the point, as we could easily lurch into the world of the absurd. My point is that "bad" witches, as commonly presented in children's literature, are merely stand-ins for a generic type of evil that is to be overcome by forces of good. When we deny children access to these books, we deny them important lessons that can be crucial to their moral development.

Some Christian writers know this. C. S. Lewis's Narnia series features a white witch that most see as an allegorical symbol for the devil. She is defeated by a band of children who harness magical powers—yet these powers, we are told by the Religious Right, are acceptable because they emanate from Christianity. The Narnia series, after all, is a Christian allegory. That is why the devout Mr. Lewis wrote them. He once observed, "I am aiming at a sort of pre-baptism of the child's imagination."

The Narnia series provides an interesting example of Religious Right double standards. By any measure, the books deal with themes of magic, special powers, and fantastic creatures—Mr. Tumnus is a faun, for heaven's sake! All of these things would be labeled part of the "occult" by the Religious Right under any other circumstances. Lewis presses them into service for Christian proselytizing; thus, they get a free pass. While I don't think any student in a public school should be pressured to read the Narnia books since they are Christian in character, I'm not for censoring them either. The series can be read as yet another simple tale of good triumphing over evil.

I found myself in the middle of a Narnia battle in the fall of 2005 when I discovered that Florida governor Jeb Bush had chosen *The Chronicles of Narnia: The Lion, the Witch and the Wardrobe* as the book in a statewide reading contest. Young people were supposed to read the book and then, depending on their grade level, write an essay or produce a video reflecting the book's themes. I wrote to Governor Bush, noting that the Narnia books are intended to teach Christian motifs, pointing out that Lewis himself hoped the books would provide young readers with a platform for better understanding Christianity when they considered it as adults. I suggested not that the state stop the contest but that it simply allow students a second choice. The governor refused.

I agreed to appear on Tucker Carlson's MSNBC program to discuss this subject. Carlson complained that I wanted to censor Lewis. He missed the point. I just wanted other options in the contest. I did not seek to have *The Lion, the Witch and the Wardrobe* removed from any school library, and to those kids who wanted to read it, I could only say, "Have at it." Occasionally, to make a point about censorship, local atheist groups have petitioned a school to remove the Bible from a school library. They never succeed, nor should they in the event they intended to. Normal school library acquisition policies should be inclusive, and both school and public libraries should have works reflecting a diversity of viewpoints. (At the school level, this does not mean that wildly age-inappropriate material—*The Best of* Hustler—should be purchased.)

Every year the ALA releases a list of the most censored books in America. Certain titles pop up over and over again. An ALA cumulative list from 1990 to 2000, for example, lists Madeleine L'Engle's *A Wrinkle in Time,* Roald Dahl's *James and the Giant Peach,* and Eve Merriam's *Halloween ABC,* as well as the Potter series. Several science-fiction titles also appear.

It's as if to the Religious Right, any attempt to even imagine an alternative world or other realities is an offense against God. This is strange because in many ways, the entire point of fiction is to transcend the normal boundaries of human thought. Certainly the genre of science fiction seeks this goal. This genre can give us mere fluff—killer robots from Saturn attack Cincinnati—but it can also produce works of staggering imagination and vision. George Orwell's *1984* and Aldous Huxley's *Brave New World,* after all, both qualify as science fiction. Yet I've had Religious Right activists tell me that any book that features aliens from space should not be read by children because it could give them the impression that God did not uniquely create life on earth!

I'll admit, some of the books on the ALA list simply stumped me. Who tried to censor *Where's Waldo?* What annoyed someone about Maurice Sendak's *In the Night Kitchen?* What got someone worked up about a book about superstitions titled *Cross Your Fingers, Spit in Your Hat?*

A little research unveiled the most flimsy reasons for attempting to censor these books. Somewhere, among the busy illustrations that populate Waldo tomes, someone claims to have seen a topless woman hiding out alongside the stripes-wearing hide-and-seek fan. In Sendak's book, apparently too much of a little boy's bottom is exposed. As for the superstitions, well, someone might believe them if they read about them.

Remember, these books appeared on a *cumulative* ALA censorship list. This means they were the most censored books over a ten-year period. It wasn't just a case of a lone crank trying to get *In the Night Kitchen* out of a school library. It happened repeatedly.

Aside from the occult, the Religious Right's favorite reason for book banning is sex. I will concede that some books are written for adult audiences and should be read by adults. I see no reason for a children's library to have a copy of Madonna's *Sex* lying around. I doubt any do.

The problem, once again, is that the Religious Right takes a reasonable assertion—some books are not intended for children—and invests it with the power to deny access to a wealth of material, some of which may in fact be fine for children and was even written for them.

The ALA list features several guides to puberty. One of them, *What's Happening to My Body? Book for Girls: A Growing-up Guide for Parents and Daughters,* has been a best seller for more than two decades and is considered a classic in the field. The book apparently bothers some religious conservatives with its frank talk about the changes that occur during puberty. I have news for them: censoring the book won't prevent those changes.

Nor will censoring books about homosexuality make gay people go away, as the Religious Right seems to believe and hope. Several titles on the ALA list are factual tomes that deal with gay-related issues. Again we see how even a factual discussion of an issue that makes the Religious Right uneasy becomes the grounds for censorship. A self-proclaimed "library activist" in Virginia named Karen Jo Gounaud has even objected to books that discuss homosexuality in a clinical manner.

Other popular young-adult titles have been attacked for dealing with mature themes. John Steinbeck's *Of Mice and Men* routinely tops ALA lists. It's number six on the cumulative list, even managing to edge out Harry Potter. Harper Lee's *To Kill a Mockingbird* is another frequent censorship target.

Both books are commonly found on high school reading lists. What is the right wing's problem with these books? Again, some research turned up a (lame) answer: Religious Right leaders think the books are "depressing" or that they deal with subject matter that is too serious, such as mercy killing, rape, and interracial tensions. ("Inappropriate language" is another common complaint.)

This leaves America's young people in a tight spot. They aren't supposed to read whimsical books featuring fantastic characters like witches and wizards because those books are "unbiblical." Yet they are not supposed to read literature anchored in the real world either, because it is too depressing and scary and some characters may swear. What exactly are young people supposed to read?

To many fundamentalists, the answer to that question used to be simple: the Bible. In the nineteenth century, it wasn't uncommon to hear fundamentalists attack all forms of literature. Reading plays, novels, and poetry, they said, just took time away from reading the Bible. I doubt this extreme view is common among many in the Religious Right today—after all, "Christian fiction," including the popular *Left Behind* series, has become a hot-selling genre—but I do believe many of them pine for other aspects of those old days, mainly the power religious leaders once had over the distribution of printed material in America.

Well into the twentieth century, local religious leaders had the ability to squelch just about any book or publication they did not like. Laws today ban the distribution of material deemed legally obscene, but in years past, the standard was much broader. Books could be banned for offending religion or violating what were deemed community morals and standards. Usually, local religious leaders established and defined those standards.

Anthony Comstock's New York Society for the Suppression of Vice held so much power in late-nineteenth- and early-twentieth-century America that it functioned as an unofficial arm of the state. The society had successfully lobbied Congress to pass a law suppressing "obscenity"—then used that law to attack basically anything its puritanical members did not like.

The Comstock Law unleashed a reign of terror. John Sumner, who succeeded Comstock as the society's chair, had birth control crusader Margaret Sanger arrested twice merely for distributing scientific information about how not to get pregnant.

Sumner's agents also went after any book that portrayed the clergy in an unflattering light. When Sinclair Lewis's *Elmer Gantry,* which deals with the antics of an amoral preacher, was published in

1926, Sumner had Boston district attorney William J. Foley ban its sale in the city. (Not all the pressure came from the government, of course. Lewis received an anonymous letter from an outraged reader in Virginia inviting Lewis to a hanging—his own.)

Sumner also engineered a ban of Theodore Dreiser's 1925 novel, *An American Tragedy.* Neither *Elmer Gantry* nor *An American Tragedy* can be called obscene. There are no sex scenes in either book. The latter volume deals with a young woman who becomes pregnant out of wedlock and is murdered by her lover; however, while sex is obviously referred to in the book—Dreiser uses the euphemism of an "intimate relationship"—sex acts are never described. Apparently, Sumner just didn't like Dreiser's realism and the serious theme of his work.

Sumner and Dreiser had tangled before. Thanks to Sumner, an earlier Dreiser novel, *The "Genius,"* was deemed "lewd and obscene" and remained out of circulation nationally for many years. *The "Genius"* deals with a young man of loose morals who seeks to become an artist. Its discussions of sex are oblique; the tome can hardly be called obscene, even by the moralistic standards of the early twentieth century. In fact, Sumner and his followers just did not like the book and did not like Dreiser or other new books in the school of fiction called realism.

Lewis, Dreiser, Frank Norris, Jack London, and others led a school of writers who believed fiction should realistically portray contemporary society and its problems in a more compelling manner. They did not shy away from depictions of the harsh realities of life at that time, and their books feature portrayals of alcoholism, family violence, hypocrisy, fraud, deceit, and betrayal. Naturally, many people wanted to keep the discussions of these issues under wraps. Yet many of the books the members of the realist school penned are now considered classics. Had the Religious Right of the time had its way, these pioneering books would have never seen the light of day. The Religious Right was wrong. We are a better society for having these books.

Religious censors used even the hint of sex to block the sale of some books. But they did not stop there. At the behest of the ruling religious establishment, antivice crusaders often targeted material that had no sexual content at all and thus could not legally be called obscene. Nevertheless, this material was often suppressed.

In her book *Freethinkers,* Susan Jacoby discusses the difficulties free-thought organizations had with the U.S. Post Office in the nineteenth century. Organizations that questioned the claims of organized religion or dared to suggest that the Bible was not true enraged the country's powerful religious elite. Their periodicals were often suppressed by postal authorities, and they were denied access to the mail system. The law may no longer have recognized blasphemy as a crime, but the Post Office did. At that time, the U.S. mail was the only game in town for distributing a periodical nationwide. Denying access to the mails could cripple an organization. The conservative religious elite knew that.

Conservative religious elements thought the American public was on their side. But people began to chafe under heavy-handed religious censorship that felt paternalistic. During the censorship battle over Dreiser's works, a Catholic priest in Chicago, the Reverend James McGill, opined that most Americans wanted censorship. "Unless I fundamentally misunderstand the American public, it will guard the morals of the people even at the sacrifice of liberty of the individual," he said. "In other words, we do believe in censorship."

But McGill did fundamentally misread the American people. We do not believe in censorship. As the twentieth century advanced, men like Comstock and Sumner gradually lost their power. Even the city of Boston stopped banning books.

In many cases, censorship just wasn't working. People usually find creative ways to dodge religious censorship. In late-eighteenth-century

Boston, society was still puritanical enough that government officials occasionally tried to ban stage plays. Yet traveling troupes of actors continually moved through the area, putting on shows. How did they get away with it? The performances were billed not as plays but as "moral lectures"—that just happened to have four or five parts. Under this type of creative thinking, *Romeo and Juliet* could easily be recast as a warning to young lovers not to get carried away.

We are long past the need for that type of deception. But some in the Religious Right argue that today we have gone too far. They point to a glut of pornographic magazines and shock television and demand that something be done about it

Sometimes the call is for direct, old-fashioned censorship. The use of state power to curtail "offensive" speech is what the Religious Right sought after the well-publicized Janet Jackson "wardrobe malfunction" during the 2004 Super Bowl. Jerry Falwell said he had to send one of his grandchildren out of the room immediately. (If that child got out of the room before the whole incident was over, he or she should already be training for the fifty-meter dash for some future Olympics.) Then, Falwell demanded that the Federal Communications Commission fine the network a staggering sum for the incident.

This led to subsequent proposed legislation to place such fines on radio and television stations on which "indecent" material (a different and looser legal standard than required under "obscenity" laws) is broadcast, as well as career-destroying fines for the talk-show host or performer who produced the offending broadcast.

Some Religious Right activists felt even this didn't go far enough. What about cable television? What about satellite radio where Howard Stern ended up? Legislation was then introduced to apply the same vague standards to services paid for by a family that chooses to do so. Doesn't this suggest that parents buying the services really have no obligation, no responsibility, to even know what they are purchasing?

I know the supporters of these measures say that even if the parents keep MTV, HBO, the "Lingerie Bowl" on pay-per-view, and so on out of the house, their children could go visit friends next door where maybe the parents allow such programs to be viewed on their cable. That's true, but it's insufficient to make a very persuasive argument. Try this analogy: I lock up my guns, but because the neighbors don't, no one should be allowed to own a hunting rifle.

For religious parents, it seems like there is a better response. Why don't we talk to our children about the violence and sexual images they will see and prepare them to respond in a reasonable fashion?

This isn't a parenting book, but I do remember two stories about my own children I would like to share. One involves my son, who once complained that he was the only kid in his class who had not seen an R-rated movie. I decided this could be a good teaching moment. We went to see what turned out to be a pretty bad Western titled *The Quick and the Dead* and shared a pizza afterward to talk about it. I knew beforehand that the film was not too intense for him—some violence, some language.

I asked my son to explain what was different about an R-rated movie. "We don't use language like that at home," he said.

"Right," I replied. "And we aren't going to start now!" We talked about violence, guns, and other issues the movie raised while sharing the final slice. The experience was not a big deal because we chose not to make it one.

When my daughter was an older teen, she knew she could see R-rated films only with parental supervision. For example, she and I had seen *Born on the Fourth of July* together, a film about a Vietnam vet I know named Ron Kovic.

One night we dropped her off at a friend's house for a birthday party. They were going to have dinner and then head down to the local multiplex for a movie. The parents had purchased tickets for a PG-13 film. When our daughter got back, I asked her how the film was. She said she had not gone in. When I asked why, she replied that her girlfriends decided to use the PG-13 tickets to gain access to the multiplex and slip into an R-rated movie. "I hadn't asked you about seeing it," she said, "so I waited in the lobby." I was proud of her because she had picked up the message we expected her to follow: if in doubt, ask your parents.

Parental supervision is the key. Government-mandated censorship will not work for several reasons. First of all, the publishing and film industries are the ultimate creatures of the free market. It is amusing to see Religious Right activists, many of whom usually praise economic deregulation, whining and moaning because that same free market brings us so much bad literature and movies.

But the simple fact is, these books and movies exist because people want to read and watch them. Conservatives sometimes complain that Stephen King's novels are gory and violent. They're right. I've read some of them. They can be gory and violent. (Indeed, several King titles appear on the ALA most banned list.) They also sell like hotcakes. The publishing industry did not hatch a conspiracy to force people to read gory and violent Stephen King novels.

Should Stephen King's books be in public libraries? Definitely. He is a popular writer, and the public wants to read what he writes. A public library should honor that request. Fundamentalist Christian pastor Tim LaHaye penned a phenomenally successful series of books called *Left Behind,* which are apocalyptic potboilers based on LaHaye's reading of the Bible. Should a public library carry those books? Absolutely. Why? For the same reason a public library should carry King's books.

Censorship campaigns fail today because the market, not sectarian interests, determines what people will read. Sure, the market is often a crude and imperfect instrument for this task. It often fails to focus on quality and more often than not elevates a slasher film over the latest Shakespeare adaptation. This is unfortunate, but I am not terribly concerned about that in the long run. The market continues to give us both. Those who want Shakespeare have little trouble finding him, even if they must pass three theaters showing slasher films to do so.

The Religious Right also seems unable to grasp that its censorship campaigns will usually just end up backfiring. Books and films that become the target of censorship often end up getting attention they otherwise would not have received. For some writers and film producers, a censorship campaign is the best thing that could happen.

Martin Scorsese's 1988 film, *The Last Temptation of Christ,* is a good example. This odd little film, based on a 1960 novel by Nikos Kazantzakis that attempted to humanize Christ, would probably not have made much of a splash if angry fundamentalists hadn't tried to censor it. After all, the public's demand for a more human Jesus has never been very high. But because fundamentalists went so apoplectic over it, the film received months of free prerelease publicity and attracted viewers who came out simply to see what all the fuss was about. On the flip side, a lot of curious people ended up seeing Mel Gibson's dreary *The Passion of the Christ* because of criticism (most of it justified, in my view) by members of minority religious faiths. As I conceded at the outset, I harbor more than a streak of this spirit myself.

If the goal is to actually restrict access to a book or movie (as opposed to, say, raise money or stir up activists), censorship campaigns almost always fail. Harry Potter has been under fire for at least six years now, yet each new book outsells the others. When Islamic clerics denounced Salman Rushdie's *Satanic Verses,* you could not buy a copy in Washington for a solid week—not because the campaign worked but because people quickly snatched up every copy, eager to read what they been told not to read.

So why does the Religious Right keep using this strategy? My guess is it has more to do with getting media attention, raising money, and motivating activists than actually achieving the goal of seeing a book or film withdrawn.

Another tactic of the Religious Right is the boycott threat. If a chain of stores sells *Playboy* and you don't like *Playboy,* then threaten to have your group stop shopping at that chain. This happened to both 7-Eleven and Circle K convenience stores. Neither stopped selling the magazine, and there was no perceptible dip in the profits of either. When a gaggle of right-wing groups decided to boycott all Disney-related products over alleged promotion of homosexuality by that company, the boycott had no measurable effect. One Baptist activist who supported the boycott said it was going too far when he discovered that Disney had an interest in ESPN, the all-sports channel.

People, including religious people, have a right to picket, protest, and call for boycotts. Sometimes, out of fear of possible success, a company will give in to the demands of the boycotters. They have a right to give in, but that usually just ends up sparking a backlash from people angry that the company caved.

Yet another tactic was developed by a Wichita Falls, Texas, Baptist minister named Robert Jeffress, who a few years ago marched on city hall, demanding that if one hundred library card–holding residents sign a petition against a children's book, it be placed on restricted access. Once restricted, the book could only be checked out by those age thirteen and older.

Jeffress had gotten in a lather after one of his parishioners spotted *Heather Has Two Mommies* and *Daddy's Roommate,* two children's books with themes of gay parenting, in the library. Jeffress checked the books out and would not return them, eventually paying a $54 fine. He then argued that the books should not be replaced. (Jeffress actually destroyed the books. What more proof do we need that the censorial spirit is alive and well in America? Also, what more proof do we need that some pastors don't understand the most obvious biblical texts like "Thou shall not steal"?)

Many in the community did not react well to Jeffress's actions. At a city council meeting, several residents spoke out against the idea of allowing a minority to have the power to restrict availability to books. Nevertheless, the city council voted 4–3 to implement the policy, although it upped the number required to limit access to a book to three hundred. The policy was later declared unconstitutional by a federal court.

I noted earlier that censorship campaigns often backfire because they end up sparking interest in the targeted book. Such was the case in Wichita Falls. The books had not attracted much attention before Jeffress's campaign and had been checked out only a few times. A gay news service later noted that not only did gay groups donate additional copies of *Heather Has Two Mommies* and *Daddy's Roommate* to the library, but "in the wake of the publicity, requests to read them had skyrocketed."

We should never forget that the Religious Right has long-term goals that it is quite happy to pursue incrementally. In the mid-1990s, Religious Right groups began agitating for what they called family-friendly libraries. The phrase struck me as odd because I've always considered libraries family friendly. They did not need to be made that way because they already were. After all, you can take your children there, load up on books, and take advantage of great programs like story hours, readings by authors, lectures, and even free movies.

It turns out what the Religious Right meant by family friendly was something very specific—and something not so friendly to families after all. These groups wanted public libraries either to toss out certain books outright or at the very least place them on restricted access. As it happens, the books Religious Right groups wanted to do this to tended to deal with the very themes that often spark controversy among their followers—the "occult," human sexuality, and gay rights.

For a period in the 1990s the Religious Right talked a lot about "local control" of libraries. I had to wonder who they think controls them now. Religious Right groups often contend that libraries bow to demands of the American Library Association, but in fact affiliation with the ALA is completely voluntary, and its policies are binding on no library in America, although many choose to adopt them.

To me, the entire scheme looked disturbingly familiar. It appeared that the Religious Right was trying to do to public libraries what it had already done to public schools: demonize them. Under this plot, the ALA would become analogous to national teachers' unions, which the Religious Right contends run public schools in America, despite the presence of democratically elected school boards in nearly every community in the nation.

Focus on the Family decided to take a lead role in pushing the new antilibrary campaign. Its magazine, *Citizen,* ran a cartoon depicting a "typical" American library. Young children sat in a section titled "ALA Reading Corner." One boy perused a *Playboy* centerfold. Another boy was reading a book titled *Pipe Bombs Illustrated.* Titles surrounding the children included *My Pal Manson* and *Naked Tennis.*

Like most Focus on the Family campaigns, this one lacked a certain subtlety. Parents were led to believe that the public library was no longer safe, that innocent children could wander in there and get their little hands on darn near anything. This outrageous situation would continue until God-fearing Christians set things right.

It's certainly true that not all material in a public library is suitable for children. This is why most libraries have a children's section. This is also why parents are discouraged, or even forbidden, from using the library as a babysitting service. Parents are encouraged to visit the library with their children, read to them on-site, and help them find appropriate titles.

While they worked to portray public libraries as corruptors of innocent children, Religious Right groups pursued a parallel tactic: insisting that there really is no censorship in America and that the ALA fans the flames of hysteria over book banning to serve its own political agenda. Focus on the Family released a report titled "Book Burning or Just Blowing Smoke?" that accused the ALA of hyping the issue.

The Religious Right's main point here seemed to be that not all censorship attempts succeed. That's true; many fail. The ALA does not try to say otherwise. What the ALA does say, and rightly so, is that even unsuccessful censorship attempts must be taken seriously. If they are not, they may not be unsuccessful next time.

At the same time, the Washington, D.C., arm of Focus on the Family, the Family Research Council, issued a paper titled "Discarded Images: Selected Classics and American Libraries" that attempted to argue that classic works of fiction were being excluded from public libraries.

The Family Research Council had no evidence to back up its claims. The report's main rhetorical device was a devious slight of hand: The organization sent a survey to public libraries asking if certain books deemed "classics" were on the shelves. The list included hundreds of books, and few libraries, especially those in small towns or rural areas, could have had them all. Some titles listed were by famous authors but considered lesser works. Naturally some libraries did not have the books on hand. This became the basis for claims that public libraries were shunning the classics. Anyone who believes, even for a minute, that there is anything to this should visit the nearest library. You will find the classics there, alive and well and much loved as always. It was highly ironic to see Religious Right groups portray themselves as defenders of the classics. In former times, their spiritual ancestors led the campaigns to ban many of these books.

A final and more recent tactic involves using the government's spending power as a club to get your way. The Southern Poverty Law Center reported in spring of 2005 that Alabama state representative Gerald Allen, a Republican, had proposed prohibiting state expenditures for the "purchase of textbooks or library materials that recognize or promote homosexuality as an acceptable lifestyle." As the SPLC pointed out, interpreted broadly, the language would make it illegal for libraries to purchase books like *The Picture of Dorian Gray, Leaves of Grass,* and *The Color Purple.*

Juanita Owens, director of the Montgomery City-County Library, told the *Birmingham News,* "Half the books in the library could end up being banned. It's all based on how one interprets the material." The SPLC pointed out that a broad interpretation of the law could lead to a ban on Shakespeare. (Don't tell Representative Allen that many of the Bard's rollicking comedies feature cross-dressing!)

In the end, I don't believe most Americans are sympathetic to the Religious Right's censorship crusade. That may be why the antilibrary campaign never got the traction that the war on public schools did. It just sounds too anti-intellectual. And it sounds that way for a reason: it *is* anti-intellectual.

Frankly, what ties almost all of these censorship efforts together is a genuine hatred of what many educators refer to as "critical thinking." Imagination, reality checks, and nuance all create the possibility that young people will start to think of parts of the moral universe not in black and white but in shades of gray. That's the havoc this could bring, they argue. It causes children to question "authority" (their parents and holy scriptures). This could unravel the whole universe.

I'll concede that if a person has been taught to read the Bible as literal truth, ambiguity can have dramatic consequences. I once met a man who had been a fundamentalist Christian until he discovered that in his translation of the Bible, two different totals for the number of Israelites returning from the Babylonian captivity were reported. This discrepancy, he said, led to questioning that eventually led him to give up his beliefs. Plenty of Christians question their beliefs and some end up rejecting them. However, the Bible reader who recognizes that he or she is reading texts written by different authors, or derived from different historical sources, can understand that chronicles of history don't always get every detail accurate. Even CBS makes mistakes.

The Religious Right needs to understand that the days of society's automatic default to prevailing religious authorities are long gone. The archbishop of Boston or the local Baptist pastor can no longer call up the district attorney and have *Elmer Gantry* yanked from every newsstand overnight. Americans simply will not stand for it.

As a practical matter, Americans also have many more choices now for finding books and other media. Community pressure is still a potent force in many parts of the country. It may very well be that a certain book, CD, or DVD is unattainable in every shop in a small city in Alabama. In years past, anyone who wanted that material had to drive somewhere else for it or try to track it down through a catalog. These days, it's just a few mouse clicks away over the Web. It can be delivered right to your door. Technology has fundamentally changed the way Americans receive information. It has also altered the ability of religious pressure groups to interfere in that exchange. This is why the Religious Right has begun to seek increased control over the Internet.

The Religious Right has a real fixation on sex. Occasionally, it is directed toward appropriate goals, such as the eradication of human trafficking and child prostitution. Unfortunately, it too often results in efforts to reduce all of the erotic imagery available to adults to what would be appropriate for children. When the Religious Right seeks controls over the Internet, they support ham-fisted approaches that block access to all kinds of materials adults in our society have a right to possess (whether the Religious Right or I think it is appropriate or not). In addition, they may support blocking mechanisms that actually keep minors from seeing material about sexually transmitted diseases or breast cancer just because the filters can't always separate sexual connotations from physiological or medical descriptions. This is always done in the name of protecting children, but to date every congressional enactment has been ruled by the Supreme Court to violate free speech guarantees for adults under the First Amendment. There are days when I wonder if the Religious Right even wants to find a practical solution to children's access or whether they just want to continue to use the "save the children" rationale for their own political purposes.

Of course children should be shielded from such material, but I don't trust the Religious Right to do the job. Religious Right groups have shown time and again that they will go too far. They may start off targeting porn DVDs but always end up attacking novels that have gay themes or books about puberty. They cast too wide a net; I do not need them to protect my children.

Who should protect America's children from a society that can seem sex obsessed? I have an idea: America's parents. To the extent that the Religious Right is calling on America's parents to be more responsible and to exercise more authority over children, I agree with them. But the Religious Right never stops there.

I once had a conversation with Donna Rice Hughes, who first came to national attention as then senator Gary Hart's mistress aboard the good ship *Monkey Business*. She has become a deeply devout Christian and is a leading antipornography crusader. We were discussing ways to prevent children from accessing sexually inappropriate material. I told her the story about my daughter and the R-rated movie that I recounted earlier. Her response was dismissive, suggesting that not all parents could get such a satisfactory result. I'm glad that the evidence to date is that my wife and I raised responsible, morally aware children. However, we worked longer days than we should have, took fewer vacations and too many more business trips than we should have, and were more tired than we should have been when dealing with our children. Nevertheless, I must stress that even hardworking parents or single parents or divorced parents not only have a responsibility toward their children in teaching them about right and wrong but will always be the front line of defense against young people picking up dangerous habits. I'm not going to leave anyone off the hook and let luminaries of the Religious Right or Washington politicians become the surrogate parents of America's children. I'd be happy if they just made sure every child had a home (one million kids in public schools every day don't have a fixed address), enough food, and some quality health care.

It is easy to paraphrase Voltaire's famous maxim and pledge to defend speech that we do not agree with. It's more difficult to actually put the maxim into action. Over the years, I have been on the receiving end of some particularly nasty attacks from the Religious Right. Jerry Falwell has questioned my ordination. Pat Robertson once called me "lower than a child molester." I've been called a fanatic, a liar, an extremist, and everything in between.

I have responded strongly to many of these attacks, and I've attempted to set the record straight when the things said about me were untrue. But I have never tried to take away the right of my opponents to speak. I value their free speech as much as mine. In fact, I treasure it. Pat Robertson has written many books over the years, and although I disagree strongly with the sentiments expressed in those tomes, I would not want to censor any of them. I believe public libraries should stock Robertson's books. I want his views spread far and wide. Robertson is so extreme, and his agenda for America is so far out of the mainstream, that I believe Americans will reject it out of hand once they understand it. The same goes for Jerry Falwell, James Dobson, D. James Kennedy, Lou Sheldon, and other Religious Right leaders. The last thing I want is for them to stop talking or for them to be muzzled. I believe in their free speech rights as a matter of constitutional law—and I also know that the more they talk and write, the more likely they are to stick their feet in their mouths.

Robertson does it on average every three months. Over the years, Robertson has threatened the city of Orlando with a meteor for flying rainbow flags on city light posts; blamed American liberals for the September 11, 2001, attacks; called for the assassination of the president of Venezuela; and opined that God smote Israeli prime minister Ariel Sharon with a stroke because Sharon gave part of Gaza to the Palestinians. Why on earth would I want to choke off this wonderful fountain of inanity?

I don't. And in the end, that's what distinguishes me from the Religious Right. They fear information. I welcome it. They believe Americans are dupes who can be easily led by what they consider bad information. I believe people are smart enough to listen to lots of ideas and make a sound judgment.

I don't fear critical scrutiny of anything—even my own religious beliefs. To me, religious beliefs that cannot stand up to investigation and questioning are not worth having. New information and un-orthodox ideas may complement and challenge genuine faith, but they can never shake it because genuine faith is always open to ex-amination and reexamination. A faith that is rooted in cement, a faith that admits no new knowledge and in fact fears new information, is not genuine faith at all—it is blind adherence to dogma.

Such thinking does not characterize my faith. That's why I don't favor religiously based censorship. Only an insecure and immature faith seeks to choke off those who would criticize its tenets. Genuine faith is confident; it can meet and answer its opponents in the public arena.

Fundamentalist Christians speak often of having God on their side or of being cloaked in a metaphorical armor that God has given them, an armor that makes them invincible in battle. Many seem to believe, based on their analysis of the scripture, that their final victory is assured. If this is so, one wonders why they are so afraid of certain ideas and trends in modern society, to the extent that they attempt to impose censorship.

Perhaps they are not so sure after all. Perhaps they are not so confident after all. Perhaps they secretly fear that their theology rests on shifting sands, not the firm foundation they claim from scripture. Perhaps they are afraid certain ideas, thoughts, or trends will cause it all to come tumbling down.

Inside every censor lies a certain amount of fear. Even as the Roman Catholic Church persecuted Galileo and banned his *Dialogue Concerning the Two Chief World Systems,* some church leaders were undoubtedly bothered by the nagging doubt that Galileo could be right. Eventually, many of us learn to embrace the nagging fears that can blossom into healthy doubt. Religious fundamentalists remain too stubborn to do that. Yet their refusal should not hold back society at large.

I support the right of members of the Religious Right to live in a dogmatic, fear-ruled world bound by suspicion of new ideas and a simplistic insistence on revealed truth, heedless of what facts or new understandings may indicate. I support the rights of those who want to live in that world, although I feel sorry for them.

What I won't accept is their use of censorship to drag the rest of us to that unhappy place against our will.

CONCLUSION

Saying No to Theocracy

ONE DAY IN THE SUMMER of 2005, I was standing outside a hotel in St. Louis looking for a taxi to take me to the airport. I had just completed a debate before a national gathering of attorneys who advise public schools, an event sponsored by the National Education Association.

A group of baseball fans wearing Cardinal jerseys walked by, and as they did one man reached out and grabbed my arm for a moment. He barely stopped as he walked by but did call out, "So, how well do you sleep at night?"

Figuring this man was not one of my fans, I merely replied, "Great. How about you?" I will admit, however, that I was tempted to use a nonpastoral response that would have been just as honest: "Sometimes not too well because jerks like you are ruining my country."

Who knows what I had done recently to upset Mr. Cardinals Fan. It could have been one of dozens of issues I debate on television.

Aside from the rudeness of grabbing a total stranger (seeing someone on television a lot does not mean you "know" that person, whether you like them or not), this fellow illustrated that the "culture war" Pat Buchanan announced in 1992 remains very much alive today.

As these previous pages demonstrate, I do fear for the continuing viability of important public institutions like our courts and our schools. I am concerned about the future of science and research. I cringe at the prospect of women's reproductive choices becoming even more constrained. But I also worry about the health of the church itself.

I don't believe that the Reverends Falwell and Robertson represent anywhere close to the majority sentiment of the American people overall or self-described Christians, either. Nevertheless, the preaching they do in pulpits, on television, and in the public square is so loud and pervasive that it tends to drown out other Christian voices. After Robertson's crude suggestion that Israeli prime minister Ariel Sharon was dealt a stroke by God for giving away land in Gaza (a move Robertson felt contradicted warnings in the biblical Book of Joel), we at Americans United saw overwhelming interest from national and international media. I was invited to appear on CNN's *Showbiz Tonight*—my first invitation to be on that particular program—and explained that Robertson is literally the only Christian "leader" many people outside North America have even seen on television. Robertson's *700 Club* program is broadcast in African nations, China (where he mutes criticism of Communist Party policies, including forced abortions, to keep a good business relationship with the government), and even Israel and other parts of the Middle East. Robertson may be increasingly seen as a reckless buffoon by U.S. commentators, yet he is genuinely important, even if frightening, because he is the "Christian voice" to the world, by their understanding.

It is no wonder that so many people cringe at the very idea that

Christian evangelists are on the way to their nation. Among other reasons, the Robertson/Falwell/Dobson God is ferociously judgmental. In sub-Saharan Africa, to preach the immorality of the use of condoms, as many fundamentalists do, is inhumane and immoral. (A recent documentary film, *Darwin's Nightmare,* is a frightening-to-watch chronicle of how international corporate greed combined with fundamentalist "moral" teachings have turned Tanzania into one of the most poverty-stricken and disease-racked places on earth.) The understanding these preachers have of "sin" is so focused on personal behavior that it shows little concern with other cultural norms or the existing religious structures. Of course, why should it? In the view of fundamentalists, there is only one way to understand God, and those who don't get on that road spiritually are doomed anyway. These are the preachers who do not object when war is seen as the tool for the imposition of "American" will on the rest of the world, who do not even flinch when the president and other figures representing him refer to our current Middle East war and policy as a "crusade."

The sense of judgment, barely tempered by the love that is central to the Christian faith, is also a reason many people in America have become skeptical of the Religious Right's claim to speak for values. Several years ago, I agreed to go to a very conservative Presbyterian church on Long Island, New York, to debate the question "Is homosexuality consistent with biblical Christianity?" My debating partner was Dr. James White of Alpha and Omega Ministries in Phoenix. I knew this event was sponsored by a conservative Christian radio station, so I had no illusions about the likely composition of the audience. The debate was very formal—opening statements, rebuttals, more rebuttals, cross-examinations, and so on. I had insisted, however, on a twenty- to thirty-minute audience participation segment that I thought might engage attendees in the process. Although the sponsor reluctantly agreed, while I was walking to the stage the moderator told me that the church's leadership had decided not to allow questions because supposedly it might lead to violence from "radical" gay rights groups.

I was speechless and felt that I had been misled, but I agreed to continue. After nearly two hours of debate, a few members of the audience in the back, representing a local chapter of Parents and Friends of Gays and Lesbians, shouted out to the moderator that they wanted to ask White some questions. They were rather rudely told to be quiet. A few minutes later, when I rose to speak, I said my biblical interpretations were over and that I had just one final comment: "I know you have been watching me all evening, but don't forget, I have been watching you also. Frankly, I have never seen more hate in a church. Your attitude toward gay people is so vindictive that it is no wonder that you have driven them away." Yes, I was being judgmental myself, and some people in the audience literally began wailing. They were shocked. I think this attitude, whether it is against members of the gay community or against women who choose to have an abortion or against Muslims or Humanists, is what stops dialogue cold in its tracks with the stench of self-righteousness.

I want to be clear: it is not, and never has been, my goal to stop Falwell, Robertson, Dobson, or even that angry Cardinals fan from worshipping and promoting God as they see fit. My goal is much simpler: I will not join them in that endeavor. At its root, it has become obvious to me over the course of several decades that we don't worship the same god. Falwell's god is so alien to me that he might as well be worshipping Baal. It is not that Falwell never preaches about a god who loves fallen humanity; it is just that this image is nearly washed away by a blinding light of retribution. Interestingly, the god of Robertson and Falwell holds, endorses, and promotes all of the same bias and political opinions held by those preachers. Somehow, I doubt this is merely a coincidence. Sometimes, I think they created their god in their own image, not the other way around.

Ditto for the Falwell/Robertson Jesus. The Religious Right's

Jesus is a distinctly American creation. He's a creature of the free market, a right-wing Republican who lives in the outer suburbs. My guess is that the Religious Right's Jesus is a member of the National Rifle Association. The Falwellian Jesus doesn't minister to the poor; he hangs out with CEOs.

It is exasperating to watch Falwell, Robertson, and other Religious Right leaders, who claim to base their beliefs on the Bible, overlook so much of what that book says. I don't want to see a government based on the Bible, but it is interesting to speculate how some TV preachers would deal with the Jesus I believe the New Testament describes. For example, I am convinced that this Jesus, if he were alive today, would walk into Falwell's church and listen uncomfortably for a few minutes. Then he would do either one of two things: walk out sadly, shaking his head, and go off to minister to the poor and forgotten or, if he were feeling feisty, pick Falwell up and bounce him down the front steps before climbing to the pulpit himself, perhaps to repeat his famous Sermon on the Mount—"Blessed are the poor in spirit, for theirs is the kingdom of heaven . . . Blessed are the meek, for they shall inherit the earth. Blessed are those who hunger and thirst for righteousness, for they shall be filled . . . Blessed are the peacemakers, for they shall be called sons of God."

The sad thing is, I believe most of Falwell's congregation would not stay to hear Jesus preach. They would get up and walk outside to follow Falwell. They have done so for years. They have listened and followed Falwell to a mean-spirited and narrow-minded place. He has led them to a dark, deep recess of American Christianity that often seems to dominate our national discourse these days.

My challenge here is not to the government, but to the Religious Right. I believe leaders of that movement have cherry-picked passages from the Bible to buttress their far-right political agenda. Their goals are primarily ultraconservative, not Christian.

But again let me stress this: while I disagree strongly with the Religious Right's version of Christianity, I fully support anyone's right to follow it. Falwell's god is distasteful to me, but Americans have an absolute and unqualified right to worship him. Those who worship Falwell's god, however, have no right to use the machinery of the government to impose that unpleasant deity on everyone else. Yet Falwell has devoted much of his career to this goal.

Falwell's authority for all of his long-sought public policy goals is not what he would have you think: that is, the Bible. Falwell's political goals spring from *his interpretation* of the Bible. The Bible and Falwell's interpretation of the Bible are far from the same thing. In my view, they simply don't have much in common.

Even if Falwell's interpretation of the Bible could somehow be proven to be correct, that would still not give him the right to impose his will on society for the simple reason that America's government is not based on holy books. The platform for our government is not the Old Testament, the New Testament, or the parables of Jesus. It is the Constitution. Plenty of theocratic states exist in the world; America is not one of them.

This is a crucial feature of American life that Religious Right groups have never been able to grasp: The United States was never intended to be an officially religious state or a country that gives official preference to one faith or even a religious view generally.

Culturally, most Americans are Christian. From a constitutional standpoint, this is irrelevant. Under our Constitution, all religions are equal. Numerical superiority, from a legal standpoint, means nothing.

It's a simple concept, but the Religious Right either cannot or will not grasp it. Time and again, when I have debated Religious Right leaders, they have fallen back on some version of the "majority rules" argument. If a majority wants organized prayer in schools, they argue, there should be organized prayer in schools.

Our Constitution simply does not work that way, and those who believe it does betray only their own ignorance of our governing document. When it comes to religion, the Constitution is explicitly *antimajoritarian*. It does not grant special rights or privileges to whatever group happens to dominate in a certain area.

Even if such a system were possible, it would hardly be desirable. Imagine a country where your religious freedom rights varied from region to region depending on demographic trends. Mormons account for 70 percent of Utah's population but haven't made much of a dent in Mississippi. Surely, a Mormon who happens to live in Provo should not enjoy more rights than one residing in Pascagoula.

I concede that culturally there might very well be differences from state to state. A Mormon in Provo is likely to be of little interest to most people. He's just another member of the majority faith. A Pascagoula Mormon may in fact be something of an oddity, an object of interest to neighbors and coworkers. The government cannot prevent the possible cultural isolation of a Pascagoula Mormon. But it must never accentuate it by adopting policies that make the Pascagoula Mormon's "differentness" an issue in his relations with the state. That is exactly what the government of Mississippi would do if it were to, say, pass a law establishing the majority religion's worship in public schools.

All of this raises another issue that the Religious Right has never been able to accept or appreciate: *what an American believes about God should be completely irrelevant to the government.*

U.S. census forms routinely ask Americans to divulge personal information. Residents who get the long form may be asked to tally the number of bathrooms in their home, disclose their race, or list relatives who live with them. But there's one thing census forms no longer ask: religious belief. Private polling firms gather all data about Americans' religious affiliations, habits, and customs. Put simply, most of us have come to an understanding in this nation that what a person believes about God is none of the state's business. As an interesting footnote, I should point out that this is a long-standing concern in America. As a member of the House of Representatives, James Madison in 1790 expressed concern about a census that proposed counting people by occupation, asserting, "As to those who are employed in teaching and inculcating the duties of religion, there may be some indelicacy in singling them out, as the general government is proscribed from interfering, in any manner whatever, in matters respecting religion; and it may be thought to do this, in ascertaining who and who are not ministers of the gospel."

The Religious Right does not accept the idea that an individual's religious beliefs, or lack thereof, should be irrelevant to the government. This is a core difference between my view and the one held by the Religious Right. Its leaders see religious belief as the be-all and end-all of human experience, and they definitely have a pecking order of religions. At the very bottom rest those who reject organized religion.

Many of the Religious Right leaders I have debated over the years have been absolutely bewildered by my assertions that a person can be good, moral, and fundamentally decent without a belief in any form of god. At first thought, this may seem like an odd belief for a Christian minister to espouse. But a moment's thought shows why it makes perfect sense. Were I to assert that only Christians could be good and moral, I would also have to believe that the adherents of entire religious systems such as Judaism, Islam, Buddhism, Hinduism, and others are not good and moral—an absurd stance. Having taken that step, it is an easy hop to the understanding that humanists, atheists, and agnostics also hew to ethical standards.

To be fair, the assumption that nonbelief equals moral license is a disturbingly widespread perception in American society and is held even by some who ought to know better. In August 2000 Democratic vice presidential nominee Senator Joseph Lieberman gave a string of speeches in which he lauded the role of religion in public life and offended some nonbelievers with an implication that faith is necessary for good behavior. Lieberman also used an inane line that drives me crazy, asserting that the First Amendment guarantees free-dom of religion but not freedom from religion. (It does both.) Lieberman's rhetoric was unfortunate, but it came nowhere close to the vituperation against nonbelievers that is common among the Re-ligious Right.

Leaders of the Religious Right certainly don't limit their attacks to nonbelievers. Too often I have seen mainline Christians attacked by the Religious Right because their views are not fundamentalist in nature. I have, with great regret and dismay, watched Falwell, who claims to hold to a superior ethical system by virtue of his Christian beliefs, attack his political opponents with lies, cheap smears, and base-less charges. I have seen him embrace a policy of the ends justifying the means, which is not a Christian doctrine. If this is an example of Falwell's superior religious morality, I'll pass.

Falwell and I have tangled about this incessantly. He once called me a liar on a CNBC program one night during the 2004 election cycle when I pointed out that one of his nonprofit groups had lost its tax exemption for partisan political activities. When we appeared on the FOX News Channel a few days after that, I had to literally wave a letter, signed by Falwell in 1997, in which he conceded his group had broken the law and agreed to pay $50,000 to the IRS. Clearly flustered for once, Falwell blustered that his attorneys made him do it. That's beside the point. I should not have to show a document on national television to get a Christian minister to tell the truth.

On a cultural level, this common Religious Right prejudice against religious skeptics feeds a form of bias that would be socially unacceptable if applied to any other American. The crude forms of anti-Semitism that plagued American society for many generations have largely withered away thankfully, but, prodded by the Religious Right, some Americans retain a residual belief that somehow one cannot be fully American without being religious. Patriotism means simply love of country. It does not include religious issues. The two concepts have been jumbled up by the Religious Right, to the extent that some Americans believe that terms like "In God We Trust" on our currency and "under God" in the Pledge of Allegiance date back to the time of the Founding Fathers when they are actually modern affectations.

This "God and country" linkage stems in part from the common insistence, again often fed by the Religious Right, that the United States has some sort of special relationship with God and is somehow prized above other nations. This is a dangerous stance to adopt, one not far removed from a common nineteenth-century view that one was not fully American unless one was a *certain type* of Christian or that this alleged national special closeness to God sprang from the adoption of *specific forms* of Christianity. In the nineteenth century, it was commonly assumed that God loved America best because of the nation's majority Protestant character. While this seems absurd today, we hear echoes of it when Religious Right leaders use the word *Christian* as synonymous with the fundamentalist, right-wing version of Christianity they have adopted—implying that only this version of Christianity is authentic or pleasing to God. More than three hundred years ago, colonial religious liberty pioneer Roger Williams boldly asserted that there could be no such thing as a Christian nation. Only individuals could make such faith professions, Williams noted. It's a lesson the Religious Right never bothered to learn. Indeed, on various occasions they have even worked with members of Congress to pass bills declaring specific days for prayer and repentance. One such measure, sponsored by that paragon of virtue Tom DeLay, called for a National Day of Reconciliation and was accompanied by a two-hour prayer service in the Capitol Building, closed to the public, that DeLay said would "lead the nation back to God."

I recognize that I am a sinner and sometimes fall short of what I believe are God's standards, but I would like to repent when and how I choose, not on some day Congress decides is appropriate.

It boils down to this: the Religious Right has narrowly defined *Christian* in such a way as to exclude millions of Americans. I was ordained in the United Church of Christ, generally recognized as one of the country's more liberal Protestant denominations, in 1973. Ours is a *Christian* faith—hence the appearance of Christ's name in our denomination. Although I am not a biblical literalist, I believe in the core Christian constructs and principles and acknowledge the power of prayer. Yet I cannot tell you how many times I have been attacked by the followers of TV preachers and accused of not being a "real" Christian. They are simply unable to understand why any Christian would advocate for the causes I do—thus, they rather arrogantly assume, I must not be the genuine item.

Sometimes perceptions work in the opposite direction, and thanks to the Religious Right, all ministers are assumed to be zealots. I had a brush with this attitude a few years ago when my wife, a physician who specializes in geriatric medicine, was invited to speak at a medical school in Grenada to give what is called the white coat lecture to the incoming class. This speech is designed to remind would-be doctors of the moral responsibility to provide health care to the poor. The medical school invited her to bring me along. We took our then-teenage son as well. On the evening following the lecture, there was a faculty dinner. My name tag read, "Rev. Barry Lynn," and I could not help but notice that I seemed to be about as popular as fire ants at a picnic. My son and I mainly sat at the end of the table and talked about going hiking.

After the meal, though, something happened that quickly reversed the climate. The president of the medical school, Dr. Peter G. Bourne, who had served as special assistant to the president for health issues in the Jimmy Carter White House, thanked my wife and then commented that he had no idea when he told her to bring her husband "that we were really getting a two-fer." He then went on to explain that he was a fan of my work, having seen me on cable television squaring off with various Religious Right leaders. People now knew (and some apologetically told me later) that the Reverend Lynn was not in the same camp as the Reverend Falwell. Suddenly dozens of people wanted to get my opinion on all kinds of topics, religious and otherwise. The perception that I was some narrow-minded sourpuss bent on imposing my faith had been formed by assumptions that all "Christians" are alike.

It's especially ironic to see all Christians lumped together in this manner, as I often have a hard time seeing the spirit of Christ reflected in the churches many in the Religious Right attend. Since the Religious Right loves to base so many of its arguments on the Bible, I would challenge its supporters by pointing out that Christ spent his time on earth ministering to the poor and disenfranchised, not hobnobbing with the rich and politically connected. Christ challenged the powers that be to provide for all people; he did not make excuses for politicians who turned their backs on the least among us. Christ certainly never entered into any type of alliance with the Roman government and in fact warned his followers to observe the separation of religion and government, telling them to "render unto Caesar the things that are Caesar's and unto God the things that are God's," an admonition that appears in the Gospels of Matthew, Mark, and Luke.

I feel compelled to point out to TV preachers that the goals of Christ and the goals of the Religious Right seem to have little in common. Christ did not spend his time trying to forge a faith-based government. He did not obsess over the sexual habits of people. Were he here today, I find it inconceivable that Christ would parade in front of abortion clinics screaming at teenage girls or picket a gay man's funeral hoisting a sign with a hateful homophobic message.

Christ would not join the Christian Coalition or sit down for a radio interview with James Dobson. (He'd probably prefer to chat with John Stewart.) Christ would not sign fund-raising letters accusing his perceived "enemies" of being anti-American fanatics opposed to all that is good and decent, nor would he lend his name to any candidate seeking political office.

But even though I have a hard time finding a place for Christ in Religious Right churches, I acknowledge it is not my job to act as final judge of these places and those who minister to and worship in them. If I am right, and Christ does feel alienated from far right houses of worship, the days will come when he will be able to explain his disappointment to every pastor who stood in those pulpits and the congregants who supported them. Christian dogma teaches that we will be judged—just not by men on this Earth.

The Religious Right and moderate-to-liberal Christians can argue about this all day and accuse one another of not being authentically Christian. I do not dispute the right of any Christian body to advocate for its point of view or even to engage in proof-texting of the Bible to support that. Such activity can lead to interesting academic debates and provide an evening's entertainment on a college campus. It's a poor platform for devising public policy.

What concerns me is when these debates spill over into the political sphere, as they do increasingly these days. The state simply has no business adjudicating competing versions of Christianity. Although I am beyond merely skeptical that Robertson's and Falwell's beliefs reflect the true intention of Jesus, that does not mean I want the government to take my side in a theological spat and use state power to enforce my particular religious views. Indeed, I oppose that as well. As I mentioned elsewhere in this book, the government must put forth *secular rationales* for all of its policies.

Falwell, Robertson, and their supporters seem to believe that whenever the government adopts a social policy that appears to be more "liberal," it is caving into the demands of either so-called do-gooders, the Religious Left, or, more frequently, radical secularists. What they overlook is that the state may in fact adopt a policy that coincides with the beliefs of religious liberals but for entirely nonreligious reasons. Consider the death penalty. Many religious liberals oppose it on scriptural grounds and point out that Jesus (who opposed it himself) was also a victim of capital punishment. If the president or a governor suddenly announced that the death penalty must be repealed because it is against biblical principles, we would have a problem on our hands.

But there are reasons that have nothing to do with the Bible that a politician could employ for ending the use of the death penalty. For example, he or she could argue that it's not effective as a deterrent or state that some people on death row have later been found to be completely innocent.

The Religious Right occasionally makes a stab at articulating a secular rationale for its policies, but these are quickly exposed as shams. There is no secular reason, for example, to pressure children to pray in school every day. What is the secular reason for teaching Old Testament narratives as scientific fact?

Religious Right groups dispute my premise because they see secularism as an evil and corrosive force. This, when all is said and done, may be my sharpest disagreement with the Religious Right: the movement does not appreciate the secular nature of our government and the religious diversity it has brought us. It continues to tar a term like *diversity* with a brush of feel-good political correctness when religious diversity is in fact a laudable goal that strengthens and enriches societies. The Religious Right insists that only certain forms of worship are pleasing to God, which it has the right to do, and then assumes that, since this is the case, its preferred forms of worship should have a public policy expression. This dangerous tautology is where the movement goes off the rails. More often than not, the Religious Right's political expression of faith takes the form of substituting fundamentalist religious dogma for sound public policy, policy that recognizes the secular nature of our government and the multifaith character of our society.

Does this mean the Religious Right wants theocracy in America? Its leaders bristle at the term and accuse me of being an alarmist when I suggest such a thing. In reply I can only recommend taking an honest look at the Religious Right's social goals for this country. Examine them and be the judge.

- The Religious Right opposes legal abortion because of its reading of the Bible (or, in the case of orthodox Roman Catholics, because of church teachings and papal decrees). Therefore, it wants to ban all abortions—for any reason—in America.

- The Religious Right says the Book of Leviticus condemns homosexuality. Therefore, it opposes even modest forms of gay rights. Many of its leaders would be happy to push gay people back into the closet or find some way to criminalize gay sex and otherwise penalize gay people.

- The Religious Right insists that the Bible stories in the Old Testament are historically and scientifically true. Therefore, it opposes the teaching of evolution in our public schools.

- The Religious Right insists that the Bible ordains men to run households and public affairs. Thus, it opposes the expansion of women's rights and helped engineer the defeat of the Equal Rights Amendment.

- Certain books, plays, films, CDs, and other forms of media are, according to the Religious Right, "blasphemous" and offensive to biblical principles. It says this material must be curbed or banned outright.

- The Bible, the Religious Right tells us, espouses a specific form of conservative Christianity. Therefore, public schools have an obligation to promote this faith.

- The Religious Right condemns sex outside of marriage and opposes certain forms of birth control. Because of these views, it seeks to end comprehensive sex education in public schools and wants to block the distribution of some methods of artificial contraceptives.

The Religious Right's policy objectives always come back, when all is said and done, to a narrow reading of biblical passages. Attempts to put a modern interpretation on ancient religious codes form the basis of their ideal government. This is not a secret. Its leaders brag about having the proper "biblical worldview." There is a term for governments based on a fundamentalist scriptural worldview. That term is *theocracy*.

Can this really happen here? Look around you. Imagine an America in which the Supreme Court, stacked with justices like Antonin Scalia and Clarence Thomas, has lowered the wall of separation to such an extent that the courts are allowed to prefer some religions over others and faith generally over nontheism. Writing in dissent in a 2005 Supreme Court ruling dealing with government display of the Ten Commandments, Scalia asserted that the government has no obligation to back only nondenominational forms of religion, insisting if that were the case, "One cannot say the word 'God,' or 'the Almighty,' one cannot offer public supplication or thanksgiving, without contradicting the beliefs of some people that there are many gods, or that God or the gods pay no attention to human affairs." Scalia went on to blithely dismiss the religious and philosophical perspectives of millions of Americans, asserting that the record of the country's historical practices "permits this disregard of polytheists and believers in unconcerned deities, just as it permits the disregard of devout atheists." It apparently never occurred to him to ask why the state might have the need to offer "public supplication," traditionally a task for houses of worship.

Imagine an America where women can no longer exercise any meaningful reproductive freedom, whether or not it is in tune with their spouses. As a judge on the U.S. Court of Appeals for the Third Circuit, Samuel Alito, now a Supreme Court justice, held that a Pennsylvania law requiring women to inform their husbands before having an abortion was not an "undue burden."

Imagine an America where young people are denied information about Darwinian evolution or the concept is neutered to meet the demands of fundamentalist pressure groups. In December of 2005, the ACLU challenged a sticker criticizing evolution that is pasted into science textbooks in Cobb County, Georgia. During oral argument, judges on the U.S. Court of Appeals for the Eleventh Circuit appeared unpersuaded that the move was a church-state violation. Judge William Pryor, a controversial appointee placed on the court by President Bush, went so far as to accuse the ACLU lawyer of getting the facts about the case wrong.

Imagine all of this being done at the behest of aggressive fundamentalist Christian groups. Such a country, our country, would be a de facto theocracy. As my colleague Rob Boston says, while government may not have the power to cut off a "heretic's" hands, we might refer to such a nation as "theocracy lite."

Some Americans are already getting a taste of things to come. In certain parts of the United States, you don't have to imagine any of this. It is already happening. Thanks to constant pressure from orthodox Christian groups, legal abortion has been so chipped away that the right is more theoretical than real in many areas. So many roadblocks—waiting periods, permission forms, mandated and paternalistic lectures—have been thrown up that women, especially poor ones, cannot exercise the "right" they still have in theory. Eighty-seven percent of American counties have no abortion providers.

Thanks to the pressure from the Religious Right, Congress has allocated federal funding for sex education that is "abstinence-based" only. Many of these programs are little more than thinly veiled religious dogma, rife with misinformation and scare tactics. Most American teenagers receive no comprehensive sex education in public schools or in taxpayer-funded programs offered in other venues. They probably know that condoms exist, but they don't hear the term in taxpayer-funded sex education class—even though poll after poll shows Americans support comprehensive sex ed. At some point, what's being offered can no longer accurately be termed sex education. It's Religious Right propaganda. The fact that it does not work sways few. Our youngsters remain in ignorance, and as a result the United States continues to have one of the highest teen pregnancy rates in the Western world.

What does your local public school teach about evolution? There's a good chance it's not much. There is a great irony here: Religious Right groups have lost every major case they have brought into the federal courts challenging the teaching of evolution in public schools. Yet they may be winning the larger war. Many schools are so fearful of generating controversy, or so fear the wrath of the local fundamentalist churches, that they don't bother to teach evolution at all or do so in such a manner that the treatment is next to useless. Some biology textbooks relegate the study of evolution—the central organizing principle of modern biology—to one or two pages. Others are afraid to even use the term *evolution,* substituting instead vague phrases like "change over time."

Some pharmacists are already refusing to fill doctor-prescribed birth-control pills. As I write this, several states are considering a legislative response to this problem—not laws requiring pharmacists to fill any prescription they are given, but statutes specifically exempting them from doing so on the grounds of "conscience"!

Gay rights have not only not advanced, they have actually been rolled back in many states, under the guise of state constitutional amendments and laws that purport to ban "same-sex marriage" but go way beyond that to attack anything that smacks of even privately arranged domestic partnerships. These measures were passed after energetic campaigns conceived, organized, and funded by Religious Right groups.

The de facto theocracy is not theoretical; it has gained a foothold throughout the country. As it does so, many Americans still sit by complacently, feeling confident that it will not reach them. For some, the Terri Schiavo case was the needed wake-up call. Others are still waiting for the alarm.

So where does that leave us? I do not believe most Americans agree with the views of Jerry Falwell and Pat Robertson. Yet too many people stubbornly refuse to believe that Religious Right groups are accumulating real political power in America. This seems to be a case of willful blindness to reality. After all, the Religious Right took credit for President Bush's election in 2000 and his reelection in 2004 as well as the growing Republican majorities in the House of Representatives and Senate. This, in turn, gave Bush the opportunity to reshape the federal judiciary, including the Supreme Court. Ultra-conservative Republican dominance of all three branches of government has handed the Religious Right a degree of political power it could have only dreamed of even ten years ago. Remember the old story about the frog placed in a pot of water that is slowly brought to a boil? Because the water heats up gradually, the frog doesn't realize what is going on and never leaps out to safety. Well, the frog has been boiling in the water for some time now and still doesn't know it.

What will it take to shock the system so that Americans really do react? Slowly but surely the wall of separation between church and state is being eroded, much to the detriment of our pluralistic democracy. Ironically, even as we smash through the wall here at home, we insist that other nations, such as fundamentalist Muslim countries, ought to erect one.

We do not honor religious freedom if we force people to financially support houses of worship. (Calling this type of church tax a faith-based initiative does not mask its intent.) We are not a free nation if we compel children to take part in religious exercises alien to them in public schools. A nation that values religious liberty does not require science to bow before rigid sectarian dogma. A country forged in liberty of conscience does not allow government, at the behest of religious groups, to make decisions about the most personal and intimate areas of human behavior.

Real religious freedom cannot exist without a separation between religion and government. The union of church and state looks like it will offer unheralded benefits to religion, but that overlooks the long view. In the end, combinations of church and state result in one of two models: nightmarish theocracies like those spawned in much of the Middle East or devitalized churches and empty cathedrals, like much of western Europe today.

Fundamentalist Christianity's alliance with the state may look like a friendly embrace at first. If history is any predictor, it won't stay that way: in time, that embrace will become so stifling as to slowly strangle the life and vitality out of genuine faith in America.

There is a wonderful Gospel song from the Christian tradition that says of God, "He would not have brought us this far just to leave us." You don't have to share my religious viewpoint to agree that we did not create a nation, spill blood of men and women to improve it, and even apologize for ignoring the contributions of the Native population and enslaving others just to leave it all to the likes of Robertson, Falwell, and Dobson.

Americans are not lemmings. We prove this all of the time. When we get to a cliff, we actually look down, ponder the distance, and conclude that once the leap is made we are going all the way to the bottom. Wisely, we often don't leap and step back to contemplate better options. This is certainly the moment for contemplation and the action that must follow, because the Religious Right is seeking fundamental changes in the way the nation functions, from the halls of Congress to the halls of your local public schools.

Those of us on the other side are starting to reclaim our heritage; we are starting to proclaim that we are the real "values" voters. We recognize that the values of the Constitution are ones we can be proud to uphold. Think about the majesty of those values; chief among them is religious freedom and the freedom to genuinely exercise our conscience in the pursuit of our own moral decisions. There are, of course, others as well: the value of equal justice under the law, the value of freedom of expression, the value of opposition to cruel and unusual punishment, the value of fair trials.

All of these values are worth protecting, but it won't just happen. The defense must be proactive. When Senator John F. Kerry conceded the 2004 presidential race, President Bush waited a few hours and then held a press event during which he said, "We have one country, one Constitution and one future that binds us." I have to disagree. It is the people who choose the future. We can move into it with our eyes on the goal of increasing justice for all, or move in the direction of a "majority wins everything" theocracy. That is up to us.

The First Amendment is only truly safeguarded when it stands for the protection of every person and every group regardless of religious or ethical background. I know that many of these battles fought together are won temporarily and then have to be fought again in another time and place. It can be frustrating and tiring. Yet I like to recall those words of Martin Luther King Jr. when he reminded us of the long view of history: "The arc of the moral universe is long but it bends toward justice."

That is why, in the end, I remain optimistic. I know that the principle of separation of church and state will face some serious tests. But I also know nothing else can guarantee our religious liberty and protect the integrity of our religious institutions. We value those principles too highly. For that reason, even if we abandon our wall temporarily, we will return to it.

In short, the arc will continue to bend—but that doesn't mean we should not help it along with an occasional push.

AFTERWORD TO
THE PAPERBACK EDITION

I KNEW WHEN I wrote this book that some people would object to its conclusions. It is a frank assessment of the power of various Religious Right groups and an assault on what I believe is their dangerous agenda for America. I'm not surprised that it bothered some readers. What did surprise me, however, was reading articles just a few months after the book came out asserting that the Religious Right was on its way to political irrelevance.

Several political pundits sounded this theme. Most notably, moderate evangelical Jim Wallis asserted in *Time* magazine that the United States has entered a post–Religious Right period. Young evangelicals, Wallis claimed, have deserted the movement. The coming years, he insisted, will see less emphasis on divisive issues like same-sex marriage and abortion and more focus on global climate change and poverty. The death of Religious Right stalwart and Moral Majority founder Jerry Falwell, on May 15, 2007, only accelerated claims that the Religious Right was on the ropes.

There is a tendency among all people—religious or non-religious, liberal, conservative, or moderate—to view the world through a lens that reflects highly individualized biases. Issues like climate change, the global fight against AIDS, and poverty concern Wallis and the evangelicals who think like him. Naturally, they would like to see these issues take front and center on the public policy stage. (I should note that their often regressive views on women's rights, same-sex marriage, and other civil liberties remain the same.)

But wishing something were so does not indeed make it so. I have opposed what I see as the dangerous agenda of the Religious Right all of my adult life. I have seen this movement secure smashing victories and suffer stunning defeats. I have sometimes watched its activists help elect presidents, members of Congress, and governors. At other times, I have watched its favored candidates face repudiation on Election Day.

Through it all, I have never made the mistake of assuming that the fate of the Religious Right hinges on one election, one vote, or one high-profile legal or political battle. That simply is not the way the American system works.

I am aware that anyone can fall into the trap of seeing the world with blinders on or allowing wish to trump reality. To keep myself out of that trap, I continue to do something many of the pundits who talk abut the Religious Right don't: I go to Religious Right meetings.

About a month before the 2006 elections, I attended a meeting of the Family Research Council in Washington, D.C. It was interesting and instructive to sit in the audience and hear myself and the organization I lead, Americans United for Separation of Church and State, attacked by podium speakers in terms that made me and the group sound unrecognizable.

At one point, Dr. James Dobson of Focus on the Family announced from the podium that he had noticed that I had signed up for the event and might be in the audience. He said he'd like to meet with me. We ended up talking backstage for about forty minutes, and I presented Dobson with a copy of this book. I doubt it changed his mind, but I appreciated the opportunity to sit down with him for a frank airing of our differences.

Dobson was offended that I have accused his organization and others of pushing houses of worship into unlawful forms of partisan politicking. He denied that that is what he wants. He claimed that he would never want that, yet sitting through the two-day "Values Voter Summit" only reinforced my belief that the goal of the FRC, Focus, and other far-right fundamentalist outfits is to elect as many Republicans who are sympathetic to their goals as possible.

During the event, Dobson told the crowd that he had considered sitting out the November elections, since he was disappointed that the GOP-led Congress had not done more for him in the previous two years. But a trip to Washington to meet with lawmakers soon changed his mind.

"I came home absolutely convinced that there is no choice because the alternative is terrible," Dobson said.

The election results in November were a bitter disappointment to Dobson and other Religious Right leaders. Their reaction was typical: Instead of accepting the fact that the American public had turned against President George W. Bush over the war in Iraq, the lackluster economy, and other issues, Religious Right leaders insisted that the Republicans would have done better if only they had pushed the Religious Right's theocratic agenda even harder!

For starters, Dobson's Focus on the Family–related groups around the country focused a major campaign on eight Senate races. By campaign, I mean they put out these bogus voter guides to make every Democrat look like Idi Amin and every Republican look like Mother Teresa. Not surprisingly, they targeted every state where there was supposed to be a close contest. In seven of those states, "their" candidate was defeated. Moreover, in two states, politicians who were on the Religious Right's dream teams for the next presidential race lost dramatically—Virginia senator George Allen and Pennsylvania senator Rick Santorum. The only Senate race they were happy about was that in Tennessee, where the Democrat, Harold Ford, Jr., had tried to prove he was more religious than the Republican, Robert Corker, by filming television commercials in a church and announcing that Jesus Christ was his campaign manager.

And the Religious Right had other major setbacks. In Oklahoma, U.S. representative Ernest Istook, lead sponsor for a decade of the effort to return government-promoted prayer to the public schools, ran for governor and was defeated by a 2–1 margin. Incumbent Kansas attorney general Phill Kline tried to build a church-based machine to boost his reelection campaign and his intimidation campaign against Planned Parenthood. (Kline had demanded patient records from Planned Parenthood clinics and tried to prosecute a doctor who performed what Kline considered illegal abortions.) It did not work. A whole slate of candidates endorsed by a pro-science group won office on the Ohio State Board of Education, thus dooming the Religious Right's efforts there to add "intelligent design" to the biology curriculum. The Religious Right even lost (for the first time) an effort to change a state constitution, in Arizona, to prohibit so-called "same sex marriages"; lost an initiative to bar all abortions in South Dakota; and found themselves on the losing side of a Missouri initiative to increase funding for stem-cell research. It was just a really bad night.

But it was worse than the mere results. Supporters of the Religious Right thought they had this election in the bag. Why? Because their leaders told them so. In early 2006, TV preacher Pat Robertson announced on his nationally syndicated television show that he had communicated with God during a retreat late in 2005 and that God had assured him that the Republicans would hold onto both houses of Congress. Moreover, just weeks before the 2006 election, Falwell assured attendees at a clergy breakfast in Washington that the GOP would hold both chambers. "I think the Lord's going to take care of that," he said.

At that same event, Falwell said he hoped Senator Clinton would be the candidate because "nothing will energize my [constituency] like Hillary Clinton. If Lucifer ran, he wouldn't."

Combine these results with two other important events occurring at the same time, and the tenor of the times gets worse for the Religious Right. First, the president of the National Association of Evangelicals, Ted Haggard, had to leave his church and his leadership of the group because of allegations that he bought methamphetamines and the services of a male prostitute during trips to Denver. Haggard admitted he was "tempted" to use the drugs but never did. He then underwent a few weeks of "therapy" and was declared "completely heterosexual." (I guess there is now a registry for that somewhere.)

More significantly, a highly placed staffer at the White House Office of Faith-Based and Community Initiatives, David Kuo, wrote a book that upset the Religious Right even more. Kuo claimed that after visits to the White House by clergy associated with the Religious Right, people in Karl Rove's office would refer to them as "the nuts." That was a betrayal, a "Judas moment" for many who had been snookered into believing that the whole White House respected them.

Most Religious Right leaders refused to learn any lessons from the 2006 elections. They are still hitching all of their wagons to stars in the Republican firmament. If anything, they are more partisan and more closely tied to the White House than ever. Perhaps seeking some solace, Bush began inviting Religious Right leaders to the White House in early 2007. He sought and largely received their support for the war in Iraq—perhaps aware that this constituency was one of the few that might still offer such a backing. (After all, Falwell said on CNN in November 2004 that Bush should "blow [the terrorists] all away in the name of the Lord.")

But as all of this played out, another political drama was emerging: an ever-expanding field of GOP hopefuls stepped forward to announce plans to seek the presidency. That field will undoubtedly be smaller by the time you read this, but it's worth remembering what every single candidate did in those early days: sought the backing and support of the Religious Right. Here we go again.

U.S. senator John McCain, a man who once derided Religious Right leaders as "agents of intolerance," practically glued himself to Falwell and was quick to issue a statement praising the Lynchburg evangelist after he died. When a questioner in Seattle asked why he was "sucking up" to the Religious Right, McCain responded, "I'm probably going to get in trouble for this, but what's wrong with sucking up to everybody?"

Mitt Romney, the former governor of Massachusetts, dropped his pro–gay, pro–legal abortion views and was reinvented as a religious conservative. Even ex–New York City mayor Rudy Giuliani, who had been both pro-choice and pro-gay rights in that capacity, felt compelled to appear on Fox News Channel and explain how much he personally loathes legal abortion and vow that as president, he would have no problem appointing more justices like Antonin Scalia to the Supreme Court.

Romney and Mike Huckabee, the former governor of Arkansas and former Southern Baptist preacher, trekked to Colorado Springs for personal meetings with Dobson. Newt Gingrich even appeared on Dobson's radio program to confess one long adulterous relationship and beg for forgiveness. They won't be the only ones to seek the blessing of the would-be patriarchal kingmaker of Pike's Peak. Curiously, absolutist social-issue conservative Huckabee was attacked by the largely Republican Club for Growth because he supported a tiny tax increase in Arkansas to improve children's health care and services for the homebound elderly.

At the same time, two other candidates—U.S. senator Sam Brownback of Kansas and U.S. representative Duncan Hunter of California—were openly seeking Religious Right support in their long shot presidential candidacies.

Watching these candidates contort themselves to appease the Religious Right, I could only wonder why people like Jim Wallis think these would-be presidents were working so hard to win approval from a dead movement.

The reason: it only looks dead. The Religious Right is like a vampire from a drive-in movie: often staked but never truly killed. There is always another sequel. No one should write off this movement at this time, because we have not yet seen the final act.

We trod a familiar path. During the TV preacher scandals of the late 1980s, several pundits were eager to proclaim the death of the Religious Right. Similar claims were heard after Falwell shut down the Moral Majority in 1989.

But the movement soldiered on. It was next pronounced dead in 1992, when Bill Clinton was elected president. But far from killing the Religious Right, Clinton's election sparked a backlash among religious conservatives, helping the GOP take Congress and propelling Gingrich to power in 1994. Undaunted, political pundits pronounced the Religious Right dead again when Pat Robertson pulled the financial plug on the Christian Coalition in 2001.

The mistake pundits make is in assuming that the Religious Right is represented by a single organization or leader. If that organization goes into decline or that leader sees a loss of influence, the assumption is that the entire movement has taken a possibly fatal hit.

Such assumptions betray an ignorance of how political and social movements are organized. In the case of the Religious Right, there is always another leader jockeying for power. When Falwell stepped back from political activity a bit in the early 1990s to shore up his university, Pat Robertson filled the gap. When Robertson cut his ties to the Christian Coalition, the Family Research Council and Focus on the Family, led by Tony Perkins and Dobson respectively, became more prominent. That's why Falwell's death didn't slow down the Religious Right: he hadn't been a major player in the movement for more than a decade.

Dobson's organization raises about $135 million every year. Should he choose to retire tomorrow, the organization is well poised to survive a leadership transition.

Would-be Dobsons and Robertsons lurk about in the wings. Two less prominent Religious Right leaders are struggling to break into the big leagues. Pastor Rick Scarborough of Texas, a protégé of Falwell's, clearly seeks the national presence that the Lynchburg evangelist has enjoyed for so many years. In Ohio, television preacher Rod Parsley has attempted to forge a political machine closely aligned with the state GOP—a model he obviously sees as useful nationwide (even though it ultimately failed to elect its favored gubernatorial candidate, Kenneth Blackwell, or reelect U.S. senator Mike DeWine in Ohio).

It is unclear if either of these men will truly achieve national status. Both are trying. Both can be engaging speakers and have authored books and done the usual round of media appearances, seeking those higher profiles.

My point is that the Religious Right, as a political movement, does not want for leadership or cash. These are powerful attributes that assure that the Religious Right will remain a presence on the political scene for many years to come. A poor showing in one election cycle—or even in several election cycles running—will not lead the Religious Right to close its doors and give up. It is not dead, nor doth it sleep.

Complicating matters politically is the atrocious advice being given to some Democratic candidates. They are being told to jettison support for separation of church and state because this will allegedly help them capture support from a mushy religious middle composed of people who, while they disagree with the strident goals of the Religious Right, still want to see plenty of evidence of faith in public places.

Mara Vanderslice, an adviser to several Democratic candidates in 2006, openly admitted that she tells them not to use the term "separation of church and state." The phrase, she insisted, "says to people that you don't want there to be a role for religion in our public life." Thomas Jefferson's terminology, it seems, has become the constitutional principle that dare not speak its name.

Meanwhile, U.S. senators Hillary Clinton and Barack Obama sometimes sound as if they are involved in a Bible-quoting contest (even as Obama had to dodge false allegations that he is secretly a Muslim). Former senator John Edwards has taken pains to explain why his faith leads him to oppose same-sex marriage.

In Congress, the first Muslim to be elected took a seat in the House of Representatives. Much to the consternation of the Religious Right, U.S. representative Keith Ellison (D-Minn.) took the oath of office on a Koran, not the Bible. This led to allegations that Ellison might be "soft" on Islamic terrorism. Less was said about the two Buddhists who were elected, but when U.S. representative Pete Stark (D-Calif.) announced a few months later that he holds no belief in a Supreme Being at all, the Religious Right shuddered. One Religious Right leader went so far as to call Stark's statement "a display of open hostility towards God" and opine, "Congressman Stark's statement is a very sad benchmark for America. It could be the moment which defines the decline of our country." The republic somehow managed to survive Stark's pronouncement.

Diversity roiled the political system, but I saw no sign that the "culture wars" that fuel so much Religious Right activity were about to abate. The issues discussed in this book continue to serve as a flashpoint for Religious Right activism.

A high school student in New Jersey had to fend off a proselytizing history teacher convinced that dinosaurs strolled about on Noah's ark. The teacher said: "If you reject [Jesus Christ's] gift of salvation, you know where you belong . . . you belong in hell." When the young man secretly taped these "sermonettes" and turned the recordings over to the principal, school officials acted quickly—by passing a policy banning the surreptitious taping of classroom lectures.

In Washington, some members of Congress talked about exercising long overdue supervision over Bush's "Faith-Based Initiative." In Ohio, some legislators were wishing they had done that years ago when it was revealed that a religious organization took tax money intended to run programs for the poor and used it to buy two jumbo-screen televisions. Newly elected governor Ted Strickland, a Methodist minister, led the charge to demand transparency and continue funding only if it was in line with the Constitution.

Americans United and the ACLU warned several municipal bodies to cease opening their deliberations with prayers that always ended "in Jesus' name, we pray." (A little diversity, please; it's 2007!) State legislators in Georgia and Texas felt compelled to advise their peers that evolution is a plot by the Jews, one even referring to a curious Web site that insists that Earth is stationary and is, in fact, the center of the universe. Why? The Bible tells us so. (No, I am not making this up.)

Public schools were besieged to institute classes in the Bible because Stephen Prothero, a religion professor at Boston University, wrote a book demonstrating that even in the most religious nation in the Western world, there is a lot of biblical illiteracy. In my view, America's houses of worship—not the public schools—must correct this. Mandatory classes on the Bible in public high schools were Prothero's solution. For me, when religious references and icons,

Christian or otherwise, arise in the course of the study of art, literature, or history, nothing prevents teachers from explaining their source
or significance. Curiously, one of Prothero's core reasons for wanting
the classes is that politicians frequently cite scripture in support of
their positions. As I told National Public Radio, "I'd rather get the
politicians out of talking about religion than interjecting religion
into public schools."

Efforts to erect the Ten Commandments in front of courthouses
and portray the Decalogue as the source of all U.S. law continued
unabated.

Debates over the appropriateness of stem-cell research reverberated through many state legislatures. Unfortunately, they often continued to sound like something out of the Middle Ages, having all
the hallmarks of an obtuse clerical debate on the nature of the Divine but little actual science.

Some evangelicals embraced activism against global climate
change. Others blasted the concept of global warming as rank heresy.
Once again, the debate in public too often seemed to rely on the
scriptures, not science. The question of whether God will allow
the creation to heat up like a pan of Jiffy Pop makes for interesting
theological debate—unless you happen to be a drowning polar bear.

So are we ready to divorce religion and politics? Not quite yet.
Are we prepared to turn to issues like climate change, stem-cell research, and the origin of humankind over to the scientific community where they belong? It does not look that way. Are we ready
to embrace full-blown diversity and be welcoming to all folks—
religious and non—in all public institutions? Not if the Religious
Right has its way. Some far-right groups, after all, did eventually
concede that Senator Obama is not a Muslim—they then proceeded
to attack him for belonging to a liberal Christian denomination! (My
own as well.)

The Religious Right was not responsible for all of the things that happened in the world of church and state since the hardcover edition of this book was published. But the movement's leaders and activists had a hand in more than a few, and the other disputes are proof of the country's squabbling over the proper role of religion in public life is not likely to die down. Indeed, only a few hours after the deadliest school shooting in American history at Virginia Tech, a local lawmaker in Oklahoma opened a council meeting with a prayer thanking Jesus Christ for a government that ". . . allows each one to have freedom of speech and to bear arms."

That is a shame. As I survey the religious–political landscape in America, I continue to see that the best resolution is the one right under our noses: complete religious and philosophical freedom for all backed by a high wall of separation between church and state.

INDEX

ABOUT THE AUTHOR

The Reverend Barry W. Lynn has served as executive director of Americans United for Separation of Church and State (www.au.org) in Washington, D.C., since 1992. An ordained minister in the United Church of Christ and an attorney, he has been involved in issues of civil liberties and social justice all of his professional life. Lynn is a frequent commentator on church-state issues in the media and serves as the host of the nationally syndicated radio program *Culture Shocks.*